WHY THE NINETIES MATTER

Books by Terry H. Anderson

The United States, Great Britain, and the Cold War, 1941–47

A Flying Tiger's Diary (with fighter ace Charles Bond Jr.)

The Movement and The Sixties

The Sixties (many editions)

The Pursuit of Fairness: A History of Affirmative Action

Bush's Wars

Why the Nineties Matter

WHY THE NINETIES MATTER

TERRY H. ANDERSON

OXFORD
UNIVERSITY PRESS

OXFORD
UNIVERSITY PRESS

Oxford University Press is a department of the University of Oxford. It furthers
the University's objective of excellence in research, scholarship, and education
by publishing worldwide. Oxford is a registered trade mark of Oxford University
Press in the UK and certain other countries.

Published in the United States of America by Oxford University Press
198 Madison Avenue, New York, NY 10016, United States of America.

Library of Congress Cataloging-in-Publication Data
Names: Anderson, Terry H., 1946– author.
Title: Why the nineties matter / Terry H. Anderson.
Description: 1. | New York : Oxford University Press, 2024. |
Includes bibliographical references and index. |
Identifiers: LCCN 2023040838 (print) | LCCN 2023040839 (ebook) |
ISBN 9780197763018 (hardback) | ISBN 9780197763032 (epub) |
ISBN 9780197763049
Subjects: LCSH: United States—History—1969– | Nineteen nineties.
Classification: LCC E881 .A53 2024 (print) | LCC E881 (ebook) |
DDC 973.92—dc23/eng/20231024
LC record available at https://lccn.loc.gov/2023040838
LC ebook record available at https://lccn.loc.gov/2023040839

DOI: 10.1093/oso/9780197763018.001.0001

Printed by Sheridan Books, Inc., United States of America

To my Bros, SK and JD—and to Rose

Contents

Preface

What are some terms that Americans did not know at the beginning of the 1990s but did at the end of the era in 2001?

Velvet Revolutions. Internet. Clery Act. Golden Visa. NAFTA. Rodney King. Gennifer Flowers. Whitewater. Ruby Ridge. Cyberspace. IMDb. Netscape. Timothy McVeigh. Infotainment. Dolly the Sheep. Laptop. Paula Jones. Information Superhighway. Browsers. Search Engines. Fox News. Google. Autocorrect. HotMail. Yahoo! MSNBC. App. Secure Sockets Layer, SSL. Monster.com. eBay. Match. com. PayPal. E★TRADE. Dayton Accords. HIPPA. Monica Lewinsky. Smartphone. Kyoto Protocol. Osama bin Laden. Digital Divide. CHIP. Selfie. Infowars. BlackBerry. *Bush v. Gore.* 9/11.

What are some terms and phrases that took on a new meaning or emphasis during that same era? Gulf War. PC. Real Time. Cold War. Global Warming. Hubble Space Telescope. Sexual Harassment. Surfing. HIV/AIDS. Amazon. Geek. Domestic Violence. Hacked. Bipartisanship. O.J. Reboot. Hip-hop. Terrorists. Connected. Social Media. Viral. Website. Device. Wired.

This book is about the American nineties, and others have expressed their views of the era. Veteran reporter Haynes Johnson wrote the first book on the epoch and gave away his interpretation with his title, *The Best of Times.* Johnson, of course, realized that his interpretation might be too positive and that the era was both "wonderful but woeful."

Over the years others joined in with their evaluations. Conservative commentator Charles Krauthammer wrote in 2004 that the nineties was "our retreat from seriousness, our Seinfeld decade of obsessive

ordinariness . . . a time of domesticity, triviality and self-absorption."
By 2008 Krauthammer was piling it on, calling it a "holiday from
history." After all, he wrote, what was Clinton's "greatest crisis? A farcical sexual dalliance." Then Krauthammer got out his battering ram,
bludgeoning the era as "the most inconsequential decade of the 20th
century."

Some years later, while running for the Republican nomination
for president in 2015, former Florida governor Jeb Bush commented
that "if someone wants to run a campaign about '90s nostalgia, it's
not going to be very successful." That provoked cultural writer and
baby boomer Kurt Andersen to blast back, "The Best Decade Ever?
The 1990s, Obviously." He reviewed the thriving economy, strong job
creation, federal budget surpluses, and the stock market increasing by
over 300 percent. He reviewed the Soviet collapse, the suppression
of AIDS, and the emergence of powerful laptops, the digital age, and
smartphones. "Plus, if you were a man and worked in an office, starting in the '90s you could get away with never wearing a necktie." And
then he smacked his readers:

> Wasn't the release of Nirvana's "Nevermind," in 1991, pretty much the
> last time a new rock 'n' roll band truly, deeply mattered, the way rock 'n'
> roll did in the '60s and '70s? Wasn't hip-hop, which achieved its mass-
> market breakthrough and dominance in the '90s, the last genuinely new
> and consequential invention of American pop culture?

Perhaps. Everyone who lived through the era would write a different volume, most likely based on what issues and events had an
impact on their own lives.

This book is not a traditional history. It does not examine all major
people, issues, and events of that era. In these pages the reader will not
find an investigation of political initiatives that failed to become law,
diplomatic proposals that did not change international relations, judicial cases with little consequences, natural disasters such as the Great
Flood of '93, or sporting events such as who won the World Series
or Super Bowls. Nor is much space spent on pop culture—Mariah
Carey or Jennifer Aniston, grunge or hip-hop, primetime TV shows,

Cheers or *Seinfeld, Late Night* with Leno v. Letterman, blockbuster films, *Titanic* or *Jurassic Park*, or best-sellers with Harry Potter. And with few significant exceptions, celebrities are not examined in this volume.[1]

Instead, this book simply asks a complex question: Why Did the Nineties Matter? Chronologically between the collapse of the Soviet Union and Desert Storm and the tragedy of September 11, 2001, who were the people, what were the issues and events, the technological innovations, and new businesses that had a profound impact—that made us what we are today—that changed the course of America?

This book begins with an Introduction that examines two events that changed American and world history—the end of the Cold War and Desert Storm. Chapter One discusses the demise of the political center in the first few years of the nineties, and Chapter Two is more thematic on the rise of angry white men. Chapter Three returns to mid-decade, when many commentators labeled the era the Nervous Nineties. Chapter Four returns to a significant theme of the era, technological advancements, especially one that changed human behavior—the cyberspace or dot.com revolution. Chapter Five examines the last years of the period when a number of events occurred that demonstrated that social and cultural forces that had been developing for years merged into Anything Goes America. The Epilogue recounts the tragedy of 9/11, and Conclusions connects the dots between the era and more recent times, answering Why the Nineties Matter.

Writing recent history is fraught with peril, but after a generation has passed it is time for this historian to ask and try to answer: How Did We Get Here?

Acknowledgments

Many buddies have helped me along this writing journey. Bobby Jones read my Chapter Four and kept me online for the cyberspace revolution, and his wife, Janet, best masseuse ever, rubbed away the lumps in my neck after my being hunched over a computer. Jonathan Carroll, who wrote an excellent PhD dissertation on Somalia, kept me on track for that unfortunate misadventure and the more successful ones in Bosnia and Ireland. My younger colleague and a "nineties guy," Brian Rouleau, read and improved Chapter Five and Anything Goes America. My brother Jeff read the entire manuscript, as usual, and forced changes for clarity, and so did my wife, Rose, who reads everything I publish. Scuba buddies Jenny Clements and Greig Rieke not only showed us their town of Toronto but invited us to sail around the Bahamas over spring break on their beautiful Catamaran Astréa 42, *Decompression*.

It is always a pleasure working with Oxford University Press. Again, my editor was Dave McBride, who answered my numerous questions, secured a good contract, kept the process moving, and found excellent reviewers who made thoughtful suggestions that definitely improved the manuscript: historians Kevin Mattson, Ohio University, and Matthew Johnson, Washington & Jefferson College. Dave was assisted by a fine project editor, Sarah Ebel, and the process moved along smoothly because of Jacqueline Pavlovic and Joellyn Ausanka, whose copy-editing improved consistency and clarity.

Back in Bryan College Station, many of my colleagues at Texas A&M University made going to campus enjoyable: Andrew Kirkendall, Brian Linn, Jason Parker, Brian Rouleau, Lorean Foote, Roger Reese,

Damon Bach, Verity McInnis, Al Broussard, Jonathan Brunstedt, Walter Kamphoefner, David Hudson, Katherine Unterman, Adam Seipp, and David Vaught. After teaching in five countries at various universities I am well aware how efficiently and amicably our department is managed, thanks Kelly Cook, Erika Hernandez, and Mary Speelman.

Other buddies improved my quality of life. David and Sharon Ogden, Kathi and Ken Appelt, Brian and Dinny Linn, and Joe and Nancy Golson shared many humorous dinner tables, besides fabulous food. Joe also humiliated me on the tennis court. Speaking of delicious food and good fun, thanks to my brothers' wives, Gini and Moey, for hosting us many times during spring hiking in Arizona and for Octoberfest in Wisconsin. Theo Kruijssen delighted in touring Rose and me around the Miami area, and Dan Eder always is on call for similar duty and good times in Los Angeles. August is hell in Texas, so thanks to my cousin, painter Leslie Anderson, and our fine friend Joanne Williams for putting us up for three summer trips to Maine, and the same for Bill and Trudy Harper and Pat Carey and Tanya Repka being great hosts in our homeland of Minnesota. Now that I have surpassed a thousand dives, I have to thank my traveling and scuba buddies: David Rolla, Leslie Ruyle and am thankful for wonderful past trips and New England visits with Dana Williams and Letha Mills.

This book is dedicated to three people who have shared good times with me for most of my life: my hiking, touring, and beer-drinking brothers, Steve and Jeff. SK taught me growing up, guided me on a two-week canoe trip into the Quetico-Superior Wilderness, and became our superb financial adviser besides being the bionic hiker and planner extraordinaire. JD shared a boyhood of laughs, visited me for life-changing personal events in Southeast Asia, and amazes me how he can swap stories as well as anyone on the planet. Also, the book is dedicated to my world-exploring companion and wife, Rose, who is closing in on seventy countries. Yes, she is packing for the next adventure even after catching her personal best brown trout in Chile Patagonia under the fabulous guidance of John Joy. And yes, she still has a sense of humor even after catching her personal best rainbow trout on Alaska's Moraine and American rivers in Katmai National Park—surrounded by hungry momma brown bears and their frisky cubs.

TA
Bryan College Station, Texas
July 1, 2023

Introduction

New World Order: Last Superpower
Standing and Desert Storm

Since the end of World War II, the Grand Alliance that crushed Hitler's Germany—the United States, Great Britain, and the Soviet Union—had dissolved into West versus East, Democratic Capitalism versus Communism, or as journalist Walter Lippmann termed the competition, a Cold War. The Soviets consolidated their hold on Eastern Europe, and the Americans formed alliances with nations in the West. Both sides competed for influence in the results of decolonialization, the new nations of Africa and Asia. Then in 1949 the Russians exploded their first atomic device, meaning that the two "superpowers" soon had the a-bombs and missiles to destroy every living being on earth.

That same year the United States and eleven other nations formed the North Atlantic Treaty Organization, NATO, to prevent Soviet expansion into Western Europe. Article five set the gold standard for alliances, stating that an attack on one member would be considered an attack on all. As the first Secretary General of the organization said, the purpose of NATO in Europe was "to keep the Russians out, the Americans in, and the Germans down."

The tense Cold War continued for over four decades. To contain communist expansion, America fought wars in Korea and Vietnam, and then in December 1979 the Soviets stumbled into their own Vietnam, a fractured nation of tribal minorities and warlords, Afghanistan. Their aim was to stabilize a friendly leftist government in Kabul. "Do not worry," Soviet premier Leonid Brezhnev said to a colleague, "we will end this war in three or four weeks."

Soon the Red Army was bogged down in a long, bloody, and costly conflict, while Americans were aiding their Islamic enemy, the Mujahedeen, or "holy warriors." The United States supplied them with stinger antiaircraft missiles and rocket launchers, and eventually the Afghans shot down more than 270 Soviet helicopters and aircraft.

Ronald Reagan became president talking tough about the Soviet Union, the "Evil Empire," and pledging an American military build-up. The old hardline Soviet leadership changed in 1982 when Brezhnev died. He was replaced by Yuri Andropov, who lived only until early 1984 when Konstantin Chernenko took charge, but he lived only until early 1985. When reporters asked the president why he didn't reduce world tensions and meet with the Soviets, Reagan quipped, "They keep dying on me."

But not the next leader, Mikhail Gorbachev, who accepted party control in March 1985 when he was young for Soviet leadership, only fifty-four. Seven months later Reagan met Gorbachev in Geneva; the next year they met again in Reykjavík, Iceland, and then again the next year in Washington. At these summits the two leaders discussed arms control, missiles, human rights, and conflicts in the world, including Afghanistan, and eventually signed the Intermediate-Range Nuclear Forces Treaty. The two men also developed a genial friendship while the Soviet leader was trying to recast his nation.

Gorbachev realized his nation was in trouble. He had inherited a stagnant economy that could not produce enough food to feed its people. In 1982 the grain harvest was a failure for the third year in a row, a disastrous sixty-six million tons short of target, meaning that the nation had to import the largest grain amounts ever at costly Western prices. Bread and meat were hard to find, butter scarce, and the government had to use food rationing to prevent massive starvation, reminding older citizens of the dark days of World War II.

Many American analysts thought that the Soviet Gross Domestic Product (GDP) was about 50 percent of the American GDP, but by the end of the decade the CIA reported that it was only about 15 percent. After all, the USSR produced few items that the rest of the world wanted to buy. It was an economy based on forcing its Eastern European satellites to buy its substandard manufactured items such as vehicles, and the rest of the world to purchase its vodka, military hardware, and its prized possessions—gas and oil.

Then oil prices plunged. In 1980 a barrel of oil sold for about $32, but new exploration resulted in surging supplies and then the "oil bust" of 1986; by the end of the decade oil was $12, deflating the Soviet budget. All the while the USSR subsidized its client states—Cuba, Vietnam, Nicaragua, Angola, and of course Afghanistan. By the mid-1980s the ailing Soviet economy was spending about $20 billion a year to support those impoverished allies.

Meanwhile, the war in Afghanistan became the Kremlin's Waterloo. Like the United States in Vietnam, after a few years Soviet citizens turned against their conflict, grumbling about its toll. Mothers and wives bombarded Gorbachev with letters demanding to know when their soldiers would come home, when the war would end. The bloody conflict continued for a decade, leading to the deaths of almost a million Afghans. The USSR spent about $2 billion a year fighting for Kabul, and some 15,000 Red Army personnel perished while about 35,000 were injured. Moreover, the rest of the Muslim world was unhappy that Russia was killing Islamic fighters, resulting in a Middle East aversion to purchasing one of the Kremlin's profit makers—military arms.

The economic burden was unbearable, and then in 1986 the Chernobyl explosion in northern Ukraine, the worst nuclear disaster in history, released more radioactive gas than both atomic bombs dropped on Hiroshima and Nagasaki. The blast killed thirty people and caused the evacuation of more than 100,000. The toxic pollution quickly expanded into neighboring Soviet states, then into Eastern Europe. This eventually caused thousands of deaths, outraged those populations, cost billions to clean up, and dramatically increased anti-Soviet feelings.

That certainly was true in Poland. In 1980 Lech Wałęsa and others founded the Solidarity trade union at the Lenin Shipyard in Gdańsk, Poland. Within a year it became incredibly popular, with some ten million members, a third of the nation's working-age population, and Poland recognized it as the first independent union in the Soviet bloc. Solidarity was a nonviolent movement, and it successfully agitated against the Polish Communist party bosses, gaining support, and inspiring other calls for social change throughout Eastern Europe.

Gorbachev responded to these troubles by declaring his policies of Perestroika and Glasnost. The former began reforming the economic and political system, especially increasing efficiency, decreasing central planning, and slowly moving toward a market economy. "We are not giving up on socialism," he announced to his citizens in 1987, "we want to make it better." Glasnost was aimed at opening the Soviet state by disseminating more information and consulting with its people. Gorbachev was beginning to pry open the closed Soviet system—he never realized the potential consequences.

"Mikhail Gorbachev had three blind spots that assured his failure at home and accelerated the collapse of the Soviet Union," wrote CIA director Robert Gates. He believed communist rule could be reformed and stay in power, that the Soviet economy could be revived, and that the people in the Soviet states and Eastern Europe would want to remain in a reformed USSR.

Gorbachev was wrong on every count. As the Kremlin struggled, activists in the Eastern European satellites struck—they began to agitate for more freedoms. The Baltic states asserted their right to protect their environment then began making claims for sovereignty and independence.

Then, Gorbachev shocked the world. He visited Paris in July 1987 and surprised listeners by declaring that "interference in domestic affairs and any attempts to restrict the sovereignty of states—friends, allies or any others—are inadmissible." He called for the reduction of tactical nuclear weapons in Europe and then declared that social and political orders in countries have "changed in the past and may change in the future. But this change is the exclusive affair of the people in that country and is their choice." In December 1988 the Soviet leader gave a speech to the United Nations and declared that his government would cut its armed forces, reduce conventional weapons, and pull more than fifty thousand troops and five thousand tanks out of East Germany, Hungary, and Czechoslovakia. Unlike all Soviet rulers after World War II, in spring 1989 he began to withdraw the Red Army from Eastern Europe.

By April 1989 Poles were calling for reforms and freedom, and that encouraged activists to make similar calls in Hungary, East Germany, Bulgaria, Czechoslovakia, and Romania. Since Stalin, the Soviet Union had crushed popular uprisings in East Germany, Poland, Hungary, and Czechoslovakia. Gorbachev ended that repression.

The Soviet leader became wildly popular in Europe—"Gorbymania"—and his visits attracted huge crowds. But his statements also opened the floodgates, and what rushed through were the nonviolent velvet revolutions. In August, Poles held free elections, and they elected a non-Communist government. The next month, Hungary opened its borders with Austria, allowing people to flee. In October the Hungarian Communist Party became socialist, in November Germans dismantled the Berlin Wall, and Bulgarians ousted their communist boss and began elections. In Prague, protesters took to the streets, and by the next month the communist bosses left, and playwright and political dissident Václav Havel became president. And in Romania, the hated communist boss Nicolae Ceausescu and his wife fled the capital and were captured by soldiers, who quickly became a firing squad and executed them.

Meanwhile, President George H. W. Bush watched from the White House. He had inherited and wanted to continue Reagan's policy of befriending and building trust with Gorbachev. To win the 1988 presidential election, however, he had to appease the hard-liners in his party, and so when he held a private meeting with the Soviet leader, he told him not to pay any attention to his tough stance on the USSR, that he fully intended to work together after the election. Gorbachev later called it the "most important talk Bush and I ever had."

After the election and while the Soviets were moving away from communism and Eastern Europeans were enacting their velvet revolutions, Bush adopted a policy of *pauza* (a pause in foreign policies) while Gorbachev pursued Perestroika and Glasnost. Bush told reporters that he did "not want to poke a stick in the eye of Mr. Gorbachev," nor did he want to "drive wedges between the Soviet Union and Eastern Europe." The United States would stay out of the way and watch the Eastern Bloc break away from Soviet control.

Simultaneously, the Soviet Union began falling apart. Gorbachev's attempts to reform the USSR led him to allow elections in March 1989 for a new Congress of People's Deputies. The results were shocking—Communist Party members lost in droves, and when the Congress convened, they did not thank Gorbachev for opening the closed system; they criticized his Soviet government.

Russians held their own elections in spring 1990, and they elected Boris Yeltsin as president, a man who shortly thereafter condemned communism. Elected democratically in the largest Soviet Republic, Yeltsin's ideas seemed more legitimate than those of anyone in memory. He proposed that Russia be granted the freedom to make its own economic and political decisions, apart from the Soviet system, which appealed to the other fourteen republics in the USSR. Over the summer all the republics followed Yeltsin's example, declaring their independence from the USSR.

Gorbachev attempted to hold his country together for the next year, proclaiming numerous proposals, but none worked—the only way previous Communist bosses had kept the nation together was by the use of force, ordering the military to crush dissent. Gorbachev didn't have the stomach for bloodshed. He watched the republics leave, take over the police and local militia, elect leaders, and become independent. And he watched the Soviet Union dissolve. It was unbelievable that the Soviet Empire, born in the Revolution of

1917, could resign from history with almost no bloodshed by the end of 1991.

"It was a rare and great moment in history," reflected National Security Advisor Brent Scowcroft. "The end of an era of enormous and unrelenting hostility had come in an instant. And, most incredible of all, without a single shot being fired."

It also was incredible that the Soviet Union, which lost about twenty-five million people in World War II, more than any other nation because Hitler's Third Reich, would allow the reunification of East and West Germany. It was, as experts noted, "the single most troublesome and dangerous issue of the Cold War." And for West Germany, also the most expensive, for to get Gorbachev to go along with reunification Bonn pledged $750 million to pay for removing the Red Army and eventually some $33 billion in financial aid to the USSR.

Events transpired quickly in summer and autumn 1990. East Germany's economy collapsed, and leaders from both sections began talks. They signed their Reunification Treaty, and by October that resulted in one Germany. The new Federal Republic of Germany then joined NATO.

Three years earlier, in 1987, President Reagan had gone to Berlin, looked into the eastern section behind the Brandenburg Gate, and declared, "Mr. Gorbachev, tear down this wall!" Reagan's supporters claimed that the speech was part of the process that reunited Germany, freed Eastern Europe, and "won the Cold War." A more accurate interpretation is that on the evening of November 9–10, 1990, the German people literally tore down the Berlin Wall. Reagan was important because he befriended Gorbachev and increased trust and decreased tensions between the superpowers. But the USSR's demise was a result of its leaders making horrible decisions (a war of choice in Afghanistan), a centralized economy that could not feed its people, manufactured goods that could not compete on the world market, and falling oil prices—and Gorbachev. Changes "in Eastern Europe," wrote Robert Gates, "were due to the leader of the Soviet Union. . . .

It was, at the end of the day, a Soviet leader who let an empire slide away peacefully."

Time magazine put Gorbachev on their January 1, 1990, cover and named him "Man of the Decade." Americans and Westerners thought so, but in his own country he became persona non grata, the leader who allowed the painful collapse of a superpower, who lost the Cold War. Twenty-five years later some Russians still resented that loss and Gorbachev. "You Americans think you won the Cold War," President Vladimir Putin said to ExxonMobil CEO Rex Tillerson. "You did not win the Cold War. We never fought that war. We could have, but we didn't."

As for President Reagan, he wasn't even in office when these monumental events unfolded. Referring to his Berlin speech, he wrote in his memoirs, "I never dreamed that in less than three years the wall would come down and a 6,000-pound section would be sent to my Presidential Library."[1]

As the Soviet Empire was imploding during summer 1990 two world events were on the horizon—one in Africa and the other in the Middle East. After years of American business and government sanctions, along with a massive internal struggle, the apartheid government in South Africa finally was collapsing. The white minority of mostly Dutch Afrikaners had settled South Africa in the seventeenth century and formally established apartheid in 1948, subjugating the Black majority to strict segregation. A few years later, in the 1950s, the African National Congress launched a Defiance Campaign, disrupting the society and government. In response the white government banned the ANC in 1960 and two years later arrested and imprisoned the prominent ANC activist Nelson Mandela. As he sat in prison during the 1980s Archbishop Desmond Tutu and Reverend Allan Boesak organized huge marches in Cape Town, Pretoria, and Johannesburg, and that provoked the international community. Many Western nations imposed sanctions, supported by the United Nations, but two world leaders resisted, President Ronald Reagan and Prime Minister Margaret Thatcher; they considered Mandela and the ANC as communists, a thought enthusiastically boosted by the apartheid regime.

Nevertheless, the US Congress and the British Parliament passed sanctions against the apartheid regime, and that put significant economic pressure on South Africa by the first year of the Bush administration. At the same time in Eastern Europe the velvet revolutions were ending Soviet domination which deemphasized communism and energized democratic forces throughout the world, including South Africa.

Mandela was released from prison in February 1990, negotiations to end apartheid began, and four months later President Bush hosted the ANC leader at the White House. Bush declared Mandela was "a man who embodies the hopes of millions," that American sanctions support peaceful change, and that "repugnant" apartheid "must end." He continued, "Oppression has ended in Eastern Europe," and "the future belongs . . . to democracy."

It did in South Africa, where eventually Mandela was elected president—but not in Iraq, where Saddam Hussein crushed all opposition to his dictatorship and had desires for his neighbors. In July 1990 the US Central Command learned that about three thousand Iraqi military vehicles were leaving the Baghdad area and heading south toward Kuwait. Saddam warned that he would attack Kuwait if that nation and Saudi Arabia did not cut oil production to increase petroleum prices and forgive Iraq's massive debts, some $130 billion, bills that he had incurred fighting an eight-year war with Iran. The dictator had told his neighbors that he had saved the Sunni Arabs from the Shia Persians and thus demanded his debts forgiven.

The Saudis and Kuwaitis refused, and on July 22 the Iraqi dictator ordered some 30,000 troops to the border, prompting Kuwait to go on military alert and US ambassador April Glaspie to meet with Saddam and discuss the situation. She had never met him before, as was typical for the dictator, and during the conversation she told him that the United States was mostly concerned about Arab–Israeli issues, not Arab–Arab issues. She hoped that this problem would be solved peacefully.

A week later, on the early morning of July 30, the CIA's satellites noticed that some three hundred Iraqi tanks were assembling on their border with Kuwait. The agency informed the White House that Iraq now had 120,000 troops poised for an invasion. Western diplomats thought Saddam was bluffing. Ambassador Glaspie flew out of Baghdad for a holiday; Secretary of Defense Dick Cheney left for his vacation in Wyoming; and Secretary of State James Baker went on a hunting trip to Mongolia. Iraq's neighbors did not think the dictator would break the code that Arabs did not attack Arabs, and they also thought Saddam was bluffing.

He wasn't. At 1 a.m. local time on August 2 the Iraqi army launched an invasion of Kuwait. More than 100,000 troops stormed into that little nation. A third of the population, along with the Emir, rushed to their luxury SUVs and drove into Saudi Arabia, while the Kuwaiti Air Force rushed to their jets and flew to friendly neighbors.

Just four hours after the invasion, National Security Council members met in the White House Situation Room. From 10 p.m. to 2 a.m. the NSC deputies discussed the American response. The Kuwaitis were asking for immediate assistance, demanding that Iraq stop the invasion and withdraw their forces. Yet the deputies noted that the main source of support was only seven US Navy warships in the Persian Gulf and that the aircraft carrier USS *Independence* battle group was near Diego Garcia, more than three thousand miles away in the Arabian Sea. Moreover, the Americans noted that it would take about three days to get targeting information for the USN's Tomahawk Cruise missiles. As for the US Air Force, it would take at least thirty-six hours to get B-52s to the war zone.

The next morning Saddam controlled Kuwait as the Bush administration's principals convened. The president, Vice President Dan Quayle, CIA director William Webster, Chairman of the Joint Chiefs of Staff General Colin Powell, General Norman Schwarzkopf, Secretary of Defense Dick Cheney, Special Assistant to the President Richard Haass, National Security Advisor Brent Scowcroft, Under Secretary of State Robert Kimmitt, and a half dozen others gathered in the Cabinet Room. The president opened with a statement for the press condemning Iraq's invasion of Kuwait. Kimmitt noted that there were 500 Americans in Iraq, 3,800 in Kuwait, with 270 at the US Embassy, and that they were reaching out to their allies to join them and freeze all Kuwaiti and Iraqi assets. The officials noted that oil production could be affected, that for the time being there should be enough, but the invasion already had increased the price, up three dollars a barrel to $23.

The men discussed options. They saw the invasion as "the first test" of the post–Cold War, and they were happy that Gorbachev's USSR would not get in the way but would go along in opposing Saddam's invasion. General Schwarzkopf noted the USS *Independence* had hit a storm with heavy seas, "has limited strike options," but should be "on station" in five days. The general stated that there are "one million Iraqi troops" and "we would need more time to build a force to attack Iraq." They talked about possible sanctions and the probable response from their allies. "Let's step back," said Scowcroft. "The most significant option economically is oil." Almost all Iraqi income came from petroleum, he continued, so we could embargo, shut down pipelines, try to stop oil tankers, "but this would be the most damaging. One-fourth of U.S. consumption is from Iraq." All were concerned that Iraq might invade Saudi Arabia and interfere with their oil shipments to America. Moreover, if Saddam invaded and seized Saudi Arabia, the dictator would own about half the world's known petroleum deposits. The president ended the conversation, "Let's talk to our allies. . . . We need to get sanctions in place before noon. We'll make leadership calls from the plane."

In just one day Saddam had captured Kuwait, and shortly thereafter he declared "a comprehensive and eternal merger," annexing the nation as the nineteenth province of Iraq.

The United States had a checkered past with Iraq. During the 1980s, Saddam, a secular Sunni Muslim, had gone to war with his hated enemy, the Ayatollah Khomeini, the Shia fundamentalist leader in neighboring Iran. President Ronald Reagan's administration played both sides, giving Saddam monetary subsidies and satellite images of the battlefield, which showed Iranian troop movements, while quietly selling arms to Iran in what became known as the "arms for hostage" scandal, more commonly called Iran-Contra. The United States and United Nations helped negotiate the end of the conflict while both nations claimed victory.

Most likely, Saddam did not think that the Bush administration would get involved in his feud with Kuwait. In 1980, when Saddam invaded Iran, Washington remained silent on the sidelines.

But not in 1990. "Naked aggression," proclaimed President Bush, "it will not stand." The president froze all Iraqi and Kuwaiti assets and property in the United States. He proclaimed Operation Desert Shield, protection of Saudi Arabia and other oil-producing nations from Saddam's aggression, and ordered the US Armed Forces to prepare for war. Bush sent Secretary of State Baker to the United Nations; that organization passed resolutions that placed economic sanctions on Iraq, curtailing their trade and oil exports. The UN told Saddam to evacuate Kuwait—or face military action.

Saddam was not moved. "Convey to President Bush," he declared, "that he should regard the Kuwaiti Emir and Crown Prince as history. . . . We know you are a superpower who can do great damage to us, but we will never capitulate."

To prove Saddam wrong Bush began a diplomatic and military response. He ordered Joseph Wilson, the US chargé d'affaires in Baghdad, to talk with Saddam. Wilson asked the dictator if he intended to attack Saudi Arabia. "We will not attack those who do not attack us," Saddam replied, a curious response since he had just attacked Kuwait, "we will not harm those who do not harm us."

The president also ordered Secretary of Defense Cheney to Saudi Arabia to meet with King Fahd and Crown Prince Abdallah. Bush needed their approval to place troops in their country. The men talked for two hours, and the king told the crown prince that they had to accept the help from the United States. Fahd turned to Abdallah and said, "Look at what happened to the Kuwaitis. They waited, and today there is no Kuwait." Abdallah muttered that there still was a Kuwait. "Yes," the king replied, "they're all living in our hotel rooms. Who'll put us up?" Then the king turned to Cheney, "Okay. We'll do it."

The president also began assembling an international armed force. In September he met with Gorbachev, who previously had sold military hardware to Iraq but now startled the Iraqis by telling them that they must evacuate Kuwait. The US Navy changed course and two more aircraft carriers steamed full speed to the Persian Gulf and Red Sea. Other nations' armed forces moved toward the Middle East. By the end of the year some 700,000 military personnel from twenty-eight countries were stationed either in Saudi Arabia or the Persian Gulf. Bush worked the phones day and night to form a UN coalition; it was brilliant diplomacy, for it eventually included the France, Germany, Britain, Turkey, and significantly, seven Arab nations, including Saudi Arabia, Egypt, and Syria.

Meanwhile, back in the United States, citizens were divided over a possible war. Many recalled that except for quick, minor skirmishes in Grenada in 1983 and Panama in 1989, Kuwait would be the first time the US Armed Forces would conduct a major invasion since the American withdrawal from Vietnam. The painful memories of that conflict prompted many citizens to begin protesting another bloody military crusade, and a number of politicians agreed with them that economic sanctions would be the most sensible way to force Saddam out of Kuwait. Others opposed a war because they felt that it was aimed mostly at benefiting the petroleum industry, which everyone knew had close ties with the Bush administration, while others wondered why the American democracy was helping the dictatorial Emir of Kuwait. By January 1991 protests blossomed in many cities across the nation; some 75,000 showed up on the Washington, DC, Mall. To one protester, a sixty-year-old nurse, the war would be "Bush's

Commander-in-Chief Bush with troops in Saudia Arabia preparing for Desert Storm, Thanksgiving 1991. Courtesy George H. W. Bush Presidential Library.

ego against Saddam Hussein's ego. . . . I don't think either is worth dying for."

Yet a majority supported Bush's policy, or simply wanted to show support for the troops. Citizens held rallies outside numerous military bases. Some 125 tractor-trailers, festooned with American flags, yellow ribbons, and banners, stretched out along the Massachusetts Turnpike: Truckers in Support of War.

The president then went to Congress, controlled by the Democrats, to ask for a resolution as required by the War Powers Act passed at the end of the Vietnam War. On January 12, 1991, Congress passed a joint resolution, and three days later the UN passed a similar resolution allowing military action—both with the same aim: to liberate Kuwait.

The "allied countries have exhausted all reasonable efforts to reach a peaceful resolution," declared the president, "and have no choice but to drive Saddam from Kuwait by force." Recalling the previous war, Bush pledged this "will not be another Vietnam. Our troops will have the best possible support in the entire world and will not be asked to fight with one hand tied behind their back."

Saddam warned that if the allies attacked, they would become involved in the "Mother of All Battles."

That was nonsense, for on the night of January 16–17 the US Navy and Air Force launched more than 150 cruise missiles. The allied air force composed of American, French, British, Spanish, and Saudi planes flew one thousand combat sorties, bombing Iraq and their military positions inside Kuwait: Desert Shield became Desert Storm.

"WAR!" screamed the *New York Post* headline: "U.S. Jets Blast Baghdad. Saddam's Palace Hit."

Next morning Baghdad's residents woke to find the Baath Party headquarters and the Ministry of Defense in rubble. The allied onslaught continued to pound Iraq for six weeks, destroying most of Saddam's command structure and demoralizing his army. "Our strategy in going after [the Iraqi army] is very simple," General Powell told reporters. "First we are going to cut it off, and then we are going to kill it."

After six weeks of horrific bombardment, the coalition force commander, US General "Stormin'" Norman Schwarzkopf, ordered some 400,000 UN forces to launch the invasion. The general had secretly deployed armored divisions over two hundred miles inland and up the Saudi–Iraq border so he could prepare for a surprise attack on the Iraqi flank, Operation Hail Mary. Back in the south, in the early morning hours of February 24, Saudi and Kuwaiti troops, along with US Marines, charged into Kuwait. Stormin' Norman then ordered Hail Mary. American, British, French, Canadian, Egyptian, and Syrian troops in the north struck a "left hook" into Iraq. That cut Saddam's communication and supply lines, forcing a retreat on the main highway north toward Baghdad and making retreating enemy vehicles and tanks easy targets for the coalition air forces.

A "turkey shoot," US pilots labeled the massacre on the "highway of death," while others called it the Highway to Hell. More than a thousand military vehicles were burning wreckage while shell-shocked Iraqi troops, mostly conscripts, came out of their bunkers, waving white flags, many bleeding from their ears.

The Mother of All Battles was over in thirty-four days, and after the bombing campaign began, coalition forces liberated Kuwait in just one hundred hours.

"Kuwait is liberated," President Bush announced to the world. "Iraq's army is defeated. Our military objectives are met. It was a victory for all the coalition nations, for the United Nations, for all mankind, and for the rule of law."

It also was a victory of the US military. At the end of the Vietnam War morale within the armed forces had sunk to its lowest level in memory. Troops came home in the early 1970s to an ungrateful nation. Many World War II veterans had sent their sons to the jungles of Southeast Asia, eventually realizing that after years of conflict victory remained elusive. In 1975 North Vietnamese tanks rolled into South Vietnam and united the nation, and American self-doubt soared. Many commentators talked about the Vietnam syndrome—many Americans loathed overseas military involvements, thinking that engagements would result in another long unsuccessful quagmire.

"By God," declared President Bush, "we've kicked the Vietnam syndrome once and for all." He was right, for when the troops came home in March and April 1991 crowds at airports applauded and cheered them. Americans began to say and have been saying ever since: "Thank you for your service."

The Bush administration painfully remembered the impact that the journalists and the media had during Vietnam. Whether true or not, many conservatives believed that the journalists played a role in our defeat, and so in this conflict the administration did not allow the media the freedom to roam the battlefield. Instead, journalists were "embedded" with troops. They would go out with the unit, make friends with soldiers, and stay close and under supervision. "What you are going to get from the Pentagon in the Persian Gulf is the good news, the success," wrote a journalist for the *Miami Herald*. "You're not going to see bodies being brought home in caskets. . . . It's OK to die for your country. The Pentagon just doesn't want too many people to know about it."

The Gulf War also was the first one that relied on new technology— high-speed computers, video cameras, satellite uplinks. Back in living rooms, Americans could actually watch a missile heading into a building and then explode in "real time," or at the same time as the detonation. "Can you believe that!" viewers declared. Watching the war in real time increased the ratings of the first cable network, Ted Turner's CNN, and that boosted their 24-hour all-news format. Soon others would follow in the nineties, like Fox News and MSNBC.

The all-volunteer military proved it was a formidable fighting force. The Defense Department's final report on the conflict noted that it tested and demonstrated the new possibilities of the "military-technological revolution in warfare," which included precision weaponry, sophisticated sensors, stealth planes, night vision capabilities, and missile defenses. That technology "greatly increased our battlefield effectiveness" and "gave the ground forces unprecedented maneuverability and reach." It was clear that the US armed forces were superior to any other on the planet, and our stunning victory helped create a myth—future wars also would be relatively short and easy.[2]

The year 1991 was momentous. The American coalition had beaten Saddam out of Kuwait, and the USSR had collapsed. The Cold War was history. It had been a "struggle for the very soul of mankind," Bush later wrote. America won.

That victory had an impact on US foreign policy during the nineties—and after. For more than four decades Americans had a focal point. The Soviet Union was "The Devil We Knew." Scores of politicians in both parties would blame the Soviets for virtually anything that did not conform to America's interests, from Korea to Vietnam to

Afghanistan. Now that demon had collapsed into fifteen new countries, the Warsaw Pact had disintegrated along with the Eastern and
Western Blocs, and that meant that American policymakers would
have to form new policies toward numerous countries based on new
relations between each nation and the United States. That would
prove to be a trying task for the last superpower standing.

The Persian Gulf War was, according to Bush, about "more than
one small country; it is a big idea; a new world order," with "new ways
of working with other nations . . . peaceful settlement of disputes,
solidarity against aggression, reduced and controlled arsenals and just
treatment of all peoples." The first time new world order became part
of the world lexicon was during the Wilsonian Moment at the end of
World War I, when the president had proclaimed his Fourteen Points,
which included the self-determination of peoples and decolonialization. That would not happen until after the next world war, and so
in the 1920s the term was abandoned when America refused to sign
the Treaty of Versailles and join the League of Nations. But with the
Gulf War and the demise of the Cold War both Bush and Gorbachev
talked about a new world order; Bush used the phrase more than forty
times, as scholars and policy advisers searched for its meaning. What
would a new world order actually look like in future diplomatic and
military challenges?

As in 1919, again in 1991 the term simply became a vague slogan,
lacking definition. "The administration hasn't fully diagnosed the
causes of disorder. We're beginning to see that the use of military
force in the gulf, for example, did not solve the problem of the Kurds,
the future shape of Iraq or even the future of Saddam Hussein," said
historian John Lewis Gaddis. Moreover, there were "new world problems" that had to be resolved, such as the disintegration of the Soviet
Union, Iraq, Somalia, and Yugoslavia.

Thus, not long after the war the administration eased back into a
traditional situation. Without the Soviet Union, the United States was
supreme, and a new group of American thinkers and policymakers,
neo-conservatives or neocons, emerged during the nineties. They

advocated that America's role in the world should be "benevolent global hegemony." It was a step back to the America First ideas of the 1930s; there was nothing new world order about that conventional stance. And the result? Our "moment alone in the sun," wrote then CIA director and future secretary of defense Robert Gates, "and the arrogance with which we conducted ourselves in the 1990s and beyond as the sole surviving superpower, caused widespread resentment."

There were other aspects of the new world order that lasted into the nineties. Instead of being focused on Moscow, US policymakers refocused on Baghdad. Thus, the UN and the Bush administration established no-fly zones over Iraqi territory. US and British airmen were stationed in Saudi Arabia to fly over and inspect Iraq, and that irritated many Muslims who did not like Christian troops in the land of the Prophet. The American fly-overs also kept the United States on a collision course with Iraq.

The new world order witnessed more economic globalization. The thirst for petroleum continued to grow, exports soared, and that boosted the international influence of the Middle East. "Let it be clear," President Bush told the nation in March 1991, "our vital national interests depend on a stable and secure Gulf."

In the nineties India and a few years later China joined the World Trade Organization, and their large populations increased manufacturing production and purchases. Moreover, the "Asian Miracle" was under way, demonstrated by dramatic economic growth in that part of the world. And as Russia and Eastern Europe turned away from communism and toward capitalism, there was an increased demand for Western goods. All these events of the era stimulated more economic globalization.

As for Russia, the economic chaos and corruption that followed the dissolution of the USSR resulted in a capitalist nation with influential billionaires who had direct ties with, and support of, the Kremlin. Democracy, in a country that never had experienced that form of government, proved impossible to establish. Furthermore, the eventual incorporation of much of Eastern Europe into NATO stimulated a continuous debate about the role of the organization; it also provoked nationalism in Russia and led to the dictatorship of Vladimir Putin.

In the United States, many citizens thought that with the end of the superpower rivalry, there would be a "peace dividend," the idea that America would cut military budgets and redirect funds toward domestic problems, while conducting a more moderate, even limited foreign policy. As we shall see, that did not happen. Although the US defense budget slowly decreased as a percentage of total spending in the nineties, it continued to grow as Congress passed larger budgets. President Eisenhower had announced in his last address to the nation in 1961 the "military-industrial complex," and he warned that the "conjunction of an immense military establishment and a large arms industry" was having economic and political influence "in every city, every State house, every office of the Federal government." General Ike warned "against the acquisition of unwarranted influence, whether sought or unsought, by the military-industrial complex."

Eisenhower was right, and the military-industrial complex became the military-industrial-congressional complex. The development of new weapons systems that were manufactured in numerous congressional districts and states ensured that a majority in Congress and the Senate would supply their votes for ever-increasing defense budgets. Military research and development became pork barrel projects with lives of their own, regardless if more aircraft carriers or fighter jets made the nation safer. That was especially true during American hegemony in the nineties—and the emerging Age of Terrorism.

As for the new world order, the president forgot the term by the end of the year while he prepared for the 1992 election. His administration never developed the slogan into a coherent policy or a global strategy. Instead, Bush returned to his old world order idea and what most of his countrymen believed since World War II: "There is no substitute for American leadership."[3]

I

Bush, Clinton, Perot, and the Crumbling Center

After the Desert Storm victory President George H. W. Bush was the most popular man in America. Polls gave him an approval rate of a remarkable 90 percent. Pundits declared that he would be unbeatable in the 1992 election, and his vice president, Dan Quayle, joked, "These days you probably have a better chance to see Elvis than you do a Democratic presidential candidate."

The ending of the Gulf War also was popular. The United Nations imposed sanctions on Iraq. That nation could not build chemical or biological weapons, possess a missile with a range over ninety miles, and US and British air forces could establish a "no fly zone" from above to monitor Iraq.

At the same time President Bush launched Operation Tin Cup, which aimed at getting the wealthier allies to share the United States' monetary burden of liberating Kuwait. Because the large majority of troops and equipment involved were American, taxpayers had a liability of more than $70 billion. The president got on the phone. Saudi Arabia agreed to pay almost 30 percent of the cost, Kuwait 25, Germany about 15, Japan 10 percent. Bush's brilliant Operation Tin Cup meant that American taxpayers paid only about 12 percent, about $7 billion.

American pride soared. "In the eyes of the world," declared the president, "the U.S. stood tall." Columnist Ben Wattenberg boasted,

"This may be the beginning of the second American Century. We are the most influential nation in history: We've beaten the totalitarians of the right, then the left, and now the bandits."

Meanwhile, the administration in 1990 signed some legislation that had a significant impact on America.

On a hot July day on the South Lawn of the White House more than two thousand advocates for the disabled, many in wheelchairs, cheered as Bush signed a law that helped over forty million handicapped people move into the mainstream—the Americans with Disabilities Act, what the *New York Times* editorialized as the "most sweeping anti-discrimination measure since the Civil Rights Act of 1964."

The president's rhetoric rose to the occasion. He thanked all those who worked so hard to pass the bill and declared that a major sponsor and wounded World War II veteran, Senator Bob Dole, "has inspired me. . . . This historic act is the world's first comprehensive declaration of equality for people with disabilities—the first," making America "the international leader on this human rights issue."

As a symbol of freedom, Bush continued, the law was no less than a "declaration of independence," and it eventually changed the lives of the disabled. Studies had demonstrated that only about 25 percent of disabled men and 13 percent of those women held full-time jobs, meaning that they earned only about two-thirds of other employees. The law banned discrimination in employment in businesses with more than fifteen employees. It prohibited discrimination against them in public life, including schools, transportation, and all places open to the public, and that resulted in special parking areas at businesses, ramps, and special automated doors at public and many private buildings. The ADA also mandated that eventually telephone companies had to provide special equipment that would enable people with impaired speech or hearing to communicate with others using ordinary phones. As a measure of bipartisan approval, only eight senators voted against the ADA. Like the dismantling of the Berlin Wall, Bush declared, it opens "a once-closed door to a bright new era."

During autumn 1990 the Bush administration was very concerned with the collapse of the Soviet Union, the velvet revolutions, and Saddam's invasion of Kuwait. Nevertheless, Bush signed the first major environmental legislation in twenty years—the 1990 Amendment to the 1970 Clean Air Act.

Concern about the environment had been mounting throughout the previous years. In 1988 the nation witnessed one of the hottest summers on record, and scores of wildfires erupted, including the largest one ever at Yellowstone National Park. Some nine thousand firefighters, added by four thousand military personnel, fought the blaze, and for the first time in history the park was closed to visitors. Almost a third of the park was burned, 800,000 acres, and only autumn rains subdued the environmental disaster. In June, climatologist Dr. James Hansen of NASA appeared before a Senate committee chaired by Democratic senator Al Gore. Hansen had been measuring the climate for years and announced that four of the warmest years on record all were in the 1980s. He declared "with 99 percent confidence" that humankind was "changing our climate now. . . . It is time to stop waffling . . . and say that the evidence in pretty strong that the greenhouse effect is here." Hansen continued that there was a clear relationship between man-made greenhouse CO_2, volatile weather, and global warming.

Hansen's remarks provoked more interest in climate change. *Time* published a cover story in 1989, "Planet of the Year: Endangered Earth," and that same year freelance writer Bill McKibben wrote what many consider the first book on global warming, *The End of Nature*. He argued that human behavior already had caused irrevocable alterations and that mankind was decades late to stop global warming, acid rain, and depletion of the ozone layer. In the past, he claimed, humans could spoil parts of nature, but the larger systems of sunlight, temperature, and rainfall remained and protected the planet; now human activity had changed the environment. It was past time to act, he argued, to get off fossil fuels, cut greenhouse gases, curb global warming, and create a sustainable future. He sounded a clarion call: "If the waves crash up against the beach, eroding dunes and destroying homes, it is not the awesome power of Mother Nature. It is the awesome power of Mother Nature as altered by the awesome power of man."

The End of Nature stimulated a tsunami of comments, and by the end of the nineties it had been translated into more than twenty languages; the book gave also additional ammunition to ecologically minded politicians such as Senator Gore. The Tennessean grew up on a farm, and his mother had him read Rachel Carson's *Silent Spring*, with its warnings about the pesticide DDT. In Vietnam the young soldier witnessed the herbicide Agent Orange, which made the jungle look like the "surface of the moon." As a young congressman he grew increasingly concerned about the chemical revolution, the massive production of herbicides, pesticides, fungicides, and chlorofluorocarbons (CFCs) that came "streaming out of laboratories and chemical plants." He organized the first congressional hearings on toxic waste, focusing on Love Canal in upstate New York, which had become synonymous with chemical pollution. At those hearings he invited a renowned scientist, Professor Roger Revelle, who had measured CO_2 concentrations in the atmosphere for three decades. He testified that higher levels of carbon dioxide would create a greenhouse effect, which would bring about "a profound and disruptive change in the entire global climate."

Thus, there was growing concern about protecting the environment and the ozone layer. "The infamous ozone 'hole' that opens each winter over Antarctica is now threatening to open over . . . a sizeable portion of North America," wrote Gore, "exposing densely populated areas for the first time to significantly increased doses of dangerous ultraviolet radiation," a major cause of skin cancer. The scientific community confirmed that the expanding ozone hole was caused by CFCs, chemicals of chlorine, fluorine, and carbon commonly used in goods such as refrigerators, air conditioners, hair spray, and aerosol cans.

Diplomats and environmentalists at the United Nations also grew concerned, and they enacted the Montreal Protocol, which was an international treaty aimed at phasing out the production of CFCs. It went into force in 1989 and since has undergone numerous revisions. Eventually, every member nation ratified the protocol, making it the first universally ratified treaty in United Nations history and prompting UN Secretary-General Kofi Annan to label it "the single most successful international agreement to date."

Back in Washington, DC, some senators were more interested in the changing environment during 1990, and a half dozen of them created the first Interparliamentary Conference on the Global Environment. Legislators from forty-two countries came to the nation's capital and called for a "global Marshall Plan" in which industrial nations would help less developed countries grow economically while protecting the environment. Delegates agreed on broad actions to meet worldwide threats, and representatives agreed on lowering carbon dioxide from the burning of fossil fuels, reducing methane from agriculture, and eliminating emissions of CFCs. The conference also called for the creation of a "green common market" that would permit trade in technology to help achieve sustainable development free of market barriers, proposed "a bank for sustainable development" to help finance growth in the developing countries, and put forward international protection of the world's forests. Senator Gore declared at the end of the conference that it represented "a sea change in the attitude of parliamentarians around the world about what is possible to do to save the environment," and a Pakistani delegate declared, "I am going away with a global vision." In the twentieth century, she continued, world issues are "democracy and security," but in the twenty-first century they will be "the environment and sustainable development."

President Bush signed the 1990 Amendment to the 1970 Clean Air Act with the goal of restoring the ozone layer, cutting acid rain pollutants by half, and sharply reducing urban smog and eliminating most of the toxic chemical emissions from industrial plants by the end of the nineties. The amendment was very popular, passing the House

401–21 and the Senate 89–11. When Bush signed the bill, he boasted that the act was "simply the most significant air pollution legislation in our nation's history."

Environmentalists agreed. The Sierra Club president described the law as "a breath of fresh air after a 10-year smog alert."

That autumn President Bush also signed other important legislation, including the Clery Act. In 1986 Jeanne Clery was a student at Lehigh University. She was in the dorm when a fellow male student raped and murdered her. The backlash against this tragedy resulted in an investigation that found that in the previous three years there had been thirty-eight violent crimes at Lehigh. As was standard then, Lehigh—and virtually all other universities—did not report them or anything negative about their institution. Jeanne's parents sued Lehigh, stating that its policies were based "on the premise that the reputation of the school is more important than the safety of any individual."

At the same time the term "date rape" was becoming common. *Ms.* magazine popularized it in 1982 and in 1985 published psychology professor Mary Koss's findings titled "Date Rape: The Story of an Epidemic and Those Who Deny It." Koss conducted a three-year study surveying more than seven thousand students at thirty-five colleges and released her landmark study on sexual assault. She reported that one in four female students had been the victim of an attempted or completed rape; later studies found one in five. The exact percentage would never be known, of course, but the number stimulated much campus and national attention. "Date rape is one crime that colleges are finding too hot to handle," declared *Time* in 1991, "but impossible to ignore."

Jeanne's parents claimed that they never would have sent their daughter to Lehigh if they had known the campus was dangerous. Congress acted, passing the Jeanne Clery Disclosure of Campus Security Policy and Campus Crime Statistics Act, which the president signed into law. The Clery Act meant that colleges that participated in federal financial aid programs, basically all of them, had to report annual security and crime statistics as well as publish information about sexual assaults, policies, and programs.

President Bush also signed a lesser known but also significant law in November 1990, the EB-5 or "Golden Visa." This stated that up to 10,000 foreigners each year could get green cards in the United States if they brought into the country $1 million to invest and put citizens to work in "new commercial enterprises." Their visa could turn into permanent resident status in two years if their investment created ten jobs. Other Western nations had similar programs to inject foreign funds into their economies, often supported by their developers, but critics called the scheme paying for residency, and since then it has been modified many times.

At the same time the Bush administration was negotiating the North American Free Trade Agreement. The aim of NAFTA was to eliminate barriers to trade and investment between the United States, Canada, and Mexico. The *New York Times* was wary of the agreement but noted that it would test America's "longstanding commitment to open trade—the primary locomotive of world growth for a half-century." Eventually, NAFTA became one of the most significant trade agreements in American history.[1]

As stated, President Bush's approval ratings in spring 1991 were in the stratosphere. There was only one way to go—down—and that began months after US troops returned home. Domestic problems mounted.

By autumn 1991 the economy sputtered, stalled, and skidded into the deepest recession since 1982. Corporations invented a new word, "downsizing," which meant cutting jobs. General Motors lost a record $4.5 billion in 1991, closed more than twenty plants, and laid off about 75,000. Ford reported its largest loss ever, $2.3 billion, and for the first time IBM lost money, some $560 million. AT&T cut 100,000 employees, but it was worse for Pan Am and Eastern Airlines. Pan Am, which had pioneered the airline industry and had been in business for

almost sixty-five years, declared bankruptcy, as did Eastern, both toss-
ing almost 50,000 out of work. Some 4.5 million Americans lost their
jobs, so by June 1992, four months before the election, the unemployment rate was edging up toward 8 percent, the highest since the 1982
recession, when Reagan's approval rate cratered at 35 percent.

"If America's economic landscape seems suddenly alien and hostile to many citizens," wrote *Time* just six weeks before the election,
"there is good reason: they have never seen anything like it. Nothing in
memory has prepared consumers for such turbulent, epochal change,
the sort of upheaval that happens once in 50 years." The magazine
noted polls demonstrated that voters had "ragged emotional edges,
so much fear and misgiving" about the future of the nation's "almost
comatose" economy. "The current slump already ranks as the longest
period of sustained weakness since the Great Depression."

There were a number of causes for the recession. Desert Storm
had disrupted oil supplies, which momentarily increased prices at the
pump. Restrictive monetary policies increased the Federal Reserve
interest rates in four years from about 6 to 10 percent, slowing investment. Moreover, Bush inherited Reagan's economic policies,
"supply-side," which promised that the federal government could cut
taxes and increase spending and balance the budget. During the 1980
primary campaign candidate Bush had correctly labeled it "voodoo
economics." In addition, Reagan had signed a law deregulating the
savings and loans companies, and that resulted in catastrophe as Bush
moved into the Oval Office. As often happens in an unregulated
economy, hucksters ran wild and created mayhem, giving out billions
of dollars in bad loans from the savings and loans companies, which
were guaranteed by US taxpayers. Some 350 S&Ls were going bank-
rupt and closing their doors, and the new administration not only
had to sign legislation reimposing regulations but also had to pay the
bailout price: $130 billion. That alone increased the annual deficit by
another $50 billion. Thus, the deficit was out of control, the highest
up to that time. Bush was paying for Reaganomics.

During the 1988 presidential campaign candidate Bush had declared, "Read My Lips. No New Taxes." But Bush was an Old School

Republican, a fiscal conservative. Like Nixon, Eisenhower, and pre-vious Republicans, he knew that the only way to balance the budget was to either cut spending, raise taxes, or both, and so in November 1990 he signed a bipartisan but mostly Democratic Omnibus Budget Reconciliation Act that increased the federal gas tax and the top in-come tax rate on the wealthiest payers from 28 to over 31 percent. The Republican supply-siders went berserk, and the *New York Post* attacked with a front-page blast: "Read My Lips. I Lied!"

Signing the small tax hike was the responsible thing to do, but since Reagan, when the federal debt increased 250 percent, most Republicans have supported Reaganomics, declaring that "tax cuts will pay for themselves." In fact, not one Republican president has balanced the budget since Eisenhower. The Democrats have under Truman, Johnson, and, as we will see, Clinton. One of Reagan's leg-acies was that Republicans abandoned federal fiscal responsibility to the Democrats. After Bush signed the tax bill, many Republicans were fuming, losing confidence in their president. In a political sense, Bush had signed his death warrant.

Besides the recession, there was another issue dividing the elect-orate. In July 1991 President Bush surprised the nation by nominating Clarence Thomas to the US Supreme Court. Thomas was an African American from Georgia who had grown up in poverty and obtained a law degree from Yale University. "Judge Thomas's life is a model for all Americans," declared the president. "He's the best man for the job."

That statement sent lots of Americans looking for facts on the ob-scure Thomas, including the first African American to sit on the Court, Thurgood Marshall, who declared he'd never heard of the nominee. Marshall, nominated by Lyndon Johnson in 1968, was gravely ill, had to retire, and was a famous civil rights lawyer who argued *Brown v. Board of Education*, before LBJ nominated the liberal icon to the court. Thomas, in contrast, had never been a judge until 1990 when Bush appointed him, instead of hundreds of experienced federal judges, to the prestigious Court of Appeals for the District of Columbia. Then only sixteen months later, Bush nominated the forty-three-year-old judge to the highest court in the land. Thomas was a conservative who President Reagan had appointed to lead the Equal Employment Opportunity Commission. At the EEOC he had done little to increase employment opportunities for African Americans and had publicly opposed affirmative action programs. Critics pointed out that it was Yale University's affirmative action plan that had admitted him into that Ivy League law school.

The nomination, thus, raised serious questions about Thomas's qualifications. The Democratic Senate Judicial Committee held hearings, liberal groups pushed back, and Thomas stumbled. When asked what Supreme Court cases Thomas thought were most significant, the candidate said he couldn't recall "off the top of my head," and when asked about his opinion of abortion versus a woman's right to choose, he changed the topic and talked about himself. Thomas's stonewalling about his judicial beliefs on controversial legal issues, unfortunately, would become much more the norm for future nominees for a lifetime position on the highest court in the land.

The Democrats had a majority on the committee, 8 to 6, so Chairman Joe Biden had the votes to stop the nomination, but the Democrats didn't want to look racist. The senator from Delaware sent it out for a vote in the entire Senate.

Then, during more hearings, the nation was shocked—by Anita Hill. The African American attorney was working for a law firm in Washington, DC, when Thomas asked her to join the law team at the EEOC. Although they were political opposites, she accepted the job. According to her measured and calm testimony, the EEOC chief had asked her out on numerous dates, had tried to talk to her on many occasions about large breasts and pornographic movies. He "referred to the size of his own penis as being larger than normal." His favorite male porno star, he told her, was a guy nicknamed Long Dong Silver.

Before 1981 Supreme Court nominations were not televised, but Hill's statements attracted an enormous audience of some twenty-seven million. People who probably paid little attention to the judicial system, to federal nominations, now tuned in and watched the show unfold. And because of the sexual nature of the allegations, both ABC and NBC televised the October 11 testimonies live in living color.

Hill declared that Thomas's statements were threatening and an invitation for sex and sexual harassment. Citizens remembered a similar incident only nine months earlier—the December 1990 date rape trail of William Kennedy Smith. A nephew of Democratic senator Ted Kennedy, and a thirty-year-old medical school student, Willie Smith, relatives, and friends went out to a bar in Palm Beach, Florida. There he met a woman, who accompanied him back to the Kennedy estate. According to her testimony, they took a walk on the beach at about 3 a.m., and Smith tackled and raped her. During the trial he took the stand and said that the sex was consensual. The female judge refused to allow three other witnesses who claimed that Smith also had assaulted them in the previous few years. The jury went to deliberate.

As a member of one of America's most famous families, Willie Smith became the subject of public scrutiny. Millions of viewers watched the nationally televised event, and reporters from around the globe converged on the courthouse. Just seventy-seven minutes after the jury began deliberating, they delivered the verdict for Smith: not guilty.

"The verdict," wrote journalist Dominick Dunne, "was a disappointment to some, a cause for delirium to others, but a surprise to no one." The nation was mesmerized by the famous family that had dominated the media for decades, and the male accused always was more important than the female accuser. Numerous Kennedys attended the trial, waving to fans, smiling for the cameras, stating over and again, "We're a close-knit family." The woman's face was obscured during the trial, and she was to viewers a nonentity, especially in contrast to Kennedy men. When Dunne asked a family friend what the Kennedys would do to Smith for causing this consternation, she responded, "They'll stick by Willie through thick and thin, but when this is over, and they're alone, they'll beat the shit out of him."

Just nine months later, in the Senate Judiciary Committee, Clarence Thomas was on trial, and on the hot seat. After Anita Hill's testimony senators began to declare that they were going to vote against Thomas, and his nomination was in grave danger. Hill took a polygraph test; Thomas refused to take one. Shortly thereafter, the nominee appeared in front of the Judicial Committee. Once divorced, he had remarried a white woman, and Ginni Thomas sat behind him as the cameras rolled.

"Absolutely nothing," he declared, his voice raising, had happened between him and Hill. He flatly denied all charges, and then called the hearings "a high-tech lynching." It "is a message that unless you kowtow to the older order, this will happen to you. You will be lynched, destroyed, caricatured, by a committee of the U.S. Senate rather than hung from a tree." So, the white senators were hanging this Black judge? No—Thomas delivered one of the most remarkable non-sequiturs in modern history. He was being lynched by a Black woman.

Thomas's nomination was in trouble. Many senators had begun to review their vote when Republican senator Orrin Hatch from Utah came to the rescue. While senators yelled at each other from the Senate floor, Hatch criticized the broad nature of harassment laws, declared that Hill wanted to make money writing a book or making a movie, that she was the "Rosa Parks of sexual harassment." Another Republican male senator pestered the witness: "How reliable is your testimony?" Asked another: "Are you a scorned woman?," and a journalist for the conservative *American Spectator* mocked Hill as "a bit nutty and a bit slutty." The circus continued, and the president joined the fray and stood by his man: "This decent and honorable man has been smeared."

Not so fast. Referring to the all-white male Senate Judicial Committee, Democratic representative Nancy Pelosi declared, "They are men, they can't possibly know what it's like to receive verbal harassment, harassment that is fleeting to the man and lasting and demeaning to the woman."

"Sex, Lies, and Politics," blared *Time*'s cover. "America's Watershed Debate on Sexual Harassment." *Newsweek*'s cover proclaimed: "Sexual Harassment. Why Women Are So Angry."

Time to vote. The nation was divided. What was sexual harassment? Who was telling the truth? Millions were considering those questions when the senators cast their ballots. Ten Democrats joined forty-two Republicans confirming Thomas by the narrowest of margins, 52 to 48, the closest vote on a justice in the century.

The nomination and hearings hurt the Bush administration. Many conservatives felt the president should have withdrawn the candidate after Hill's charges that questioned his moral behavior. African Americans didn't back this judge who did not support affirmative action. Many women felt Bush was insensitive to the new publicized issue of sexual harassment.

The Anita Hill episode, along with the Kennedy date rape trail, publicized male behavior toward vulnerable women. The female response dispelled the myth that most rapes were conducted by strangers on their victims; instead they proclaimed that the vast majority of women knew their attackers and did not consent to sexual activity. And they reacted legally. After Thomas had been confirmed, Congress passed and the president signed the Civil Rights Act of 1991, which strengthened Title VII of the 1964 act; it allowed women to collect damages for sexual harassment or discrimination. Women began to file boatloads of legal suits. There had been fewer than 7,000 suits claiming sexual harassment by 1991, but by 1998 there were 15,500 a year—some sixty new cases every working day.

The Senate hearings also had an impact on some feminists. The first wave of feminism was after the 1848 Seneca Falls conference, the second was in the late 1960s and 1970s when women marched to end discrimination and obtain equality. The "fight is far from over," wrote the twenty-two-year-old African American writer and activist Rebecca Walker. She found the televised Senate hearings "too painful" to watch. After all, Thomas was promoted to a lifetime position on the Supreme Court, where he would rule on women's rights. Hill was "repudiated. Men were assured of the inviolability of their penis/power. Women were admonished to keep their experiences to themselves." Walker continued to all women and especially those of her GenX cohort:

Let this dismissal of a woman's experience move you to anger. Turn that outrage into political power. Do not vote for them unless they work for us. Do not have sex with them, do not break bread with them, do not nurture them if they don't prioritize our freedom to control our bodies and our lives. I am not a postfeminism feminist. I am the Third Wave.

The Third Wave would be difficult to define in the nineties, but one central idea was "intersectional," that women and especially African Americans experienced "layers of oppression" caused by gender, race, class, and sexual orientation. These ideas would percolate in various forms, and in pop culture they were occasionally heard in music by Cyndi Lauper, Madonna, and Destiny's Child, or might be written about in the new feminist magazine *Bitch*. In the long run Anita Hill stimulated American women to fight back harder, and in that sense, she planted the seed that later would bloom into the "Me Too" movement.[2]

Right after Clarence Thomas took his seat on the Court, the justices in April 1992 heard arguments for and against an important case, *Planned Parenthood v. Casey*. In anticipation of that case some 500,000 mostly women streamed down Washington's main streets for the March for Women's Lives. Being an election year there were scores of candidates, but the speakers were all women who urged the crowd to organize and get out the pro-choice vote, including California Senate candidate Dianne Feinstein, NOW president Patricia Ireland, author Gloria Steinem, actress Jane Fonda, and former New York representative Bella Abzug, adorned with her trademark straw hat. The demonstrators carried signs—"We Won't Go Back," "I Have a Uterus and I Vote"—and one woman marched with two infants in a stroller bearing a sign, "In Vitro Babies for Choice."

In June the Court decided *Casey*. The justices voted 5 to 4 to uphold the right to have an abortion as established in 1973 by *Roe v. Wade*. During the two decades after *Roe* many states had passed laws restricting the procedure, raising the question of what constraints were and were not Constitutional. In *Casey*, the Court affirmed what it called the central holding of *Roe*, that states could not prohibit abortions before fetal viability, the point when a fetus could survive outside the womb, about twenty-three weeks. The majority wrote "a state may not prohibit any woman from making the ultimate decision to terminate her pregnancy before viability."

During this debate over abortion and sexual harassment, and during the economic recession in March 1991, Rodney King and two other African American men were driving through Los Angeles. Police attempted to initiate a traffic stop, and King started a chase with speeds over 110 mph until the officers pulled over the car. King got out, and four policemen arrested the two passengers. The police tasered King, tackled him, and while he was down kicked him seven times and hit him fifty-five times with their nightsticks. "Oh, my God, they're beating him to death!" a horrified woman cried from her balcony—while another resident took out his camcorder and videotaped all twelve minutes of the brutality. The resident gave the video to the television station, and it went viral.

Thirteen days later, as the Black community was digesting King's brutal beating, another cruelty toward an African American appeared, this time in South Central Los Angeles. On a Saturday morning fifteen-year-old Latasha Harlins entered a Korean-owned market, walked over to a refrigerator, took out a bottle of orange juice, and put it in her backpack. She approached the counter with two dollars in her hand. Behind the counter was the owner's wife, Soon Ja Du, who did not see the cash in Latasha's hand and who accused the girl of stealing a $1.79 bottle of OJ. A scuffle ensued. According to two young witnesses, and a security camera, Du grabbed Latasha's backpack; she swung and hit Du twice. The OJ fell to the floor, and Latasha picked it up, gave it Du, and turned to walk out of the store. Du reached under the counter, pulled out a handgun, and fired, shooting Latasha in the back of the head, killing her instantly.

Horrified, the two other kids ran out of the store, and shortly thereafter police arrived and arrested Du, charging her with manslaughter. Tension between African Americans and Koreans in South Central always had been high but grew exponentially as they awaited the trial that began that November. Du pleaded self-defense, but the witnesses and security camera convinced the jury that Latasha was walking away from the confrontation; they found Du guilty of voluntary manslaughter. The white female judge could have sentenced Du to up to sixteen years, but instead sentenced the Korean only to probation, community service, and a $500 fine.

The light sentence outraged South Central African Americans. Blacks started a slogan, "No Justice, No Peace," and they continued chanting during the Rodney King trial—and after. The four police officers who beat King were charged with assault and use of excessive force, and after a year of preparation the trial commenced in April 1992. The judge allowed the trial to be moved to a white suburb, Simi Valley, and the jury was composed of ten whites, one Latina, and one Asian American. No Blacks.

The jury acquitted the officers, and within half an hour angry Blacks were taking to the streets. Los Angeles African American mayor Tom Bradley held a quick press conference and declared, "We will not tolerate the savage beating of our citizens by a few renegade cops." President Bush told reporters, "It's sickening to see the beating that was rendered. There's no way in my view to explain it away. It was outrageous." The mayor called for calm, but it was too late.

South Central exploded. Television viewers witnessed violent scenes. African Americans rushed into Koreatown and began stealing and beating Asian businessmen, who armed themselves, often shooting wildly to defend their properties. Two-thirds of attacks were against Korean businesses, and the store in which Latasha was shot was burned to the ground. Looters rushed into stores, carried out bags of groceries, cases of beer, televisions and boom boxes, Air Jordan shoes. Overhead, one of the most graphic sights was filmed by a TV news helicopter. Reginald Denny, a white truck driver who stopped at a traffic light, was dragged from his semitrailer by a mob of Blacks and beaten savagely with a tire iron and a brick. Fortunately, four African American strangers emerged from the crowd, got Denny back in the truck, and drove him to a local hospital, saving his life.

The mayor declared a state of emergency, set curfews, and the governor sent in 10,000 Army National Guard personnel. South Central employers told workers to stay home, mail delivery was halted, and schools were closed. Bush addressed the country, denouncing "random terror and lawlessness" and declaring the "urgent need to restore order." He continued that the "brutality of a mob" would not be tolerated, and he would "use whatever force is necessary." In the first time since the urban riots of the 1960s, a president invoked the Insurrection Act of 1807 that empowered him to deploy military troops within the United States in emergencies such as civil disorder, insurrection, and rebellion. Soon, the US Marines patrolled in combat vehicles.

Days later Rodney King, the topic of the "most endlessly replayed videotape ever made," appeared on television, hesitant, almost sobbing. "Stop making it horrible," King begged the rioters. Almost dazed by the violence, he mumbled, "just not right . . . just not right," and addressed race relations: "Can we all get along?"

The South Central Riot, 1992, the most destructive in US history. AP Photo/ Reed Saxon.

After six days the riots came to an end. Criticism mounted, and the Police Commission held an investigation: fifty-four people died and nearly $1 billion of property was damaged or destroyed. Rioters destroyed at least 3,800 buildings and vandalized, looted, and burned another 10,000. It was the largest—and worst—riot in American history.

South Central also was significant. After the urban riots of the mid-1960s few thought that such resentment was still simmering in African American lower-income communities. But this was a stand against the white power structure, white policemen, white juries. To local African Americans, it was a conspiracy; they could get no justice during the Reagan–Bush era. Nor equality, for Blacks had higher unemployment and poverty, poorer schools, and more drugs in their neighborhoods. Yet it was no accident, *Time* wrote, "that nearly all the great ghetto riots since the 1960s have been triggered by some incident involving arrested blacks and white cops. To an extent that whites can barely even imagine—because it so rarely happens to them—police brutality to many blacks is an ever present threat to their bodies and lives."

Few things illustrated the extent to which whites and Blacks lived in different worlds than their reactions to police brutality. "Oh, my god!" African American congresswoman Maxine Waters exclaimed as she watched the police beat King on TV. Waters said the uprisings in her congressional district were a milestone in the history of Black people demanding justice. "Because of Rodney King's beating," local people were saying, "We're here. You can't do this to us. Look what you're doing." In a press conference the day after the acquittal, Waters continued, "There are some angry people in America and young black males in my district are feeling . . . if they could not get a conviction with the Rodney King video available to the jurors, that there can be no justice in America."

As the riots and trial smoldered in March 1992, Los Angeles rapper Ice-T and the heavy metal band Body Count released a self-titled album dedicating it to the "LAPD," including the song "Cop Killer." In the music video the singer puts on black gloves and a ski mask, turns off his headlights, and prepares for violence. "I'm a cop killer," he declares, "fuck police brutality!" The refrain is sung over and again, "Fuck the police," and the message is ominous, "tonight we get even!"

To de-escalate the unrest, the most popular civil rights leader of the era, the Reverend Jesse Jackson, arrived in South Central, walked blocks for hours, trying to bring African Americans, whites, and Koreans together, preaching tolerance and love. Along with him, Waters urged the Justice Department to file civil rights charges against the acquitted cops. Bill Clinton, Democratic presidential hopeful, appeared with Waters, and after Clinton became president, two of the policemen were convicted of violating Rodney King's civil rights and served short prison terms.[3]

In the wake of South Central the candidates stumped the nation for the 1992 presidential election. Republican Bush blamed the riots on the "failed liberal policies of the 1960s." Democrat Clinton responded that the rebellion resulted in part from "12 years of denial and neglect" of mounting social problems under two Republican presidents. "It's just amazing," rebutted Clinton. "Republicans have had the White House for 20 of the last 24 years, and they have to go all the way back to the 60s to find somebody to blame. I don't care who's to blame. I want to do something about the problems." Vice President Dan Quayle joined the fray, declaring that he was going to go after liberals and be the "pit bull terrier" of the campaign. Reporters rushed to Clinton and got his response: "Quayle's claim would strike terror into the heart of every fire hydrant in America."

The Republicans bashed the Democratic candidates. Bush referred to Democratic vice presential candidate Al Gore as "Ozone man," Clinton as a "draft dodger" during Vietnam, and as a "womanizer." Even the Arkansan admitted that he had caused "pain" in his marriage. And when the Republicans called Clinton a "pot smoker" during his college years, he responded tongue-in-cheek, "but I didn't inhale."

The pain in his marriage had been revealed earlier in the year— Gennifer Flowers. A woman with an enormous head of blond hair and wearing bright red lipstick, she had been a cabaret singer and an Arkansas state employee. She claimed in February 1992 during the New Hampshire primary that she had a twelve-year affair with Clinton. That quickly became front-page news and gave late-night talk show hosts ammunition. "Clinton is pretty kinky," said Jay Leno. "The other night he blindfolded Hillary, then tied her up, then he went out with another woman."

To stop the hemorrhaging, Bill and Hillary appeared on CBS's *60 Minutes*. With some fifty million tuned in, they saved the campaign, just barely, and soon thereafter he got the message back on the recession. Eventually six years later, in 1998, Clinton admitted to having sex "one time" in 1977 with Flowers, while over the years she had amassed a half million dollars on TV talk shows and with magazine interviews. *Penthouse* cover, "GENNIFER FLOWERS, TELLS ALL, SHOWS ALL."

Flowers wilted from the scene, but the Clintons had more problems than just Bill's womanizing. They had a land deal in the headlines—Whitewater.

Bill and Hillary Clinton had joined Arkansas businesspeople Jim and Susan McDougal in 1978 and purchased 230 acres of land on the scenic White River. The intent was to develop the riverside property, sell land or homes, and make some money for their newly established Whitewater Development Corporation. But the economy of the late 1970s got in the way, with inflation and very high interest rates, and the company fell on hard times. Everyone lost money.

A decade later, during the presidential campaign in early March 1992, the *New York Times* published an article that the former governor and his wife had invested and lost money on their Whitewater scheme. In the meantime, Madison Guaranty Savings and Loan, also owned by the McDougals, collapsed during the savings and loan scandal. Madison Guaranty was one of numerous S&Ls that shut down, and it cost the taxpayers about $60 million. An attorney for the S&L was Hillary Clinton.

During the media frenzy of a presidential campaign, politicos and journalists made all kinds of statements, accusations, charges, and countercharges: there was some link between the Clintons and the McDougals (which they both admitted); the Clintons made money from Whitewater (they actually lost); Hillary had worked for Madison Guaranty S&L (which she admitted).

Eventually, none of that mattered during the campaign. Clinton's character was not a critical issue because the nation had moved on. In 1960 Americans elected their first Catholic to the Oval Office; the media had made John Kennedy's religion an issue, quoting talking heads, "He'll take orders from the pope!" Other so-called barriers to the presidency had fallen. In 1976 citizens elected the first "born again Christian," Carter, and in 1980 the first previously divorced man, Reagan.

What doomed Bush? "The Economy, stupid" was a sign hanging at Clinton's Democratic campaign headquarters. The GDP declined in 1991, the first since 1982, and unemployment mounted up and stayed high before the November election. The president's approval rate sank with the economy, down to just 29 percent in July. Vice President Quayle also hurt the ticket, with his culture war attacks and numerous verbal gaffes. "I found him dumber than advertised," quipped Texas humorist Molly Ivins. "If you put that man's brain in a bumblebee, it would fly backwards." Quayle had become the most unpopular VP in modern history. Political critics and pundits complained that the Bush administration had become "a ship without a rudder," and two men stepped forward to take the helm—Democratic nominee Bill Clinton and independent billionaire H. Ross Perot.

William Jefferson Clinton would become the nation's first baby boomer president. Born in 1946 in Arkansas, he was from a humble background and was raised by his mother. Clinton worked hard, got into Georgetown University, and became a staffer for Democratic senator J. William Fulbright. He avoided the Vietnam War partly by being out of the country where he couldn't be drafted; he attended Oxford University in England as a Rhodes scholar. He returned and went to Yale Law School, where he met his future wife, Hillary Rodham. Clinton took her back to Arkansas where he quickly got involved in politics, was elected attorney general and then in 1978 was elected governor—age thirty-three.

The election of Ronald Reagan and especially the overwhelming reelection in 1984 had an impact on Clinton. He and other young Democrats such as Al Gore realized that their party would have to move away from the liberal policies of the 1960s and toward more moderate and nonideological positions. They began to think that their party would be doomed unless it changed its focus from the left to the middle and made a strenuous effort to woo white voters back to the party. In 1985 Clinton was one of the founders of the Democratic Leadership Council, a group of centrists, and the DLC began advocating welfare reform, a tougher stance on crime, smaller government, a middle-class tax cut, and a strong defense. Clinton embraced those themes and began presenting himself as a "New Democrat," picking Gore as his running mate in his march to the White House.

During the campaign Clinton avoided speaking on issues that would divide potential white and Black voters, such as affirmative action. But when pressed, the New Democrat opposed "racial quotas," called for more "personal responsibility," and proposed a "two years and out" welfare plan, which countered attempts to label the Democrats the party of "handouts for minorities." Giving a speech to Jesse Jackson's Rainbow Coalition the candidate condemned rap singer Sister Souljah for her remark, "If black people kill black people every day, why not have a week and kill white people?" And the Democrat criticized rapper Ice-T's recording of the song "Cop Killer." He would be tough on Black and white criminals, and he declared his support for capital punishment, which resulted in a feud with Jackson but cheers from blue-collar whites. "The day he told off that fucking Jackson," said one white worker, "is the day he got my vote."

Bush tried to appear as the commander-in-chief who had won the Cold War and the Gulf War while the conservatives hammered away at Clinton's so-called character flaws—philandering and avoiding military service during the Vietnam War. At the Republican convention, conservative pundit Patrick Buchanan delivered his "Culture War" speech, blasting Clinton's wife: "Hillary believes that 12-year-olds should have the right to sue their parents, and Hillary has compared marriage and the family as institutions to slavery and life on an Indian reservation." The Democratic ticket was the "most pro-lesbian and pro-gay ticket in history."We're at war with the liberals, he concluded, we "must take back our cities, and take back our culture, and take back our country." After hearing Buchanan, Molly Ivins quipped that the speech "probably sounded better in the original German."

Most voters were not concerned about a culture war or Clinton's character, but they were alarmed about the hapless economy. Giving Bush four more years to run the economy, Clinton quipped, would be "like hiring General Sherman for fire commissioner in Georgia."

Boyish Clinton jogged on the campaign trial. He appealed to masses, especially the youth, by appearing on popular talk shows, especially late night. He appeared on ninety-six of them, even MTV. Future candidates learned and employed new technology; Obama used the internet and YouTube, and Trump would become the Tweeter-in-Chief. Clinton even played the saxophone on the *Arsenio Hall Show*, after which the host declared, "Great to see that a Democrat can blow something besides an election!"

While Clinton and Bush traded jabs the campaign suddenly got interesting—H. Ross Perot. After attending the US Naval Academy and serving as an officer, he became a promoter of relatively new computer systems in the 1960s. He soon owned his own company, Electronic Data Systems in Dallas, and made large profits helping states set up their first computer systems and programs for the new Medicare and Medicaid. He took the company public in 1968 and was worth millions on paper before he sold it to General Motors for $2.5 billion, making him a billionaire when they were rare.

The "Man from Texarkana" was pugnacious. Standing tall at 5 feet 5 inches, weighing in at 140, Perot spoke in an East Texas twang and continually barked out orders. Molly Ivins labeled him "Chihuahua" while talk show host Rush Limbaugh labeled him a "hand grenade with a bad haircut."

Perot's campaign demonstrated that many former Reagan supporters were disillusioned with Bush. Perot announced his candidacy
in February 1992 and volunteers went to work, especially after he
declared that he would not accept campaign donations over $5 and
that he would fund most of his own campaign. The billionaire spent
$400,000 in the first month, and by the end of spring his grassroots
campaigners had him on the ballots in all fifty states.

The independent needed a vice presidential candidate, of course,
and could find no popular Democrat or Republican, so in March he
picked retired Vice Admiral James Stockdale. The admiral had been a
Navy fighter pilot who had been a prisoner of war during Vietnam
and had been awarded the Medal of Honor. Yet he was no politician,
played little role in the campaign, and would be remembered for his
statement when he appeared in the vice presidential debates, "Who
am I? Why am I here?"

Few could answer, but it made little difference because the real
show was Perot. He appealed because he was fresh, direct, and spewed
out homespun quips. Like Reagan before him, he often attacked
Washington, DC: "If you see a snake, just kill it. Don't appoint a committee on snakes." The nation's capital, he declared, "has become a
town with sound bites, shell games, handlers, media stuntmen who
posture, create images, talk, shoot off Roman candles, but don't ever
accomplish anything. We need deeds, not words, in this city.

"What we have now is a system where if you have potholes in your
city, all the politicians hold conferences on potholes," Perot said. "If
and when I ever have to do this job, we're going to get hot asphalt,
get a shovel, fill potholes, move on to the next one and skip the press
conference.

"We've got a patient whose heart has stopped beating and has broken fingers and toes, and all the politicians want to talk about is the
fingers and toes," he said. "I want to go straight to the heart."

The *New York Times* saw the "potential for an explosive form of
political combustion" mixing "an angry, frustrated electorate" with
"Perot's iconoclastic, take-no-prisoners, personal and anti-politics

politics." It did; by June, polls had Perot at 36 percent, ahead of both Bush and Clinton.

That same month CBS News anchor Dan Rather asked the Man from Texarkana, "Can I quote you as saying, 'Read my lips: no new taxes'?" "No," Perot declared, "you can't ever quote me as saying anything that stupid."

Then in July Perot stumbled. His authoritarian style irritated his campaign workers. He wouldn't listen to political advisers, began sending out mixed messages, and his poll numbers slid. He fired his campaign director, Ed Rollins, who later wrote that the candidate was "the ultimate control freak," labeling it "The Campaign from Hell." Perot quickly and foolishly ended his campaign, which irritated many grassroots volunteers who had worked so hard for him. *Newsweek* placed him on their cover: "The Quitter."

Perot stayed out of the campaign for over two months while popular pressure mounted. On October 1 he announced he was re-entering the race. He had lost momentum but regained it by using a unique marketing strategy: he paid millions to buy half hour and hour-long infomercials on major television networks boosting his campaign. On October 6 he aired his first infomercial, which surprised commentators when more than sixteen million people watched him as he presented numerous charts explaining the budget deficit: "We got into trickle-down economics, and it didn't trickle."

He appealed to his frustrated supporters: "Our President blames Congress, Congress blames the President, the Democrats and Republicans blame each other. Nobody steps up to the plate and accepts responsibility for anything." A couple of days later he aired an ad campaign. One commercial, titled "Red Flag," displayed a waving red flag. "While the Cold War is ending another war is upon us. In this new war, the enemy is not the red flag of Communism, but the red ink of our national debt, the red tape of our government bureaucracy. The casualties of this war are counted in lost jobs and lost dreams."

Perot's polling numbers increased and qualified him for the presidential debates that month, the first ones with all three candidates on the stage. The billionaire continued hammering on his economic themes. Concerning NAFTA he declared that if the trade agreement was signed there would be a "giant sucking sound" of manufacturing jobs from America to Mexico. He mocked the "gridlock" in Washington. "It's not the Republicans' fault, of course, and it's not the Democrats' fault," he said. "Somewhere out there there's an extraterrestrial that's doing this to us." In concluding remarks Perot said he was the "results" guy, the "action" candidate, and if people want to "slow dancing and talk about" the deficit, and not do anything about it, "I'm not your man."

On election day, Perot wasn't their man, but he did have a respectable showing for a third-party candidate, winning about twenty million votes and almost 19 percent of the electorate. It was the strongest third-party showing since 1912, when former president Theodore Roosevelt ran as a Bull Moose Progressive. In the end it was "The Economy, stupid," as the American people searched for a way out of

Candidates Clinton, Perot, and Bush share a laugh at the end of their debate on October 19, 1992. Mark Cardwell/Reuters.

the recession and thought that it was time for new ideas from the first baby boomer presidential candidate. Perot helped Clinton, for his run secured defeat for George H. W. Bush. Studies estimated that about 70 percent of Perot's supporters came from people who had voted for Bush in 1988. Bush won only 39 percent—some ten million votes less than in his victorious election. Clinton won 43 percent of the vote but easily won the Electoral College votes, carrying prize states such as California, New York, Ohio, and Illinois. Importantly for him and for future Democrats, he split the South, winning Louisiana, Tennessee, Georgia, and Arkansas, and the Southwest, where he won New Mexico, Colorado, and Nevada. He won a surprising 57 percent of the women's vote and about 90 percent of African Americans, who gave him the edge in Illinois, Michigan, Ohio, and New Jersey. Clinton won almost the same percentage of the white vote as Bush, 39 to 40 percent. The Democrats also won majorities in the House and Senate. Thus, for the first time since the 1970s the Democrats were in power; now all they had to do was fix the economy. "My God," remarked Democratic senator Daniel Patrick Moynihan, "now it's our deficit."

Bill Clinton moved into the White House, walked into the Oval Office, and found on the presidential desk a letter.[4]

Dear Bill,
When I walked into this office just now I felt the same sense of wonder and respect that I felt four years ago. I know you will feel that, too.

I wish you great happiness here. . . .

There will be very tough times, made even more difficult by criticism you may not think is fair. I'm not a very good one to give advice; but just don't let the critics discourage you or push you off course.

You will be our President when you read this note. I wish you well. I wish your family well.

Your success now is our country's success. I am rooting hard for you.
Good luck —
George

Bush's gracious letter would be the exception, for the election of Bill Clinton demonstrated that the center of American life was crumbling. The Cold War was history and so citizens no longer feared and focused on communism and the Soviet Union, meaning they could turn inward to domestic issues, politics, and social and cultural matters. Concerning politics, Clinton broke a twelve-year Republican White House, which naturally made him the target of many conservatives. The youthful forty-six-year-old president himself would be the epitome of conservatives' wrath with his baby boomer values, self-assuredness, and support from youth, liberal intellectuals, and Hollywood. In the three-way race Perot's strong showing made a statement that the two parties were not representing some twenty million voters in the electorate. Furthermore, and as we shall see, the culture wars that had been festering since the 1960s returned with a vengeance in the 1990s over topics such as affirmative action, diversity, political correctness, the racial divide, and a new emphasis on issues such as sexual harassment. During the nineties a culture emerged that was even more steeped than usual in sex, money, fame, and sensationalism—Anything Goes America. It was broadcast on the talk shows, and by mid-decade on a new network and on the internet. That changed citizens' perceptions, promoted combative opinions, spread information and misinformation, and created conspiracies—all of which intensified division in the nation.

During the campaign Clinton contributed to the crumbling center by pledging to make his appointments more diverse than those of the two Republican administrations. His nominees would "look like America," which energized minorities and women but irritated many white men. And by Clinton's inaugural address it was clear that the era was becoming the age of diversity, sometimes called multiculturalism, which conservative critics charged was led by a movement they mockingly called "political correctness," or PC.

PC had been emerging in the late 1980s. No one knows exactly the origins of the term, but apparently politically correct in the 1960s and '70s was a "kind of in-joke among American leftists—something you called a fellow leftist when you thought he or she was being self-righteous." That changed by the end of the 1980s. Instead of being "a phrase that leftists used to check dogmatic tendencies," PC was hijacked by conservatives who used it as a talking point, declaring that it "constituted a leftwing political program" to seize control of "American universities and cultural institutions—and they were determined to stop it." In its best sense, being politically correct was using neutral descriptive references to avoid words and actions that offend certain groups of people. For example, some women might think that "fireman" is a sexist term and prefer the politically correct "firefighter."

PC caught fire in the early nineties. In 1992 Henry Beard and Christopher Cerf published *The Official Politically Correct Dictionary and Handbook*, which confused many because it mixed real PC terms with fictional ones, and the next year Comedy Central launched Bill Maher's talk show *Politically Incorrect*. The University of California, Berkeley, created an "American Cultures" requirement in which students studied the contributions of minority groups to American society. The University of Texas faculty voted to have freshmen no longer write essays on literary classics but rather on discrimination, affirmative action, and civil rights cases. Many professors praised the change for giving the curriculum more relevance to current concerns, while more conservative faculty saw the change as enforcing liberal academic orthodoxy. "You cannot tell me," said one professor, "that students will not be inevitably graded on politically correct thinking in these classes."

Conservatives coined political correctness as a label for a broad range of liberals who generally supported expanded rights for women, gays, and minorities, along with affirmative action, while abandoning Western classes and classics in favor of multicultural curriculums. "Would be Jacobins who stormed the barricades in 1968," wrote conservative Charles Sykes, became professors and "today hold earnest seminars on 'Empowering women with eating disorders through Fairy Tales and Dance Movement Therapy' and 'Feminism and Animal Liberation: Making the Connection.'"

At the academy, PC alarmed some traditionalists. Roger Kimball published *Tenured Radicals*, which went on the attack. As one reviewer noted, "This book will breed fistfights." English professor Allan Bloom published his broadside on PC classes, with the damning title *The Closing of the American Mind*. These faculty viewed PC as "a new kind of intolerance: a McCarthyism of the left."

PC on campus also was an appeal to curb racial slurs and hate speech. After a racial incident at Stanford in 1989, the university adopted a code prohibiting offensive speech. During the next two years a hundred colleges and universities followed suit, which critics complained often restricted freedom of speech and was leftist censorship. In 1990 and the next year, for example, Brown University expelled a student for shouting racial slurs, the City College of New York rebuked two professors for making comments about racial superiority, and the University of Connecticut ordered an Asian American student to move off campus after she put up a sign on her dorm door listing "people who are shot on sight": "preppies," "bimbos," "men without chest hair," and "homos."

"Thought Police," *Newsweek* headlined, "Watch What You Say." By 1991 the PC debate was so newsworthy that President Bush mentioned the topic during a commencement address at the University of Michigan, declaring that "political correctness has ignited controversy across the land. And although the movement arises from the laudable desire to sweep away the debris of racism and sexism and hatred, it replaces old prejudice with new ones. It declares certain topics off-limits. . . . Such bullying is outrageous."

The PC debate would continue for years and later would morph into "cancel" and then "woke" culture, as would the discourse about another vogue term of the early nineties: diversity. Like PC, diversity did not suddenly emerge and in various forms it was a very old concept. "There are not more than five primary colors, yet in combination they produce more hues than can ever been seen," wrote the ancient Chinese strategist Sun Tzu in *The Art of War*. "There are not more than five cardinal tastes, yet combinations of them yield more flavors than can ever be tasted."

The meaning of diversity, of course, continued to change in America. Before the civil rights movement diversity meant geography, religion, and class. Presidents might fill their cabinets with a wealthy Californian Protestant banker, a working-class New York Irish Catholic, a southern planter of English descent, or a midwestern manufacturer. Everyone knew a politician's religion, heritage, and background. On the NBC *Today Show* in the 1950s diversity meant three white male announcers—one with dark hair, one blond, and one redhead.

Because of civil rights and subsequent empowerment movements, during the 1970s corporate employers and college deans were calling for racial, gender, even ethnic diversity in their workforces and student bodies. Diversity continued to emerge and by the early nineties had become a significant attempt to rectify previous discrimination. Management consultants, along with corporate human resource officers, increasingly promoted the view that workforce diversity was socially and morally responsible, would increase creativity while it staved off possible discrimination lawsuits, and was good for business in the future global economy. In 1991 the first annual National Diversity Conference was held in San Francisco, attended by more than fifty corporations and over twenty federal government agencies, and shortly thereafter bookstores were filling up with titles such as *Managing a Diverse Workforce*, *Profiting in America's Multicultural Workforce*, *The Diversity Advantage*, *Managing Diversity Survival Guide*, and *The New Leaders*. Meanwhile, editors were publishing scores of articles in business journals and the mass media. "The Diversity Industry," declared *The New Republic* in a piece on the new "diversity management consultants" for business, while *Fortune* told readers "How to make diversity pay." *Working Woman* described "Changing the face of management," and the *National Review* responded with "Workforce diversity: PC's final frontier."

The movement also slammed into the academy. "How will cultural diversity affect teaching?" asked one scholar, and another answered, "Multiculturalism can be taught only by multicultural people." "The Cult of Multiculturalism" had arrived at the Ivory Tower, and that was having an influence in educating the public. When the National Endowment for the Humanities commissioned a group of historians to write national standards for teaching US history, some hailed the subsequent book as promoting the "rainbow history" of all races while the more conservative *U.S. News* declared it was biased, PC "propaganda," the "hijacking of American history." On campus, declared *Time*, the diversity controversy was bringing about "the politics of separation," while minority students were wearing t-shirts with the slogan: "Diversity. Embrace It."

During the nineties diversity was the winner. Democrats understood that as a political tactic, supporting diversity was less risky than endorsing affirmative action—it redefined the issue not as a preference for minorities or women but as a public good that supposedly utilized the potential of all citizens. While affirmative action drew heat, diversity drew praise, which made it popular on campus and in business. In 1995 a survey of the top Fortune 50 corporations found that 70 percent had established diversity management programs, 16 percent were developing them, and only 12 percent had no such program. By 1996 the GOP also had jumped on the diversity bandwagon. At their convention, New Jersey governor Christine Todd Whitman declared Republicans the "party of diversity," while on ABC's *Nightline* the Republican Speaker of the House, Newt Gingrich, boasted, "Diversity is our strength!" By the end of the decade the federal government was giving out 50,000 permanent resident visas a year for a "diversity lottery" to immigrants with a high school degree or two years of work experience. The only criterion was that they came from countries with underrepresented populations in the United States, which included about 150 countries, from Angola to Uzbekistan. "In the '90s, affirmative action recast itself as 'diversity,'" wrote conservative columnist Charles Krauthammer, "the colorless, apparently unassailable euphemism for racial, gender and ethnic preferences."

During the campaign Clinton had pledged a diverse cabinet. Like President Carter, who put new emphasis on the old American ideal of human rights, Clinton placed fresh importance on diversity. In 1992 the sixteen-member Bush cabinet had only two women and two minorities. Only about 10 percent of the federal judges were either minorities or women, in a year when minorities made up over 25 percent and women were over 50 percent of Americans. In response, Clinton appointed the most diverse cabinet in history—half were women or minorities. During his two terms he named seven African American cabinet secretaries, and women made up 44 percent of his appointees, including the first to serve as attorney general, Janet Reno, and in his second term, secretary of state Madeleine Albright. Clinton appointed more African Americans, women, and Hispanics to his administration and to federal judgeships than any previous administration—a trend continued by future Democratic presidents.

"Bill Clinton did what he promised," wrote columnist Ellen Goodman. "The class photo of his cabinet presented a more diverse portrait of Americans than had ever been assembled around a presidential table." Comedian Al Franken added, "Clinton stocked his administration with an adulterous Hispanic, a couple of mildly crooked black guys, a six-foot-one woman whose mother used to wrestle alligators, and a four-foot-tall Jewish guy. Which doesn't look like America at all, but it's an exceptional model of diversity."[5]

When Bill and Hillary Clinton moved into the White House, most felt that he would be able to move the country quickly since he had Democratic majorities in Congress, 258 to 176 in the House and 57 to 43 in the Senate. Instead, the new president quickly divided the nation. Just a week after his inauguration Clinton began discussing gays in the military with Congress and the Joint Chiefs of Staff.

Gays had strongly supported Clinton, at a time when AIDS had reached epidemic proportions in the gay community. The Center for Disease Control (CDC) reported in 1992 that HIV infection was the number-one cause of death among men aged 25–44 years, and some 200,000 Americans had died. Moreover, employers often fired those ill workers. California and a few other states responded by passing antigay discrimination laws. Later that year Hollywood produced an exceptional film about AIDS, *Philadelphia*, and the media focused on gay employees with TV specials and articles. *Business Week* examined how one professional was the "very model of a company man" at Shell until it was discovered that after hours, he had used the office computer to send invitations to a gay party. The oil company fired him, he sued, and under California law he won, the judge finding Shell's behavior "outrageous." *Fortune* penned an article quoting a lesbian who declared that in the "company closet is a big, talented, and scared group of men and women. They want out—and are making the workplace the next frontier for gay rights."

In fact, there was no federal law that prohibited discrimination against gays, lesbians, or transsexuals, and many experts considered that this unprotected class was about 10 percent of the workforce; in almost every state discrimination against them was legal. For years gay activists had lobbied for a "sexual orientation" amendment to the 1964 Civil Rights Act that would protect them nationally, as it did for race, color, religion, sex, and national origin, later amended to include age and the disabled.

Congress was not interested, but a few officials in the Defense Department were because they had commissioned experts to conduct studies concerning gays in the military. The studies suggested that gays and lesbians in uniform were not more likely to be security risks than heterosexual troops, that training and then discharging them was an expensive waste of personnel, and that many field commanders were not particularly concerned about gay sex; in a military with many more women they wanted all sex banned in the foxholes.

Thus, it seemed like an appropriate time to begin a discussion about gays in the armed forces. Clinton asked the Joint Chiefs of Staff why the government should be spending money to train, then kick out 17,000 gays from the military during the previous decade. The JCS in 1993 used the same argument as they had made in 1948 when President Harry Truman ordered the desegregation of the armed forces—Blacks then, gays now, would hurt unit cohesion and morale.

Only a week after assuming office the new commander-in-chief announced that he was ending the armed forces' policy of discriminating against gays. That prompted a vociferous response from social conservatives, talk show hosts, televangelists, and conservative politicians such as the powerful Senate Armed Forces Committee chairman, Democratic senator Sam Nunn, and the South Carolina Republican senator Strom Thurmond. They went on a tour of military bases. At Norfolk Naval Base, Senator Thurmond lectured a USN lieutenant who had admitted he was gay. "Your lifestyle is not normal," the senator thundered. "It's not normal for a man to want to be with a man or a woman with a woman." Sailors applauded wildly, and the senator asked if the lieutenant had sought "medical or psychiatric aids."

Other powerful men disapproved of Clinton's proposal, including influential generals such as Colin Powell, and many more at the Pentagon and in Congress. The American public also was opposed to allowing gays to serve. Polls demonstrated that about 47 percent opposed gays in the military while fewer than 20 percent approved. The House passed a resolution opposing gay service three to one, and the Senate also passed a resolution, all of which dragged on in the news until July, when the president finally announced his policy: Don't Ask, Don't Tell.

It was a terrible way to begin a new administration; ever since Franklin D. Roosevelt, most understood the importance of the First Hundred Days. Not Clinton, for Don't Ask, Don't Tell was a lose-lose. "In the short run," wrote Clinton, "I got the worst of both worlds." The gay community was very critical of the compromise, just a "fresh coat of paint," said Keith Meinhold, who in 1992 was discharged from the Navy for admitting his sexual orientation. The only servicemembers penalized "were people who told, often in very circumspect ways. No one who asked ever got punished." Conservatives were outraged and so were evangelicals. The Reverend Jerry Falwell used his *Old-Time Gospel Hour* program to produce 24,000 signatures on a petition in opposition, and in just one day some 400,000 people called to express disapproval to Congress. The American public, who thought they elected a president to work on the faltering economy, were wondering why he was spending his time on a small percentage of the population instead of a recession that affected everyone. At the end of Clinton's first hundred days, 70 percent of those polled thought the nation was moving in the wrong direction. "The Incredible Shrinking President," *Time*'s cover proclaimed in June, asking, "Is Clinton up to the job?" *Newsweek*'s cover asked, "What's Wrong?"

The usual media "honeymoon" with a new president quickly evaporated. Coverage of Clinton "was both more hostile and more volatile than that of any president since at least Harry Truman," wrote journalist James Fallows. This was going to be a stormy relationship, which humorist Dave Barry made fun of a month *before* Clinton was inaugurated with an article about the "failed Clinton presidency."

Nevertheless, "Don't Ask, Don't Tell" began a national debate that would continue for the next seventeen years and eventually result in a sea change concerning sexual preference in the military—and in America.

Another Clinton action did not receive nearly the amount of attention as gays in the military—medical abortion. During the early 1980s the French developed an abortion drug, RU 486. A woman in the early stages of pregnancy would take two pills in the privacy of her home and the drug would break a fertilized egg's bond to the uterine wall and induce a miscarriage. Presidents Reagan and Bush banned the drug from America, but just two days after the inauguration the new president ordered his administration to "promote the testing, licensing and manufacturing" of RU 486. "If there is a safe and effective medical alternative to a surgical procedure," said the FDA commissioner, "then we believe it should be available in this country." Eventually it was; in 2000 the FDA approved RU 486 (also known as mifepristone) as a method of early abortion, and by 2020 medical instead of surgical had become the primary method.

Perhaps Clinton's most popular legislation in his first hundred days was signing the Family and Medical Leave Act. FMLA had a significant impact on the workplace, for it guaranteed workers up to twelve weeks of unpaid time off when a baby is born or adopted or when a family member was ill. "In the next eight years in office," Clinton wrote, "more people would mention it to me than any other bill I signed." Indeed, during Clinton's two terms more than thirty-five million Americans utilized FMLA.

Not only new mothers, but also new fathers. "Valerie's asleep now, having snacked most of the morning, fussed and finally closed the brightest blue I eyes I've ever seen," said a proud dad. "Quiet moments like these are rare when you are taking care of a 4-month-old. . . . Because of this legislation my life is richer. Much richer."[6]

Two weeks after Clinton signed FMLA, tragedy struck in New York City. "BLAST HITS TRADE CENTER, BOMB SUSPECTED," headlined the *New York Times*. "Thousands Flee Smoke in Towers."

"It depended on where you were in the towers when it came," wrote a journalist. "For some the warning was a trembling underfoot or just a blank computer screen or flickering lights. For others, it was a shocking noise. One woman was blown out of her high heels. . . . And then, instantly it seemed, came the billowing smoke and the chilling realization that you had to get out of there."

This was a troublesome change for the nation. While the rest of the world, especially the Middle East, had become accustomed to acts of terrorism, Americans seemed to think that it happened somewhere else, "a safe distance over the horizon," wrote *Time*. Then "in an instant, the World Trade Center in New York City became ground zero."

A group of terrorists had detonated an enormous truck bomb in the basement garage of the North Tower of the World Trade Center. The architect of the plan was Ramzi Ahmed Yousef, a Kuwaiti-born militant who was repulsed by Desert Storm and eventually moved to Afghanistan, where he became an expert bomb-maker and traveled abroad to work as a recruiter for the emerging al Qaeda organization. In September 1992 Yousef flew to New York City, where he contacted the radical Egyptian-born cleric Omar Abdel Rahman, the Blind Sheik, who originally entered the United States on a tourist visa and by early 1993 was giving anti-American sermons at mosques in the New York City area. Also included in the group were five other extremists who received funding from Yousef's uncle, Khalid Sheikh Mohammed, later instrumental in 9/11.

The 1,300-pound bomb was supposed to send the North Tower falling into the South Tower, collapsing the entire WTC and killing thousands of people. The WTC withstood the blast, but it killed six people and injured over a thousand. That evening Ramzi Ahmed Yousef boarded an airplane bound for Pakistan, where for the next two years he devised plans to put bombs on American planes in Asia, help Islamic rebels in the Philippines, even assassinate the pope. Two years after the WTC bombing Pakistani police captured Yousef and flew him back to the United States, where he stood trial and remains in federal prison for life without a chance for parole. His coconspirator, Abdel Rahman, aimed to have his followers set off bombs at the United Nations, the Lincoln and Holland Tunnels, the George Washington Bridge, and an FBI building. An informant videotaped radicals mixing bomb ingredients, and four months after the WTC attack the FBI arrested the Blind Sheik and his followers, and they were tried and sentenced to life in prison; Abdel Rahman died there in 2017.

The WTC bombing had an immediate and significant impact on the Clinton administration. The president looked for an expert on terrorism and found Richard Clarke. He had been in the federal government for twenty years, working on security matters for previous administrations. By 1992 President Bush appointed him to the National Security Council. Clinton kept him on the NSC and eventually appointed him National Coordinator for Security, Infrastructure Protection, and Counter-terrorism, or Terrorism Czar. Working from an office in the White House, Clarke went to work on terrorist attacks on America, wondering "who are these guys?"

It was much easier to find and confront Saddam Hussein. Clinton's policy changed little from that of his Republican predecessor. The Democrat also would try to contain Saddam, and he told the dictator to abide by UN sanctions. But the dictator did not listen to Clinton—instead he attempted to kill former president Bush.

The Emir of Kuwait had invited the Bush family to visit Kuwait, and many of them arrived in April 1993. Son George was not with them because he wanted to attend to his baseball business, the Texas Rangers. During the celebrations in Kuwait the local police discovered a plot: Saddam had ordered Iraqi agents to drive a Toyota Land Cruiser, loaded with ample explosives, along the path of the motorcade; when detonated it would have assassinated the former president and the Emir. The Toyota was involved in a traffic violation, and the police uncovered the plot. Kuwaitis arrested the Iraqis, and the CIA sent forensic experts to examine the bomb; they concluded it was made by Iraq's Intelligence Service, the Mukhabarat. The FBI sent agents to interview the potential assassins and told Clinton, "We're certain." The Iraqis admitted that they were "tasked specifically to kill President Bush."

Kuwait convicted and hanged the Iraqis, and Clinton responded by ordering the US Navy to launch twenty-three Tomahawk missiles during the night; they blew up the Mukhabarat headquarters in Baghdad. Secretary of Defense Les Aspin said that the attack was intended to send a message to those who serve Saddam that "following this man is not good for your health." Saddam got the point—according to Clarke, that was the last time that Saddam attempted any aggression against the United States.

Back home, Clinton tried to sell his health plan, which flopped, but the New Democrat had better success with his budget. The problem was that the annual federal deficit had been growing; the last balanced budget was Lyndon Baines Johnson's final budget in 1969. The annual deficits in the late 1970s were about $60 billion, during Reagan's administration they were about triple that, and they had peaked in 1992 at $290 billion. At that rate of growth, Clinton maintained, the annual deficit would be more than $600 billion at the end of the decade, and interest on the debt would become America's largest budget item.

Alarmed, Clinton and his economic advisers—Alan Greenspan, Robert Rubin, and Secretary of Treasury Lloyd Bentsen—all advocated abandoning a campaign promise of a middle-class tax cut and instead balancing the budget. Clinton gave an address to Congress and spelled out his plan. He would decrease the number of federal workers through attrition, no layoffs but few rehires when workers left service, while he would increase the corporate tax rate from 34 to 36 percent, begin a new energy or BTU tax, and raise the highest tax rate on the top 1 percent of annual incomes (over $250,000) from about 31 to 39 percent.

The fight began. Republicans refused to entertain any tax increases, period. Although Clinton wanted to shrink the federal government, they declared that was not enough; it was time to "starve the beast." Republican congressman Jim Bunning quickly labeled it a "tax-and-spend bill," which "won't reduce the deficit, but will injure the country and decimate the economy. It's a job killing bill from the word go."

Most Democrats got behind the plan, yet when the bill was called for a vote in August 1993 it passed in the House by only the narrowest of margins, 218 to 216, and in the Senate 50 to 50. Vice President Al Gore broke the tie, and Clinton's plan became law. Not one Republican voted in favor.

Bunning was way off the mark. Clinton's budget plan would become one of his finest accomplishments. By 1997 the deficit had shrunk 90 percent to only about $20 billion, and the next four years all had surpluses, averaging $140 billion a year. For the first time since the 1920s the federal government ran a surplus four straight years, and economists speculated that if that trend continued the nation would be able to pay off its entire debt by 2010.

Another significant Clinton policy was more bipartisan—NAFTA. George H.W. Bush's administration had initiated the talks with Canada and Mexico. Clinton advocated that the agreement had to ensure labor and environmental standards that would be binding in Mexico, but that was not sufficient for Democratic labor supporters. They agreed with Perot that NAFTA would result in a "giant sucking sound" of American manufacturing jobs going south of the border. They also contended that supporting the trade agreement would alienate trad-itional Democratic supporters—unions—which had been part of the New Deal coalition since the 1930s—labor, small and medium-sized farmers, and African Americans. Apparently, many Democrats, such as House Majority Leader Dick Gephardt, refused to recognize that most white working-class and union members had been leaving their party for the Republicans since the Reagan presidency. Opinion polls

Presidents George Bush and Bill Clinton kicking off their NAFTA effort, September 14, 1993. Working together, they created what became the largest trading bloc in the world, and changed the economic future of the United States, Canada, and Mexico. Courtesy Clinton Presidential Library.

and focus groups after Reagan's 1984 landslide noted that most white working men felt that the Democrats did not help them and only supported women and minorities.

Clinton was aware of those focus groups and as a New Democrat was moving away from traditional supporters and policies. "I was a free-trader at heart," he later wrote, but was surprised at what he called "the vociferous organized opposition of the nation's unions" to NAFTA. "We see this as a life-and-death issue," said the president of the ladies garment workers' union, and the leader of the electrical workers bluntly declared, "We're going to go out and defeat every congressman" who votes for the trade agreement.

Clinton had no option, and he reached out to Republicans, where he found ample support. In fact, more Republican congressmen and senators than Democrats voted for NAFTA. Clinton signed the new trade agreement, and it went into effect on January 1, 1994.

Trade increased rapidly. In 1999 Mexico became America's second-largest trading partner, surpassing Japan, and eventually our southern and northern neighbors competed with China to be number one for the United States. The agreement had a profound effect on American-Canadian-Mexican commerce—and on the three neighbors' way of life.[7]

NAFTA was foreign and domestic policy, and as Clinton said, "Foreign policy is not what I came to do." But he had no choice, for his predecessors had been attempting to promote better relations between Israel and the Palestine Liberation Organization. The PLO was led by Yasser Arafat, and the group demanded an end to Israeli occupation of Palestinian lands in the West Bank. To achieve that, the PLO in 1987 had started an intifada, an armed uprising, and that resulted in violent protests and riots on the West Bank, Gaza Strip, even within Israel. With Norway's negotiating help, the president in September 1993 brought Arafat and Prime Minister Yitzhak Rabin to the South Lawn of the White House, where the two antagonists met.

With Clinton smiling in the middle, Rabin and Arafat shook hands and signed the Oslo Accords.

The accords temporarily ended the intifada and began the transition of parts of the West Bank and the Gaza Strip to the Palestinians. For their part the PLO renounced terrorism and recognized the right of the Jewish State to exist. Just two years later, at a rally to support the Oslo Accords in Tel Aviv, an Israeli ultranationalist assassinated Rabin.

Another foreign policy Clinton inherited concerned the African "country" of Somalia, which various colonial powers had established by cobbling together almost twenty clans. In December 1992, just after losing the election, Bush sent a US-led coalition to Somalia dubbed Operation Restore Hope. It was the right thing to do, for more than 350,000 had died in a bloody civil war and subsequent widespread famine. International observers were calling the country the world's first "failed state." "Somalia these days is a name on a map, and a nightmare," reported the Associated Press, "but it is no longer a country." Another labeled it the "land of the living dead," and a *New York Times* journalist wrote about Somalis with "rib cages protruding," lining up at soup kitchens for food, while "hundreds, too feeble to eat, died while they waited." The place was lawless, with one observer noting that "virtually every male over the age of 12 in Somalia was armed." Another added, "Flights are sometimes diverted at the last minute due to gun battles on the tarmac at the main airport in Mogadishu. One German with the United Nations had his house burgled so frequently he had concrete furniture made."

American and coalition forces began to stabilize and feed the nation. In May 1993, the UN took over in Somalia, with an aim of nation-building, a mandate supported by the new Clinton administration. The peacekeepers went to work, but the next month violence erupted. After a confrontation over who controlled Radio Mogadishu, warlord Mohammed Farah Aidid's militiamen launched a vicious attack on Pakistani UN troops, killing twenty-five and wounding fifty-seven—the deadliest single-day attack on UN peacekeepers since the Congo in 1961. Some casualties reportedly had their eyes gouged out and limbs severed, including one peacekeeper's testicles. It was a shocking slaughter, and it marked the start of a campaign of violence between UN peacekeepers and the United States against Aidid's followers and other armed militias and looters.

Clinton, his generals, and the UN felt that Aidid had to be brought to justice and that the country had to be pacified. Thus, the president decided to send 450 US Rangers supplemented by Delta Force to capture either Aidid or his lieutenants, who they thought were meeting at a hotel in downtown Mogadishu. According to the plan, sixteen helicopters would fly to the city, including eight Black Hawks carrying troops, followed by a convoy of trucks and Humvees. Since it was difficult for the helicopters to land in the narrow city alleys, the Rangers would slide down ropes, take their prisoners, load them on trucks, and drive out fast. The entire mission was to take only thirty minutes, so they took no food and little water.

The Black Hawks flew into the capital—and everything went wrong. Aidid's militia unloaded, shooting machine guns and rocket-propelled grenades, downing two helicopters. The Rangers went in to recover their injured. Soon, some ninety US soldiers were on the ground, facing hundreds of rebels in a massive shootout. The UN sent a multinational relief force, which encountered heavy resistance. Three other US helicopters were hit, one crashed in the port, and eventually the tally was eight damaged or destroyed. The bodies of dead American soldiers littered the battleground. Eighteen Americans were killed and more than five hundred Somalis. Americans turned on their televisions to see screaming Somalis dragging the battered body of a US soldier through the streets of Mogadishu. Another dead soldier was stripped naked and surrounded by an elated Somali mob chanting "Victory!" and telling reporters, "Come look at the white man!"

"Confronting Chaos," declared *Time*, asking on the cover, "What In The World Are We Doing?"

The agonizing battlefield fiasco had an impact on the Clinton administration. Many officials began to question the military tactics of going into a large city with a tiny attack force to capture an elusive general, especially two years after Bush, who had an enormous army in Iraq, did not try to capture Saddam. Within six months Clinton ordered a withdrawal from Somalia.

The attack also prompted the administration to rethink plans to use American troops for UN peacekeeping operations in other troubled spots in 1994 such as Haiti, Bosnia, and Rwanda. And it again questioned Clinton's foreign policy knowledge and experience. During the presidential campaign the Bush administration continually made the claim that the youthful governor was "a closet dove masquerading as a hawk and that his experience in world affairs is limited to breakfast at the International House of Pancakes."

Conservatives kept up the "Clinton has no foreign policy" mantra for years, which certainly contrasted with Bush, who had built up America's credibility with the thunderous victory of Desert Storm. To them, Bush's New World Order had become Clinton's New World Disorder.

Yet that chant was flawed. As stated, Clinton and his foreign policy team did not have the luxury of a focal point for policy—the USSR—so his administration struggled to find the most appropriate policies toward each new situation that appeared on the international horizon. Mogadishu was a disaster for all concerned—the United States, the UN, and especially Somalia.

Also, as Americans later learned, the United States' hasty exit from Mogadishu emboldened a little-known terrorist at the time—Osama bin Laden. The terrorist boasted that the United States was weak for withdrawing after losing G.I.s in "minor battles" in the African Muslim country, and that the "superpower" had been humiliated. "It is true that al Qaeda was emboldened by 1993," said former senator Bob Kerrey, who served on the 9/11 Commission. It was "their first successful attack on us and we were unaware of bin Laden's involvement until later."

The Clinton team shied away from interventions, especially in faraway Africa, and that included Rwanda. During spring 1994 that country was being torn apart by a civil war between the two main ethnic groups, the minority Tutsi, which occupied most government positions, and the majority Hutu. It was brutal, with Hutu armed bands slaughtering innocents, often using machetes to slash Tutsis to death. *Time* put the carnage on its cover, declaring "There Are No Devils Left In Hell, The Missionary Said. They Are All In Rwanda."

Clinton did nothing. His secretary of defense, William J. Perry, recalled that Somalia "foreclosed" acting in Rwanda. "Congress would have exploded," Perry remembered. "Had anybody proposed it to them, they would have been summarily dismissed as smoking dope or something." The president later lamented that he and his team did not consider sending troops to stop the genocide of more than 800,000 people, which was "one of the greatest regrets of my presidency."

A more successful foreign policy experience was in Haiti. During winter 1990–91 Haitians went to the polls and voted overwhelmingly for Catholic priest Jean-Bertrand Aristide. After years of various dictators, he was the nation's first democratically elected president. He also was a proponent of liberation theology, which advocated social and economic equality for the oppressed, meaning he would have strong opposition from the political and military elites. He did. Just seven months after the election, General Raoul Cédras staged a coup, forcing Aristide into exile and beginning a reign of terror. Over the next three years the junta killed some five thousand Aristide supporters. Many of the victims were "tortured and made to lay in open sewers before being shot."

Clinton was cautious, wary, later writing, "The battle of Mogadishu haunted me." But the carnage in Haiti finally convinced the administration that General Cédras had to go. Clinton told the public in September 1994 that he had tried to restore democracy in Haiti, but the "dictators rejected all of our efforts, and their reign of terror, a campaign of murder, rape, and mutilation, gets worse with every passing day," he said. "Now we must act."

The UN agreed and supported a possible invasion. To avoid bloodshed, and get Cédras to give up power and allow Aristide to return, Clinton dispatched former president Jimmy Carter, Senator Sam

Nunn, and General Colin Powell. They arrived and began intense discussions. The Americans gave Cédras a three-hour deadline to leave; he stalled. The Americans told the dictator that the Pentagon was ordering paratroopers to board aircraft, that two aircraft carriers were steaming to Haiti. The dictator relented—one hour before the skies would have been filled with parachutes. The next day fifteen thousand troops from the multinational force arrived on the island without firing a shot, and the next month the dictator left for exile. Aristide and democracy returned to Haiti.

Meanwhile, a humanitarian crisis was brewing in Southeast Europe—Bosnia—which was the result of the collapse of the Soviet Union, the velvet revolutions, and end of the Cold War.

During the Cold War, Josip Broz Tito in Belgrade led communist multiethnic Yugoslavia with an iron fist, perhaps the only way one could keep together the nation of Catholics, Orthodox Christians, and Muslims. While Yugoslavia was made up of federal republics that were ethnically and religiously diverse, Serbians, from their capital of Belgrade, dominated Yugoslav affairs. Tito died in 1980, and nationalistic forces in the nation's six republics began emerging and supporting their own independence from Belgrade. In June 1991 Slovenia and Croatia, both predominately Catholic, declared independence, and eventually so did Bosnia-Herzegovina and Macedonia. The Serbian president, Slobodan Milošević, moved to sustain a powerful "Greater Serbia," which included parts of its neighbors where Serbs lived; fighting broke out between Serbia and Croatia. Violence spilled into Bosnia, the most ethnically diverse province of former Yugoslavia, where about 45 percent were Muslims, 30 percent Serbs, and over 15 percent Croatians. In March 1992 Bosnia held a referendum on whether the area should become independent, where all ethnicities and religions would be treated equally. It passed with two-thirds of the vote. But Bosnian Serbs boycotted the polls and then unleashed their paramilitary forces, who began attacking one Muslim neighborhood then another, driving them from their homes, slaughtering them, creating some 140,000 refugees. The bloodshed continued, as commentators began calling this murder a new term: ethnic cleansing.

The Serbian government in Belgrade put Ratko Mladić in charge of the new Bosnian Serb army, and the conflict turned even more bloody. Mladić's artillery surrounded the Bosnian capital, Sarajevo, and pounded the city in spring 1992, hammering the Muslim citizens as he whipped up his gunners, yelling, "Shell them until they're on the edge of madness!" After the siege laid waste to parts of central Sarajevo, Mladić's forces moved into town and became snipers, killing virtually anything that moved—men, women, children. Mladić became known as the Butcher of Bosnia.

European leaders and the United Nations attempted to stop the killing, non-governmental organizations (NGOs) tried to provide food and shelter to the growing humanitarian crisis, and the UN sent eight thousand troops to protect aid convoys into Bosnia. In spring 1993 Clinton discussed plans with the British, French, and Germans, but they split on who they supported. The president aimed to make the current arms embargo more effective while the UN created a no-fly zone over Bosnia, which deprived the Serbs of their monopoly on airpower. Clinton sent Secretary of State Warren Christopher to Europe, and the administration began discussing forcing the Serbs to accept a cease-fire, lifting the arms embargo against the Muslims, and launching airstrikes against Serbian military targets. Serb leaders were eager to avoid US missiles and agreed to sign a UN peace plan. They did, but nobody believed it would end the crisis.

It didn't; scattered fighting continued, and so did the shelling and siege of Sarajevo. Clinton considered sending US troops into the imbroglio, prompting a *Time* cover, "Bosnia, will it be Clinton's Vietnam?"

"The challenge of dealing with complicated problems like Somalia, Haiti, and Bosnia," Clinton later wrote, inspired him to agree with one of his advisers: "Sometimes I really miss the Cold War."[8]

Another pressing issue was gun violence. As President Ronald Reagan was leaving the Hilton Hotel near Dupont Circle in

Washington, DC, in 1981, a deranged John Hinckley Jr. suddenly approached with a revolver and quickly fired six shots at the president. One bullet hit Reagan, who was rushed to the hospital, others hit two Secret Service officers, and another hit the president's press secretary, James Brady. He survived, and for the next seven years he and his wife campaigned for gun control, specifically background checks so the mentally ill and felons would not be able to buy a firearm. President Bush vetoed an early version of the bill under intense pressure from the National Rifle Association.

The NRA began after the Civil War to teach sharpshooting and gun safety, but the organization had changed radically after the 1960s assassinations when politicians began calling for gun control. It became the lobbyist for gun and ammunition manufacturers, receiving large donations and contributing to the campaigns of politicians who opposed gun control and supported the NRA's extreme version of the Second Amendment.

Like most Democrats, Clinton did not accept NRA contributions, and he was alarmed that in 1993 gun homicides peaked at a new annual record, more than eighteen thousand. The president invited Jim and Sarah Brady to the signing of the Brady Bill. The NRA sued on Second Amendment grounds, the Supreme Court upheld most of the act, and by the end of the nineties background checks had been computerized and almost 90 percent of citizens approved of them.

There were other firearm problems. On a bright, beautiful winter day in January 1989 a troubled twenty-four-year-old man, Patrick West, got out of his car and walked onto an elementary school playground in Stockton, California. He was armed with two handguns and a Russian-designed AK-47 rifle. There were over four hundred pupils from the first to third grades playing at the noontime recess. West fired into them. In just three to four minutes he shot thirty-four children, killing five, before he shot himself in the head. There had been some isolated school shootings in previous years, of course, but the Stockton act marked the first mass shooting of schoolchildren in American history.

The carnage continued. In October 1991, unemployed George Hennard drove his pickup truck through the plate-glass front window of a Luby's Cafeteria in Killeen, Texas. Hennard, a belligerent racist who also hated women, yelled, "This is payback day!" and opened fire with two semiautomatic pistols. He stalked, shot, and killed twenty-three people, ten of them with one shot to the head, fourteen of them women, before the police arrived. They engaged Hennard in a shootout, wounded him, and he committed suicide. At that time, it was the deadliest mass shooting in American history.

Back in California, the next year in Olivehurst, Eric Houston arrived at Lindhurst High School with a shotgun and a rifle. He entered the school and shot his former teacher, Robert Brens, who previously had failed him in civics class. He walked the hallways shooting students and then into a classroom filled with students; eventually he held eighty hostages and engaged in an eight-hour standoff with police before surrendering to authorities. Houston killed four, wounded ten, stood trial, and was given the death penalty. Over one hundred miles to the southwest, on California Street in San Francisco, failed businessman Gian Luigi Ferri entered an office building, took the elevator up thirty-four floors to the law firm Pettit & Martin. He hated lawyers, told friends he had been "raped" by them. He exited the elevator and opened fire with semiautomatic pistols. After wounding scores, he moved down staircases to lower floors and continued shooting. When police closed in, he committed suicide, leaving eight dead and six injured.

These horrific shootings of innocent children and adults, along with the stunning increase in homicides, prompted Clinton and his supporters to get to work in Congress. The result in September 1994 was the passage of the largest crime bill ever signed, the Violent Crime Control and Law Enforcement Act. In the House it was sponsored by Democratic congressman Jack Brooks of Texas, and the Senate version was written by Senator Joe Biden, who worked closely with the National Association of Police Organizations. This enormous bill supplied federal funding for 100,000 additional policemen for American cities and new prison construction, and it established a variety of new offenses relating to immigration, hate, sex, and gang-related crimes. The bill created more federal crimes that could receive the death penalty, including acts of terrorism, murdering a federal law enforcement officer, and causing deaths by using weapons of mass destruction.

The act also incorporated a relatively popular notion then into federal law: Three Strikes and You're Out. Numerous states passed these laws that declared that if someone was a repeat offender and had committed two violent or serious felonies, then the third one would result in an automatic long sentence or life in prison. By the end of the nineties almost half the states passed such laws—and the result was what some call mass incarceration. In 1970 about 300,000 citizens were behind bars, a number that soared in the 1990s to some two million by the end of the millennium. Three Strikes and You're Out later became controversial when it was demonstrated that they didn't actually decrease crime rates as they greatly increased the number of citizens incarcerated, especially Black men.

Another significant part of the enormous crime bill was the Violence Against Women Act. Sponsored by Senator Joe Biden and Utah Republican senator Orrin Hatch, the bill had three goals, said Biden. To "make streets safer for women; to make homes safer for women; and to protect women's civil rights." In part, the bill was prompted by the 1994 rape and murder of Megan Kanka, a seven-year-old from New Jersey. The assailant was a thirty-three-year-old neighbor who had two previous convictions for sexually assaulting girls, and that prompted the New Jersey General Assembly to pass Megan's Law, which required a state sex offender registry, community notification of offenders moving into a neighborhood, and the possibility of repeat offenders receiving life in prison. Nationally, the Violence Against Women Act required states to establish registries for sexual offenders and the federal government to create the National Domestic Violence Hotline and Office on Violence Against Women within the Department of Justice. The federal government also established numerous programs to train victim advocates, police officers, prosecutors, and judges on gender-based violence. Since then, federal grants have provided for programs that prevent domestic and dating violence, sexual assault, and stalking, and promote women's shelters.

While prohibiting violence against women generally had bipartisan support, a more controversial part of the Violent Crime Control and Law Enforcement Act was the Assault Weapons Ban. In May 1994 former presidents Gerald Ford, Jimmy Carter, and Ronald Reagan wrote to the US House of Representatives in support of banning "semi-automatic assault guns." Previously, in 1989, Reagan had been asked about guns and replied that he supported background checks. "I do not believe in taking away the right of the citizen to own guns for sporting, for hunting, and so forth, or for home defense, but I do believe that an AK-47—a machine gun—is not a sporting weapon, or needed for the defense of a home." The three presidents cited a 1993 Gallup Poll that found 77 percent of Americans supported a ban on the manufacture, sale, and possession of such weapons. The resulting Assault Weapons Ban was a compromise that would be in effect for only ten years, and eventually citizens realized that there were two loopholes: someone could buy these weapons without background checks at gun shows and eventually over the internet. Nevertheless, for the first time, the federal government defined assault weapons, those that could fire automatically and hold more than ten rounds of ammunition, along with certain brands and models, such as AK-47s and Uzis.

The vote demonstrated the crumbling center, for the ban passed the House by the narrowest of margins, 216–214, and 52–48 in the Senate.

While a majority of Americans supported the ban, Wayne LaPierre of the National Rifle Association proclaimed "a full-scale war to crush your gun rights. . . . This final assault has begun . . . to eliminate private firearms ownership completely and forever."

In September 1994, Clinton signed the Assault Weapons Ban into law; it's been debated ever since, and in 2004 the next president, Republican George W. Bush, let it expire.

The gun debate would continue throughout the nineties and for years after, of course, but for now the last word goes to the late Texas humorist and journalist Molly Ivins: "I am not anti-gun. I'm pro-knife. Consider the merits of the knife. In the first place, you have to catch up with someone in order to stab him. A general substitution of knives for guns would promote physical fitness. We'd turn into a whole nation of great runners. Plus, knives don't ricochet. And people are seldom killed while cleaning their knives."[9]

Some laughed with Molly and supported the Assault Weapons Ban, but not Francisco Martin Duran—he was armed and loaded, driving his pickup to Washington, DC.

2

Angry White Men

A month after President Clinton signed the Assault Weapons Ban in October 1994, Francisco Martin Duran got into his pickup truck and drove to Washington, DC. He was an army veteran who had been dishonorably discharged for aggravated assault, a twenty-six-year-old upholsterer from Colorado Springs, and when he arrived in the nation's capital he checked into a hotel and waited. After a couple of days Duran put on a trench coat and approached the North Lawn iron fence of the White House. It was Sunday, and inside the president was watching a football game in the living quarters. Duran saw a group of men on the lawn, thought one looked like Clinton, took out an SKS assault weapon, and opened fire. The gunman quickly emptied a clip of thirty rounds as bystanders scattered in panic. Five bullets hit the mansion's sandstone facade, and three shattered a window and chipped a stone of the West Wing. When Duran stopped to insert another clip, a male bystander tackled him from behind. As they struggled, another man jumped in, and they subdued the assailant as Secret Service officers arrived and cuffed him. Astonishingly, no one was hurt.

Duran was deranged, was sentenced to forty years in prison—and he was angry. As Clinton later wrote, "He protested the crime bill by opening fire on the White House."

In the early nineties there were many angry white men, and in modern times the seedbed for that was on July 2, 1964, when President

Lyndon B. Johnson signed perhaps the most significant law in the twentieth century—the Civil Rights Act. After signing it, the president turned to aide Bill Moyers and said, "I think we have just delivered the South to the Republican Party for a long time to come." Later that year, South Carolina Democratic senator Strom Thurmond resigned from his party and declared himself a Republican. That process continued for the next eighteen years until the Reagan era. By the early 1980s, the formally solid Democratic South had become the solid Republican South.

Richard Nixon understood the transformation, and after he became president, he and his attorney general, John Mitchell, devised their "Southern Strategy." They were well aware that in the 1968 election former Democrat and Alabama governor George Wallace ran as an independent for the presidency, won more than 13 percent of votes, and carried five Deep South states. Nixon was determined to win those forty-five southern electoral votes in 1972, and so his administration opposed public school busing to achieve integration, tried to appoint southern judges to the Supreme Court (two were rejected by the Senate), championed states' rights, and declared that liberal northern Democratic policies had declared war on the South.

At the same time Nixon was withdrawing troops from Vietnam, which contributed to the rise of angry white men. During the next generation many were veterans who believed that the federal government had sent American boys to Vietnam and denied them the military force to win it. They had gone to war, many felt, with one arm tied behind their backs; liberal politicians had not let them win. They had seen their colleagues die or be maimed and then come home to an ungrateful nation that provided no recognition, no homecoming parades. Moreover, now a draft-dodging president sat in the Oval Office. The enemy to them had been on the Mekong—and now was on the Potomac.

To make matters worse, the stagflation of the 1970s meant that many could not find decent jobs, and then the Jimmy Carter administration admitted hundreds of thousands of Vietnamese "boat people" into the United States. Many Vietnamese settled on the Texas Gulf Coast, where they often continued their profession of fishing for crab and shrimp. White power journals and Klansmen spread rumors: the shrimp population was declining; the newcomers had smuggled American gold out of Vietnam; they were eating neighborhood pets; they actually were Vietcong! "There are a number of Vietnam veterans like myself who might want to do some good old search and destroy right here in Texas," wrote veteran Louis Beam. "I'm ready." Violence ensued, forcing federal and state authorities to step in and protect the refugees.

Also during the 1970s Carter supported affirmative action and minority and female equality, but that diminished during the Reagan era. During the 1980s Republicans increasingly claimed that Democrats only helped women and minorities and by inference not white men. Conservative politicians were aware of a Democratic focus group in white working-class Detroit that found that the area voted a 20 percent victory for Lyndon Johnson in 1964 and in 1984 a twenty-point margin for Ronald Reagan. Thus, the Reagan administration opposed affirmative action hiring plans, the extension of the Voting Rights Act of 1982, and establishing Martin Luther King Jr. Day—but eventually signed the last two because Congress had passed them with veto-proof margins.

Reagan himself, of course, helped to fuel the antigovernment feelings. "In this present crisis," he declared during his inaugural address, "government is not the solution to our problem; government is the problem." Once in office the president continued such rhetoric. "The top nine most terrifying words in the English language are: I'm from the government, and I'm here to help." He continued, "Either you will control your government, or it will control you."

To many white men the Reagan years planted and fertilized the idea that the government could be, or was, the enemy, as the Carter years had sowed the idea that minorities and women could be on the other side, could be "Them." By the late 1980s some Republicans were running the race card full speed. In the 1988 Bush campaign, political adviser Lee Atwater ran an ad against the Democratic candidate, Massachusetts governor Michael Dukakis. He, like many governors including former California governor Reagan, allowed state prisoners who had exhibited good behavior to have weekend furloughs. One was William Horton, renamed "Willy" for the ad, who broke into a home, knifed its owner, and raped his fiancée. Atwater's ad, the "Revolving Door," which showed Black men walking through a turnstile, conjured up white fears of Black crimes. In 1990, North Carolina Republican senator Jesse Helms ran for reelection against a Black Democrat. Helms ran an ad known as "Hands." It showed only a pair of white hands with the voiceover, "You wanted this job, but because of a law they had to give it to a minority." Actually, there was no such law, but that made no difference—white working-class men wanted to believe it. Helms won reelection.

During the Reagan–Bush years the Republicans increasingly associated "liberal" with terms such as malevolence, elitism, softness, irresponsibility, and the perceived failures of LBJ's Great Society and Jimmy Carter. In Reagan's last year in office, he began talking about the "L-word" as a word that one should not say in polite company. Other conservatives kept up the chant, and few Democrats stood up and defended their term; instead, they started calling themselves "progressives."

Regardless of political labels, during the 1980s the nation witnessed growing white resentment, which was being felt from the South to the Great Plains. During the previous generation the farmers of the fertile prairies also were leaving the Democrats—even though they had benefited from the New Deal policies of federal rural electrification, crop subsidies, and insurance. In tough years, many farmers made more money from federal payouts than from corn or cattle, and the mid-1980s were tough years on the farm. Smaller farmers in the Midwest were getting battered by low commodity prices, global competition, and the continued emergence of agribusiness that controlled more and more of the markets. Feeling their pain in 1985, musicians Willie Nelson, John Mellencamp, and Neil Young organized the Farm Aid benefit concert in Champaign, Illinois. It raised some $9 million, which only momentarily helped the plight of the farmer. Many sold out to corporate agribusinesses, and because they wanted to remain in the country, they found employment in feedlots, meat packing plants, or as tenant farmers, working land they used to own, which spiked their resentment.

One could understand why white men in the Old Confederacy resented programs that helped Blacks, but it was and is more difficult to grip why midwestern small and middle-sized farmers would switch their political alliance from being New Deal Democrats to conservative Republicans. Yes, rural people always are more individualistic and conservative than many other citizens, but the GOP generally favored large agribusiness, not family farmers. Of course, country folks usually held traditional views and beliefs, God and Country, and were offended by those marching or protesting status quo America and by "liberal Hollywood," which produced an endless stream of movies and television programs that emphasized sex and not family values.

Whatever the case, many farmers shifted their political alliance to the Republicans, which continued during the nineties. By the 2000 presidential election, Republican candidate George W. Bush carried the small towns and farms of the Great Plains by an astonishing 80 percent. A bumper sticker at a Kansas gun show declared, "A working person that supports Democrats is like a chicken that supports Col. Sanders!"

Thus, by the early nineties there were many angry white men, and many felt mistreated. "Something extraordinary is happening in American society," wrote conservative Charles Sykes. "American life is increasingly characterized by the plaintive insistence, I am a victim." The culture had shifted, he continued. Instead of the traditional American self-reliance and individualism, the new culture focused on blaming others, resentment, claiming that everybody's getting something but me, being a victim. Examples flourished. *New York* magazine featured a cover story, "The New Culture of Victimization," with the headline: "Don't Blame Me." *Harper's* asked, "Victims All?" *Time* ran a cover story, "Crybabies: Eternal Victims," and *Esquire* penned "A Confederacy of Complainers." "Indeed," Sykes declared, "the new culture seems to grow by feeding on itself. . . . The National Anthem has become The Whine."

And whine they did, as primetime media reported a splurge of stories about employment complaints and lawsuits. Partly a result of the 1991 Civil Rights Act and the 1990 Americans with Disabilities Act and Older Workers Protection Benefits Act, the EEOC's jurisdiction was expanded, and the agency witnessed the largest number of complaints and lawsuits in its history. Many were serious, but the agency admitted in 1994 that 60 percent of complaints were rejected for lack of sufficient evidence and that 25 percent were closed because the worker withdrew the complaint, declined to cooperate, or could not be found: hit and run. About 12 percent were settled in the worker's favor by the agency but without a formal charge of discrimination against the company. Surprisingly, only 3 percent had enough evidence to deserve legal intervention in conciliation or court.

Unfortunately, many complaints were unreasonable, and they became headline fodder. Donald Keister, at 640 pounds, sued Baltimore, claiming that the city unconstitutionally refused to recognize his obesity as a disability entitling him to preferred status in bidding on city contracts, and a Chicago man complained that McDonald's violated federal law because their restaurants' seats were not large enough for his sixty-inch waist and enormous posterior. Other complaints came from the Madison Men's Organization, which filed suit charging gender discrimination when local pubs gave the first beer free to college gals but not guys on "ladies nights"; African American Tracy Walker, an Internal Revenue Service employee, who filed suit after she was fired, claiming that her Black boss, who had dark skin, dismissed her not for poor performance but because of her light skin; the chap working the cosmetics counter in a Dillard's department store, who filed a complaint with the EEOC claiming that he was discriminated against in sales contests—the prizes were makeup and perfume. In Chicago, a group of men filed a lawsuit claiming that they had been discriminated against by the hiring practices of Hooters, the restaurant chain known for scantily clad waitresses in tight fitting t-shirts and hot pants. When the EEOC agreed to investigate, the company held a press conference and a march with a hundred "Hooters' girls," many with signs: "Men as Hooter Guys—What a Drag."

In Boston, eight men made a complaint against the Jenny Craig weight loss organization, claiming that they were asked to do manual work and bombarded with "girl talk" in the office, "who to marry, who is pregnant, how to get pregnant," which they claimed was offensive. They hired a public relations firm, filed suit, and the story was reported in the *Wall Street Journal*, followed by appearances on CBS *This Morning*, *Entertainment Tonight*, and the *Today* show. As the "Jenny Craig Eight" awaited the trial, female journalists took aim. "We are asked to believe that these men's having to listen to jokes about push-up bras or being asked to lift a heavy box makes for a winning case," wrote Margaret Carlson in *Time*, "when women have been listening to penis jokes and making coffee for decades."

The "hypersensitive society," declared journalist John Leo, in which a flood of "accusations keep a constituency alive with resentment."

That resentment appeared forcefully in the early nineties in the form of the angry white men. This group had been emerging for years, of course, and in 1990 sociologist Frederick Lynch declared, "One of the sleeper political forces in America is the growing sense of grievance among younger working-class and middle-class white males." Many of these men were not college graduates and were the first hurt by recessions and anxious over tough competition for good-paying jobs in the global economy; they felt that they had been losing economic and political power to women and minorities, and even family authority to their working wives. Lynch noted that opinion polls, newspaper reports, and sociological research supported his claim that whites felt "frustrated and unfairly victimized by affirmative action."

That feeling had been expanding as these males vented their anger on minorities, immigrants, welfare, and preferences. All the Blacks do, said a white builder, is "scream, 'We want, we want.' . . . Our tax dollars go to support people just to have kids. They don't care—they have kids just to get the checks." When columnist Anthony Lewis examined why so many whites in Louisiana voted for former KKK leader David Duke for state legislature and then for governor, he noted that Duke was not just a representative of the Old South. A New York college-educated white male wrote the columnist that he backed Duke because he represented the "deepest anger we have with race quotas and welfare mothers."

David Duke emerged as one of the first angry white men of the nineties. As a student at LSU in 1970 he formed the White Youth Alliance, occasionally wore a Nazi uniform, and attended an American Nazi Party conference. By mid-decade he founded the Knights of the Ku Klux Klan (KKK) in his state and soon became the grand wizard. He advanced a new, more educated, and genteel image of the Klan, appearing on talk shows in suit and tie, advocating separation of the races, and not violence toward Blacks. He declared that whites should have the right to associate only with their own race; to him, integration was an evil. People of color had been misled by communists and Jews.

During the 1980s Duke ran unsuccessfully for various political offices. In 1989 he emerged as a Republican running in a special election for the state legislature, and although many in the GOP repudiated him and supported his opponent, Duke won by a little more than one percentage point and served in the State House from 1989 until 1992.

Duke used elected office as a springboard to continue neo-Nazi attacks on Jews and on African Americans, condemning school busing, affirmative action, and other terms associated with white resentment. He founded the National Association for the Advancement of White People and promoted Holocaust denial. In 1990 he ran in the Republican primary for the US Senate, receiving 43 percent of the vote, and the next year in the primary for governor, winning 32 percent of the overall vote—but a surprising 55 percent of the white vote.

During that campaign President Bush called Duke a "charlatan unfit to hold public office because he has espoused racist and neo-Nazi beliefs"; Duke even linked the "extermination of Jews in Nazi Germany with affirmative action programs in the United States."

Affirmative action was a flash point, and conservatives labeling the program "quotas" had taken its toll. *Newsweek* reported a "widespread impression that minorities and white women have hopped on a government-protected, quota-fueled gravy train," and that had resulted in "a deep-seated feeling that affirmative action is no longer a device to eliminate discrimination against minorities but a means of discriminating against white males." Not surprisingly, a 1993 poll found that about half of white males felt that they should "fight against affirmative action," and two years later 57 percent of whites agreed that affirmative action had resulted in "less opportunity for white men." Years before, in 1987, only 16 percent of white men felt that "equal rights have been pushed too far," but by 1994 about half of them felt that way.

On college campuses many white male graduate students and professors held similar feelings, especially as universities openly advertised for "targets of diversity." California State Northridge, for example, announced that it was setting aside faculty positions for "departments that identify well-qualified minority candidates" while California State Sacramento set aside funds for "opportunity appointments," defined as Blacks, Asians, Hispanics, or Native Americans. The academy knew that these positions excluded all white men, although they were funded by all the taxpayers and most likely in violation of Title VII of the 1964 Civil Rights Act. Often the result of such policies was what a political science professor, Robert Weissberg, called the "gypsy scholars," white males who "wind up with endless temporary positions at third-rate schools" while "black, Hispanic and female job candidates, many of whom are not very well qualified, are on national tours going from one campus to the next receiving the most outrageous offers." These white men were bewildered, Weissberg continued, for they never had practiced discrimination and now felt that they were being discriminated against. Affirmative action hires, he concluded, were creating a "dangerous pool of highly educated . . . angry young white men."

On campus it was not PC to hold and publish views opposing affirmative action and diversity programs. Debate over such hires, wrote a tenured sociology professor, "so easily become melodramas of moralistic self-presentation and recriminatory denunciation that sweep aside the whisper of reason." Weissberg, who also owned a men's clothing store, had hired Black and female managers, Hispanic salespeople, female accountants, and even had given family leave to one employee so he could participate in the Miss Gay USA pageant. "None of this counts with my academic colleagues," he claimed, for because he did not embrace their ideas about diversity, "I remain the Racist Satan Himself, the Great Insensitive One."

Actually, it was difficult to determine the amount of reverse discrimination throughout the nation. African American Roger Wilkins scoffed at the idea: "The only place in America where blacks have taken jobs in a major way from whites is the National Basketball Association."

The numbers indicated only a minor problem. The EEOC reported that less than 2 percent of discrimination charges had been made by white males, who were not shy about making most of the age discrimination complaints. One researcher found that in more than three thousand discrimination opinions by federal courts from 1990 to 1994, fewer than a hundred cases concerned reverse discrimination and that charge was upheld and awarded compensation in only six cases. Many of the complaints were brought by disappointed job seekers who the courts ruled were less qualified than the women or minorities who were given the jobs.[1]

Reverse discrimination and affirmative action were topics of discussion at the same time domestic extremists and white power activists were emerging. These extremists were stimulated by the end of the Cold War. Anti-Communist rhetoric had focused many of them, as well as most conservatives, but with the collapse of the Soviet Union that no longer seemed valid. Some refocused their dislike and distrust. "Washington has replaced communism as the glue for conservatives," said one Republican official. "These are people that love their country but hate their federal government. Where is the evil empire? The evil empire is Washington."

Moreover, conservative evangelicals who had felt that the world was going to end in a Soviet nuclear apocalypse began to search for a new enemy, perhaps the Zionist "New World Order," or the Deep State, secret and unauthorized networks operating independently of elected government, often in pursuit of their own agenda, such as confiscating guns. Another event that encouraged white militants was the 1992 South Central riots, with visions of angry Blacks pulling whites from cars and trucks, beating them bloody.

Some felt it was time to arm themselves and prepare for the Apocalypse, and one of these was Randy Weaver. He joined the US Army in 1968, trained as a Green Beret, and was discharged honorably. He married Vicki Jordison, started a family, and moved to Idaho, building a home on top of Ruby Ridge. They were survivalists who didn't have electricity, running water, or telephone, and on some occasions attended Aryan Nation meetings at Hayden Lake. It was a compound for government resisters and for white separatists and supremacists that had a sign at the entrance: WHITES ONLY. The Weavers never joined the organization but held similar beliefs opposed to race-mixing and the oppressive federal government. Vicki followed the Bible's Old Covenant Laws, canned her own food, and home-schooled the children while her husband tried to work odd jobs.

Strapped for cash, Randy made the mistake of selling two illegal sawed-off shotguns to a government undercover agent. The ATF tried to enlist Weaver as an informant; they wanted to know more about the white power adherents at Hayden Lake, promising to drop the gun charges, but Randy refused and was indicted by a grand jury.

Weaver failed to appear in court, and federal agents issued an arrest warrant.

Tension increased between the Weavers and the federal marshals who had been told to bring Randy to justice. They set up a camp on the road at the base of Ruby Ridge and waited. "I don't care what you do," Weaver declared, "I'm not coming off my mountaintop." Agents knew that the family was armed. Pressure and frustration mounted. In August 1992 federal agents in camo uniforms appeared at Weaver's twenty acres, and when they began walking up the hill, the family dog began barking. The agents shot the dog, and a gun battle erupted: federal agents versus Weaver's fourteen-year-old son, Sam, and a family friend. Sam was killed and so was a US marshal.

Randy moved Sam's body into a shed, and the next day as the Weaver family was going to visit the body, an FBI sniper shot Randy in the arm. A second shot went through the door and struck Vicki in the head while she was holding her ten-month-old daughter.

The siege was on. Some four hundred federal agents outfitted in military gear arrived and began a stakeout at Ruby Ridge. They employed armored troop carriers and helicopters and were joined by National Guard troops. The press swarmed the marshals' roadblock at the bottom of the hill and reported that Sam had been killed, prompting outraged neighbors and friends to confront agents. "You bastards!" one angry woman yelled as she marched up to the agents. "Are you proud of yourself? You're going to kill all the children to get one man? . . .You're going to have nightmares about this! You're going to burn in Hell!" Men began shouting, "Baby killers! Baby killers!"

The blockade continued. Neither side would budge, and there was no way to communicate with Randy. Then Bo Gritz showed up, a former Green Beret lieutenant colonel who had become a hero of the radical right. He was running a lackluster campaign in the 1992 presidential election as a Populist, using the slogan "God, Guns and Gritz." He offered to negotiate with Randy, saying that they could talk to each other, two Green Berets. Bo went up to the house and Randy talked to him. When Bo learned that Vicki had been killed, he

Ruby Ridge protesters. Federal agents' behavior expanded the number of angry white men and the militia movement. Photo Archive/The Spokesman-Review.

returned and told of her death, prompting a protester to shout at the marshals, "We're going to war!"

On the eleventh day, Gritz again returned to the house and told Weaver that it was time to stop. Weaver hesitated, Bo pushed him, and then Weaver said, "Girls, get your things together. We're going to follow Colonel Bo down the hill." The siege was over.

Weaver surrendered. He was charged with murder in the death of the marshal, but an Idaho jury acquitted him; he spent sixteen months in jail for the original gun offense.

A sign posted at the Ruby Ridge site declared what a growing number of angry white men felt: "Randy Weaver: True White Patriot." For them, the eleven-day standoff contributed to a rising rage against the government. "I warn you calmly, coldly, and without reservation," Louis Beam of the Aryan Nations told his audience of 160 white men two months after Ruby Ridge. You "will come to hate government more than anything in your life." He continued, "We must cry out that we will not tolerate their stinking, murdering, lying, corrupt government. Men, in the name of our Father, we are called upon to make a decision . . . will it be liberty, or will it be death?"

The next confrontation was just six months later, with a different set of actors: Branch Davidians.

On February 28, 1993, officers from the ATF approached the Branch Davidian ranch, Mount Carmel, nine miles northeast of Waco, Texas. The six dozen Branch Davidians were Protestants who believed they were living before the Apocalypse. Their leader, thirty-three-year-old David Koresh, thought of himself as the final prophet, the lamb who would lead his followers in a holy war against the outside world of Babylon.

Koresh forced strict rules on his followers. No alcohol, but he drank beer in his private quarters. Men had to have short hair, but his fell to his shoulders. His followers slept in primitive dorms, but his quarters had television, stereo, heat, and air conditioning. The "Living Prophet" forced celibacy on male followers but then claimed almost twenty females as "wives." Some were married to husbands living at Mount Carmel, while others were daughters, one fourteen years old, another only twelve. He fathered more than a dozen children who he claimed would inherit the Kingdom of Heaven.

Rumors ran rampant about Mount Carmel—polygamy, child sex, guns. Because of a few cult defectors authorities knew that the compound had an enormous armory of guns, AK-47 assault weapons, thousands of rounds, even hand grenade launchers. Attorney General Janet Reno ordered the ATF to present a search warrant that listed weapons, sexual assault, and child abuse. The ATF officers advanced toward the compound, knocked on the front door, and then placed ladders alongside and climbed up on the roof. Suddenly an intense gun battle erupted, the cause of which still is debated, but not the outcome: the death of four officers and six Davidians. With twenty agents dead or wounded, it was the worst day ever for ATF.

The siege began. Eventually more than seven hundred law enforcement personnel were on the scene and about two hundred reporters from all over the world. Hundreds of curious onlookers appeared, some selling t-shirts and other souvenirs. Authorities ordered them to retreat a mile away, for no one knew when another battle might erupt. The FBI took over with armored vehicles and with negotiators who tried to talk Koresh and his followers into coming out peacefully. The possibility that Koresh and his followers would surrender was doubtful, since they knew that they would be tried for murdering and wounding federal agents. The cult would be broken up, some going to jail. Moreover, they had enough food and water to last months.

The FBI on the scene and many citizens were becoming concerned about the children, and eventually fourteen of them were evacuated from the compound. On March 9 federal officials cut the electricity, which only reinforced the Branch Davidians' conviction that the Apocalypse was coming and they would be transported to Heaven.

Waco became the longest siege in American history. After fifty-one days, at about 6 a.m. on April 19, FBI armored vehicles approached the compound with a loudspeaker: "We are in the process of placing tear gas in the building. This is not an assault. This is not an assault. Come out of the building with your hands up. You are under arrest." A battle erupted. The cultists shot more than eighty rounds at the FBI. Turmoil continued for the next six hours. Then around noontime the Davidians ignited Mount Carmel.

"Oh, my God," exclaimed an FBI officer. "They're killing themselves!" The compound burst into flames, killing seventy-five people, including two pregnant women, more than twenty children, and David Koresh.

The Waco siege was a defining moment for Americans who distrusted government, valued guns, and wanted to protect themselves from what they thought was federal aggression: Don't Tread on Me. In the crowd outside the compound were a number of gawkers; one was hawking antigovernment bumper stickers and t-shirts, FEAR THE GOVT THAT FEARS YOUR GUN, and would get even with the feds—Timothy McVeigh. The memorial service for the Davidians was attended by a young conspiracist from Austin—Alex Jones. Another witness, a member of the National Rifle Association, bluntly wrote to the attorney general: "And Miss Reno, I say to you: If you send your jack-booted, baby-burning bushwhackers to confiscate my guns, pack them a lunch—it will be a damn long day. The Branch Davidians were amateurs. I'm a professional."

Right-wing talk show hosts piled it on the ATF. Former Watergate conspirator G. Gordon Liddy on his show *Radio Free D.C.* claimed the ATF had "run amok" and was conducting a "terror campaign." Liddy told his listeners what to do if attacked by those agents: "Head shots, head shots—kill the sons of bitches!" And if you missed, then "shoot them in the groin."

The fiery conclusion fit into what was becoming the right-wing narrative of an overreaching government that crushed individuals— and that expanded the militia movement. By 1995 the federal government reported that there were approximately 450 militias, while one expert, Kenneth S. Stern, estimated that there were 15,000 members in forty states. These hate groups did not target just the traditional victims, racial and religious minorities, but government. One militia advertised on the new internet that they needed volunteers to march on Washington and arrest Congress—at gunpoint.

Militias advocated conspiracies: government had plans to marshal dissidents into forty-three concentration camps; black helicopters were going to attack and blind them with top-secret lasers; Clinton was training Hong Kong police and Gurka troops in the Montana wilderness so they could swoop in to take away all guns; there was a plot to give parts of the Cascade Mountains and Washington State to the United Nations. Militia members spread their theories openly and felt comfortable enough to protest at courthouses and statehouses armed with assault weapons and bayonets and wrapped with belts of ammunition.

The Waco "raid had gone terribly wrong," Clinton later wrote. "I was furious with myself, first for agreeing to the raid against my better judgment, then for delaying a public acknowledgment of responsibility for it." Citizens agreed, as Clinton's approval rating took a beating, sinking to just 37 percent by the end of spring.[2]

The Republicans saw their chance and jumped on the bandwagon, and one of the most vociferous critics was Newt Gingrich.

Gingrich began his political career at just age thirty-five by winning a congressional seat from Georgia in 1978. He had earned a BA degree in history from Emory University and a PhD in European history from Tulane University. He became a history professor at West Georgia College but was eager for political life. On the campaign trail in 1978 he had a conservative message: "One of the great problems we have in the Republican Party is that we don't encourage you to be nasty," he told his audience. "We encourage you to be neat, obedient, and loyal, and faithful, and all those Boy Scout words, which would be great around the campfire but are lousy in politics." The next generation of Republicans, he continued, would have to "raise hell" and realize that politics was a "war for power."

The young congressman headed for Washington and soon found ways to get attention. C-SPAN had installed cameras in the House chamber, so Newt began delivering tirades against Democrats when virtually no one was there. He didn't care, for to the television audience it looked like the congressman was delivering a masterful oration, with eye contact, pauses, gestures to a packed House. He was one of the first congressmen to understand that the audience that really mattered was not in the chamber but in the living room. He knew that his remarks would be televised to news outlets and eventually viewers across the United States.

As his profile grew, Gingrich took aim at the moderates in his own party and baited Democratic leaders, insulting them as pro-communist and un-American. In 1984, one of Newt's floor speeches provoked Democratic Speaker Tip O'Neill: "It's the lowest thing that I've ever seen in my 32 years in Congress!" The episode landed them both on the nightly news, and Gingrich got what he wanted, declaring, "I am now a famous person." The more outrageous his rhetoric became, the more times he appeared on the nightly news. "We are engaged in reshaping a whole nation through the news media," Gingrich declared. "Newt's used the media from the beginning," said his press secretary, Tony Blankley, and he boasted that Newt's style and approach predated the rise of another angry white man—Rush Limbaugh.

Newt found success in the Republican Party, and in 1989 he became House Minority Whip. His intention, he declared, was to "build a much more aggressive, activist party." He told a group of college Republicans, "I am essentially a revolutionary," and he wrote for his colleagues, "If House Republicans are ever to become a majority," the party needed a "fundamental change" in election strategy; they had to stoke anger against the government and arouse "discontent with Congress." He organized young conservatives on Capitol Hill with the aims of attacking the Democrats, advancing a bold new agenda, and taking control of his own political party. Only two things stood in his way, he said, "the Democrats and the Republicans."

To Newt, politics was a blood sport. When Clinton announced his health care plan Gingrich went into high gear in a maximum effort to deny an administration success. Killing the Democratic plan, he said, would be "their Stalingrad, their Gettysburg, their Waterloo," allowing Republicans to "defund the government," "destroy the liberal constituent groups," and win back the House. Newt claimed that Democrats were "enemies of normal people," that they had sold out to "a coalition of big-city machines, trial lawyers, union leaders, left-wing activists and political incumbents." The brash congressman even went after some Republican colleagues. When Senator Bob Dole supported a tax raise because he wanted a balanced budget, Gingrich attacked him as the "tax collector for the welfare state."

Before the 1990 midterm elections, GOPAC, a political training organization associated with Gingrich, supplied Republicans with a working paper titled "Language: A Key Mechanism of Control." It told candidates to memorize and label Democrats with words like "failure," "lie," "sick," "crisis," "pathetic," "liberal," "radical," "corrupt," "betray," "decay," "welfare," "anti-family," "anti-jobs," and, of course, "taxes." For themselves the document told them to define Republicans with "moral," "courage," "flag," "opportunity," "common sense," "hard work," "freedom," and "truth."

Throughout the ensuing elections when Republicans lost, and without proof, many of them emphasized the term "voter fraud," a tactic continued to and beyond the 2020 presidential election.

Heading into the 1994 midterm elections, Gingrich rallied Republicans around the idea of turning Election Day into a national referendum at a time when the Clinton administration was sinking into political trouble. He was a minority president whose New Democrat policies had irritated many Old Liberal Democrats—union men who had opposed NAFTA, the poor who did not like his idea to "end welfare as we know it," civil libertarians who were dismayed by his support for capital punishment. Clinton's health care plan, which would have helped his middle-class constituency, failed in Congress, and the president angered many other supporters when he spoke out for gays in the military instead of daily calls for equality for women and minorities in the workforce.

Moreover, his conservative enemies had been on the attack as soon as he moved into the White House. They claimed that the administration's solicitor general was "soft on child pornography," and they alleged corruption concerning "Whitewater," the land-buying scheme a decade before Clinton became president. Then, in February 1994, the conservative magazine *American Spectator* introduced Paula. Ms. Paula Jones charged that Clinton had made sexual advances as late as 1991. He denied it, didn't recall meeting her, and she sued for an apology and $700,000. Pretrial questioning kept the Paula story and character issue in the news for years.

Conservative talk show hosts such as Rush Limbaugh had a field day and so did late night TV hosts. "President Clinton said that there were powerful forces threatening to bring down his administration," quipped Jay Leno. "I think they are called hormones."

By late summer 1994, as the midterm election loomed, Clinton's low approval ratings opened the door for attacks from Gingrich. No stranger to hyperbole, he labeled Clinton the most left-wing president of the twentieth century. While that was laughable, Gingrich had a more realistic sense of the electorate in 1994. During the summer he and his colleagues presented their Contract with America. The document wisely reached out to former H. Ross Perot supporters while it avoided racial issues such as affirmative action or socially divisive ones such as abortion and school prayer. Instead, the contract declared core principles of accountability, responsibility, and opportunity, and it proclaimed policies aimed at the angry white men—a Personal Responsibility Act that would limit welfare to unwed mothers, a Taking Back Our Streets Act that would boost law enforcement and cut crime in cities, a Family Reinforcement Act that would provide stronger child pornography laws—along with tax cuts on capital gains, term limits, a line item veto, and a balanced budget amendment. Newt's aim was to replace FDR's "liberal welfare state" with a "conservative opportunity society."

Clinton fought back and took to the campaign trail, crisscrossing the nation to help struggling Democrats. His advisers realized that when he stayed at the White House and acted presidential, he helped his party, not when he showed up to raise money or appear on talk show programs. But as one said, "Advising Clinton to stay off the campaign trail in October was like asking him not to breathe."

The November election resulted in a Republican sweep. "Angry white men is a phrase with a certain ring to it these days," declared the *Washington Post* after the election. "They've changed the political face of America by voting disproportionately GOP.... They've had it with Democrats." "To say that the electorate is angry," Said a Republican consultant, "would be like saying that the ocean is wet," and *Time's* cover proclaimed, "Mad as Hell Newt Gingrich Has Perfected the Politics of Anger."

"Call it what you want," said the chairman of the Democratic National Committee, "an earthquake, a tidal wave, a blowout. We got our butts kicked." White men voted in droves, and more than 62 percent of them picked Republicans, flooding the House with fifty-four Republican freshmen and electing eight new senators, making the first Republican Congress since 1952. The new freshmen voted Rush Limbaugh an "honorary member of the Class of '94," while Gingrich became the new Speaker of the House and Bob Dole the Senate Majority Leader. The Republican sweep also had state implications, for they did not lose one governor's race. In New York the previously popular governor, Mario Cuomo, named by pundits as a possible presidential candidate, went down in defeat to George Pataki, and in Texas, Governor Ann Richards was beaten by a political newcomer, George W. Bush. One commentator saw the election in historic proportions, labeling the GOP takeover of Congress "The completion of what Ronald Reagan began" and "the End of the New Deal." Others felt Clinton was, like Carter and Bush, doomed to be a one-term president. Pundits wondered if Clinton still was "relevant" or if the New Democrat only could be reelected as a "Newt Democrat."

"The election of 1994," Newt reflected, "brought to Washington a new generation and breed of congressmen. They were not ordinary politicians but rather ideologically fervent," and they were "determined people." Indeed, the election boosted the idea that "real" conservatives should not compromise with liberals to pass legislation. In fact, with many hard-right politicians the term "compromise" became a dirty word. The future of the Republican Party would increasingly be energized by many more uncompromising conservatives.

Newt moved into the Speaker's office, and *Time*'s cover labeled him "King of the Hill." He informed the new Republican congressmen not to meet with the Democratic colleagues, not to form friendships across the aisle, and he handed out a list of slogans demonizing the liberal party. "Politicians flourish by sowing discontent," said *New York Times* columnist Russell Baker. "They triumph by churning discontent into anger. Press, television and radio also have a big financial stake in keeping the [country] boiling mad."

It was one thing to keep the public angry, but the new Speaker soon discovered it was an entirely different thing to pass legislation. The Fiscal Responsibility Act was going to amend the Constitution to require a balanced budget; it never was passed by the Senate. Part of that act was passed, the line item veto, and the first time Clinton used it New York State sued and the Supreme Court ruled it unconstitutional. Not surprisingly, Congress refused to pass an amendment to the Constitution that would have imposed twelve-year term limits on representatives and senators—on themselves. Yet, there were a few Republican victories. The Taking Back Our Streets Act funded more prison construction. The Personal Responsibility Act aimed at cutting funds to Aid to Families with Dependent Children (AFDC) at first was vetoed by Clinton, but in 1996 he surprised liberals by signing a revised act that limited AFDC to five years. Most of the Contract did not pass in Congress, or if Clinton did sign on, the policies were significantly altered. The president referred to Newt's proposals as the "Contract on America."[3]

The new Republican Congress also pleased many angry white men by attacking affirmative action. Senate Majority Leader Dole wondered if affirmative action discriminated unfairly against white men, if they should "have to pay" for discrimination practiced by generations "before they were born." Other conservatives agreed. "Affirmative action has not brought us what we want—a colorblind society," William Bennett said. "It has brought us an extremely color-conscious society. In our universities we have separate dorms, separate social centers. What's next—water fountains?"

Shots at affirmative action continued during the winter and spring of 1995. Two white male professors in California who claimed "widespread reverse discrimination" at state colleges began collecting the 700,000 signatures needed for the California Civil Rights Initiative that would ban the use of race, sex, or national origin as a criterion for either discriminating against, or granting preferential treatment to, any individual or group in public employment, education, or contracting. "Count me among those angry men," said Professor Thomas Wood. "I know the sting of affirmative action. I was once passed over for a teaching job because, I was told privately, I was white and male. The worm has turned."

Advocates for the policy squirmed as Republicans exploited this wedge issue that divided two usual Democratic voting groups, the white working class and African Americans. "It's a winner for us any way you look at it," said Republican strategist Bill Kristol. A *Newsweek* poll found Kristol correct. By a 79 to 14 percent margin whites opposed racial preferences in employment or college admissions, while an ABC poll found that between 77 and 81 percent of males and females opposed preferences for minorities and women. Minority support also was on the wane, only by a 50–46 margin. Should qualified Blacks receive preference over equally qualified whites in getting into college or getting jobs? No, said 75 percent of respondents. Affirmative action, *Newsweek* proclaimed, "is tearing at the Democratic Party."

Clinton and Gore were listening. The president ordered an "intense, urgent review" of all federal affirmative action programs.

That spring of 1995 there was one angry white man who was on his own intense, urgent mission to change the future of the nation—Timothy McVeigh. He grew up in the Buffalo area of western New York State. He was an average student in a middle-class family, graduated from high school, but was not interested in college. As a teenager he was fascinated with guns. By age twenty, he was making and exploding bombs and shooting guns on a wooded lot that he described as a survivalist bunker. After some dead-end jobs, McVeigh joined the US Army. The army trained him, and he was assigned to the First Infantry Division, famous as the Big Red One. He was a rising star in his company and was one of the first to become sergeant, but he had one blind spot: race. McVeigh made derogatory remarks about Black soldiers and often assigned them to undesirable work assignments. He also felt uncomfortable around women, and when his buddies tried to set him up with a date, he was embarrassed and turned red. He decided to try out for the Special Forces, the Green Berets, and trained compulsively for the punishing physical exam, doing four hundred push-ups a day, fifty at a time. When others relaxed after drills, McVeigh loaded his rucksack with eighty-pound sandbags and marched around the post. But his tryout was canceled.

McVeigh began training for war in the Persian Gulf after Iraqi president Saddam Hussein invaded Kuwait. The sergeant was a Bradley Fighting Vehicle gunner but only engaged in one firefight before the enemy surrendered. Nevertheless, the army awarded him the Bronze Star, and he again applied for the Green Berets. This time, however, he was not in condition to pass the grueling physical test and washed out on the second day. That broke him, and although he had excellent evaluations from his superiors, he left the army frustrated and bitter.

He moved back to his father's home. He wanted to be a US marshal but never heard back after he applied, eventually returning to his premilitary job as a security guard. He became moody, veering from passivity to anger. His supervisor had to move him from the front door so he would not come in contact with people. He moved to Michigan, joined survivalist groups, and moved around the country selling his enormous gun collection and attending gun shows. A lone wolf, he felt that America had let him down and that other people were getting the benefits, but not him. He wrote a letter to a newspaper, a listing of grievances, complaining of rising crime, high taxes, self-serving politicians: "The 'American Dream' of the middle class has all but disappeared, substituted with people struggling just to buy next week's groceries. . . . What is it going to take to open up the eyes of our elected officials? AMERICA IS IN SERIOUS DECLINE. . . . Is a Civil War imminent? Do we have to shed blood to reform our current system? I hope it doesn't come to that! But it might."

"Timothy McVeigh was preparing to teach the government a lesson," his biographers wrote. "He was preparing to strike back for Waco, for Ruby Ridge, for U.S. military actions against smaller nations, for no-knock search warrants. It was a list of grievances he'd been amassing for years: crooked politicians, overzealous government agents, high taxes, political correctness, gun laws. . . . This is payback time."

The payback came on a beautiful April 19 morning—exactly the second anniversary of the Waco siege. McVeigh and his army buddy Terry Nichols used fertilizer to construct a 7,000-pound bomb in a Ryder truck. McVeigh drove it and parked it in front of the Alfred P. Murrah Federal Building in downtown Oklahoma City. The building housed the offices of seventeen federal agencies, including the ATF, as well as a day care center for employees' children. McVeigh lit a timed fuse and hurried away to his getaway car.

The truck detonated with a tremendous roar, shooting a red-orange fireball into the sky, collapsing ceilings and walls, ripping a hole in the building's façade, and collapsing all nine floors, which came down in a gigantic cascade of concrete, steel, and shattered glass. It was so powerful that it damaged more than three hundred structures up to sixteen blocks away, and the concussion was so potent it turned over parked cars while it propelled shards of glass missiles. The blast killed 168 people, including nineteen children at the day care center, and

An Oklahoma City police car near the Alfred P. Murrah Federal Building in Oklahoma City, April 24, 1995. AP Photo/Rick Bowmer.

injured 680 others. It was the worst domestic terrorist act in US history, and it demonstrated that terror wasn't just a problem caused by foreigners or in other lands—it had arrived here.

One by one local residents mumbled the same thing: "This does not happen here." "We're just a little old Cowtown," said one firefighter at the scene. "You can't get no more Middle America than Oklahoma City." Terror in the Heartland.

McVeigh was a couple of blocks away, heard the blast, was protected by a building, and kept walking to his 1977 Mercury. He started the car and went out of town north on Interstate 35. The car did not have a license plate, which was why eighty miles later a state trooper pulled the car over and ordered the driver to get out and show his license, insurance, and registration. McVeigh wondered what to do, for he had a Glock semiautomatic pistol, but decided not to fire. Instead, the officer frisked the driver, saw the concealed pistol in McVeigh's belt, disarmed him, and put on handcuffs for having a concealed weapon and the automobile misdemeanors. The trooper booked him into the Noble County jail, without realizing who they had behind bars.

The homegrown terrorist spent two days in jail while rumors swirled. Just two years after the 1993 attack on the World Trade Center many Americans thought that an Islamic jihadist had committed the crime. The *Wall Street Journal* compared the event to car bombs usually seen in Beirut. Others claimed Black Muslims did it, another alleged it was the CIA, while numerous experts claimed it was right-wing militia. "TERROR IN OKLAHOMA: THE FAR RIGHT," headlined a *New York Times* article. "Bomb Echoes Extremists' Tactics."

That was closer to the truth, for meanwhile federal authorities had tracked parts of the truck to Ryder and learned that it had been rented to a "Robert Kling," which was one of McVeigh's aliases. Two employees described McVeigh, and officials composed a sketch. The local judge was about to release McVeigh when federal officials called, drove to the courthouse, and walked him out in an orange jumpsuit. No, he was not a Middle Easterner; he was an angry white man from upstate New York. The crowd yelled, "Murderer!" "Killer!"

Clinton rushed to Oklahoma City, and with the damaged building in the background he spoke for the government employees who died as people "who worked to help the elderly and the disabled, who worked to support our farmers and our veterans, who worked to enforce our laws and to protect us." They were our "neighbors and friends," folks who we would see "at church or the PTA meetings, at the civic clubs, at the ball park." Next day Clinton got tougher, speaking out against "those who hate." Although basically opposed to the death penalty, he declared that "justice for these killers will be certain, swift and severe. We will find them. We will convict them. And we will seek the death penalty for them."

Nichols turned himself in to the police, and in the subsequent trial the jury gave him life in prison for conspiring with his partner and involuntary manslaughter. McVeigh received death.

When Ruby Ridge's Randy Weaver was asked about McVeigh's sentence, Weaver said, "He is a folk hero of ultra-right-wing groups." When asked about McVeigh's impending execution, he declared, "There should be a bunch of federal agents lying right beside him on the gurney." McVeigh, he continued, "was going to be judge, jury and executioner. No different from the federal government. One has a badge and one don't."

While McVeigh waited in his cell, there were the usual conspiracy theories swirling across the nation, especially that such a tragedy had to be caused by more than a couple of men. *Time* and CNN found in 1997 that 77 percent of respondents thought that other coconspirators had not yet been arrested. A Gallup poll five years after the tragedy still found that two-thirds of those asked said that McVeigh had not informed officials of all those involved in the bombing, a theory that novelist and celebrity Gore Vidal repeated in a popular article in *Vanity Fair* in 2001. That year the angry white man was executed by lethal injection.

To fight terrorism, Clinton significantly increased funding for the FBI and CIA, ordered them to work more closely together, and in 1996 signed the Antiterrorism and Effective Death Penalty Act. That bill and subsequent amendments tightened the standards for habeas corpus and increased the protection around federal buildings. The bill gave law enforcement greater access to financial records, more electronic surveillance of suspected terrorists, made it easier to deny them entry to the United States, and made it possible to trace explosive materials.

Weeks after the bombing the National Rifle Association dispatched a fund-raising letter that attacked federal agents, calling them "jackbooted thugs." Former president Bush, a life member of the NRA, called the letter a "vicious slander. . . . your broadside against Federal agents deeply offends my own sense of decency and honor; and it offends my concept of service to country." He resigned from the NRA.

Also within weeks, the "Main Street" of America, Pennsylvania Avenue, which runs in front of the White House en route to the Capitol, was under construction. Workers were putting up barricades so vehicles could not park or pass in front of the presidential mansion.[4]

Angry white men also included the emerging conservative media that developed as a force against the Clinton administration. Of course, there always had been conservatives of one degree or another on the airwaves. There were many demagogues during the second decade of radio, the Great Depression, and most of them were liberals in the sense that they were promising more than President Franklin Roosevelt was offering in his New Deal. In contrast, the first era of conservative talk show hosts appeared in the 1950s after Senator Joe McCarthy whipped up the nation over the fear of communism. Businessman Robert W. Welch Jr. founded the John Birch Society to oppose regulations, socialism, and especially communism. One of their primary financial supporters was Fred C. Koch, who cofounded Koch Industries. The Birchers focused more on totalitarian threats at home than abroad, and like McCarthy, many JBS attacks were based on conspiracies and preposterous ideas. They attacked President Eisenhower as "a dedicated, conscious agent of the Communist conspiracy."

Their radical message was too far right for other important conservatives of the era, including William F. Buckley Jr. who founded *National Review* and was instrumental in forming the Young Americans for Freedom in the early 1960s as a bulwark against the numerous protesters and demonstrators for civil and student rights and against the Vietnam War. Paul Harvey was one of the most popular commentators. His *Paul Harvey News and Comment*, and later, *The Rest of the Story*, was on the air for over half a century and reached more than twenty million people; he spun folksy stories and gave his news stories a conservative slant. On the death of Harry S Truman, for example, he called historian Richard S. Kirkendall and asked him some "what if" questions about the former president, then went on the air and told his audience exactly the opposite of what Kirkendall had said on the phone.

Conservative talk radio increased during the Reagan years and was fueled by some technological changes. The opening of the FM spectrum, which was not as susceptible to static, led station owners to move away from AM and go to FM, leaving space and time to be filled on AM stations. In the early 1980s, AT&T introduced direct dial toll-free calling, which made it easy and inviting for listeners to pick up the phone. And talk shows were greatly stimulated after 1987, when the Federal Communications Commission voted to abolish the Fairness Doctrine. That doctrine had required radio stations to present opposing views, but this more conservative FCC stated it contradicted the First Amendment, eliminated it, and all-talk shows proliferated. In 1960 there were only two stations with the talk format. Then came the end of the doctrine, and by the mid-1990s there were more than 1,100.

The next year the nation was introduced to Rush. Limbaugh's show in 1988 entered national syndication on AM and FM radio stations, and he quickly emerged as a powerful force. "His style," wrote the

New York Times, "a schizoid spritz, bouncing between earnest lecturer and political vaudevillian . . . his exuberance, his energy, his volume, his sobs, giggles, sighs, coughs, snatches of song, simulated trumpet fanfares and other vocal effects." After only two years on the national dial, he had five million listeners a week, more than any other talk show host on nearly three hundred stations, growing weekly.

Rush was an attack dog on liberals. During the early nineties he had proclaimed: "Evidence refutes liberalism," and "Liberals measure compassion by how many people are given welfare." And "some of them—many of them, perhaps—are just plain diabolical and dishonest to the core." Rush claimed, "No nation has ever taxed itself into prosperity." Don't blame conservatives, he said many times, blame liberals. "Lee Harvey Oswald came back from Moscow, a communist, blows away JFK. Sirhan Sirhan, Robert Kennedy, leftists. James Earl Ray, if anything, a leftist, assassin of Martin Luther King. It's not right-wingers doing any of this."

Rush continued and surprised no one when he declared: "Ronald Reagan was the greatest president of the twentieth century." Women liberationists were "Feminazis," and women "should not be allowed on juries where the accused is a stud." He claimed that "feminism was established as to allow unattractive women easier access." And he goaded:

> We know that women in groups—same office, same dormitory, same barracks—eventually have synchronized menstrual cycles. We also know that there is this thing called PMS, and we know that it turns a woman into a hellion. We know that PMS has been used as a defense against a charge of murder. Here's my proposal: We have 52 battalions. We can prepare the nation so that we have on any given week of the year a combat-ready battalion of Amazons to go into battle. . . . And there is Sgt. Maj. Molly Yard leading a battalion of Amazons with PMS over the hill! That would be enough to scare the pants off anybody.

Rush had other ideas. As for education, "The way to improve our schools is not more money, but the reintroduction of moral and spiritual values, as well as the four 'R's': reading, 'riting, 'rithmetic, and

Rush." "I am not arrogant," he claimed, later adding, "Too many Americans can't laugh at themselves anymore."

Rush lambasted mainstream media: "In this battle for the soul of democracy, it is more and more clear that the press . . . can't be trusted, cannot be counted on." He made fun of the poor, "the biggest piglets at the mother pig and her nipples," and minorities, "stupid, unskilled Mexicans."

As for the Clinton administration, Rush condemned the government's "attack" on Ruby Ridge, stoked anger with reports of the "Waco invasion" and Janet Reno's "murder" of citizens who were Christians. He called the Clintons' thirteen-year-old daughter, Chelsea, the "White House dog."

Like many angry white men, Rush was keen on conspiracies. "That is a myth," he declared about the dangers of smoking, and then claimed, "That has been disproven at the World Health Organization and the report was suppressed. There is no fatality whatsoever. There's no . . . major sickness component associated with secondhand smoke. It may irritate you, and you may not like it, but it will not make you sick, and it will not kill you." (In 2021 cigar-smoking Rush died of lung cancer, age seventy.)

In 1995, in the days after the Oklahoma City bombing, President Clinton denounced the "promoters of paranoia" on talk radio, remarks that were widely seen as aimed at Limbaugh. "We hear so many loud and angry voices in America today," said Clinton, "whose sole goal seems to be to try to keep some people as paranoid as possible and the rest of us all torn up and upset with each other."

During the nineties Limbaugh transformed talk radio into a relentless right-wing attack machine, his voice a regular feature of daily life. He was a showman who fermented mistrust and grievances to his base. He pushed groundless claims and rumors—all of which made his show remarkably popular. His program attracted almost twenty million listeners a week on more than 650 radio stations, more than any other radio show in the United States. His fans gleefully called themselves "dittoheads," because they apparently agreed with everything he said. "Limbaugh's fact-challenged dittoheads are men," wrote comedian Al Franken. "Limbaugh has tapped into the resentments of 'the angry white male,' which are quite legitimate. I mean, if you think about it, what chance for advancement have white men really had in this country?"

Rush and other conservative commentators had a field day with Clinton. Allegations surfaced about girls, murder, and land deals. The girls, of course, were Gennifer Flowers and Paula Jones. More would follow, and the "murder" was in 1993: Clinton's deputy White House counsel Vincent W. Foster was found dead in Fort Marcy Park outside Washington, DC. A number of official investigations ruled it a suicide, but it was much too juicy and stimulated numerous conspiracy theories. Roger Ailes, a longtime Republican operative and then president of CNBC, accused the administration of a "suicide cover-up—possible murder." A former Republican congressman called for congressional hearings on the "frightening" number of people who knew Clinton and had died "under other than natural circumstances." Televangelist Pat Robertson asked on his *700 Club*, "Was there a murder of a White House counsel? . . . It looks more and more like that." Limbaugh joined in, claiming that Vince had been murdered in an apartment Hillary owned and his body had been moved to the park. The seed was planted: Vince was killed in Hillary's apartment.

The land deal was Whitewater, as mentioned. The Whitewater Development Corporation was a failed business venture in the late 1970s. Then-governor Clinton and McDougal Associates were involved and lost money in Whitewater. End of story. No, the 1992 *New York Times* article stimulated renewed interest: the search for a conspiracy was on. In August 1994, a three-judge panel appointed Republican Kenneth Starr to head the Whitewater investigation, which continued on and in the news until the end of Clinton's presidency.

Meanwhile, conservatives were relating Whitewater with Clinton's failing health care plan. "Whitewater is about health care," declared Rush without explanation, while Republican representative Joel

Hefley said the president "promised health care reform, but delivered an unworkable socialist health care scheme. He promised the most ethical White House in history, but has delivered the most scandal-ridden administration in memory."

While Rush was exciting his base, another conservative talk show host took to the airwaves—Michael Savage. He grew up in the Bronx, attended Queens College, the University of Hawaii, and University of California, Berkeley, where he earned a PhD in nutritional ethnomedicine and thought of himself as the "herbal doctor." A prolific writer, he wrote many books on his academic specialties, even on topics such as nutritional cooking, planting trees, and beer-tasting, before he began writing on controversial conservative causes. He had given up on liberalism in the 1970s and turned more conservative during the Reagan years. In 1991 he published *The Death of the White Male*, arguing against affirmative action, which he labeled "reverse discrimination." Shortly thereafter he tried to publish a book linking illegal immigration and epidemics, but publishers rejected it as too inflammatory. Aware of Rush's popularity, Savage recorded a demo talk radio tape for 250 stations. In March 1994, he began his radio career on a San Francisco news/talk radio station as a fill-in and weekend host. His slogan: "To the right of Rush and to the left of God."

The show quickly became a local hit, and nine months later he had his own show, *The Savage Nation*. He bludgeoned "America's enemies"—liberals, gays, homeless, immigrants, feminists, minorities, CNN, Muslims, and, of course, the Clintons. Filled with energy, he was on the air three hours a day, five afternoons a week, playing to the angry white men's darkest fantasies. He suggested routing illegal immigrants: "If we had a government, we'd blow them out of the desert with airplanes!" As for commies, perverts, and other undesirables, "I say round them up and hang 'em high!" And as for the ACLU and other civil rights advocates, "When I hear someone's in the civil rights business, I oil up my AR-15!" He egged on his critics and other "brownshirt groups." "You stinking rats who hide in the sewers! . . . You think I'm going to roll over like a pussy? You're wrong!"

Like Rush, Savage wouldn't go away as many other conservatives hurried to the airwaves. Ken Hamblin, an African American conservative who called himself the "Black Avenger," was syndicated to sixty-three stations nationwide in 1995. "Being a bigot does not void your First Amendment rights," he declared, and he railed against gun control and even against James Brady, "the cripple guy," for promoting the Brady Bill. Neal Boortz, morning commentator for Atlanta's WSB, talked about the arrest of three boys for attempted robbery and the ensuing quarrel involving the mother: "When the police came to her welfare house and knocked on this welfare queen's door and took her little predators away, this woman, who by the way was about the size of a phone booth—she obviously puts her food stamps and welfare checks to good use!—she was screaming like a stuck pig because the police were taking her little predator welfare tickets away!" He continued talking about the mom: Your kids will "be home in a few days, and when they grow up, they'll probably kill somebody! Maybe even somebody you know!" On another Atlanta station was Sean Hannity, who criticized the Democratic proposal to raise the minimum wage: "How much more can you pay to someone who flips burgers for a living? Are you willing to pay more for a hamburger?" The Democrats, he continued, "can get a lot of mileage out of this because they can create this class envy and strife—which they're masters at."

Many other media conservatives were listening, including Roger Ailes. He grew up in a working-class family in Warren, Ohio, and majored in radio and television at Ohio University before he went into television production in Philadelphia. "I've had a broad life experience that doesn't translate into going to the Columbia Journalism School," he boasted. "That makes me a lot better journalist than some guys who had to listen to some pathetic professor who has been on the public dole all his life and really doesn't like this country much."

By age twenty-seven Ailes was working for *The Mike Douglas Show*, where in 1968 he met presidential candidate Richard Nixon. The Republican had been shy of the camera ever since the media declared he lost the 1960 televised debates to Democrat John Kennedy. "It's a shame a man has to use gimmicks like this to get elected," Nixon told Ailes, and the young producer shot back, "Television is not a gimmick, and if you think it is, you'll lose again." Nixon hired him a few days later.

Nixon's 1968 campaign was Ailes's first venture into politics, followed later in 1984 for Reagan and 1988 for Bush. The TV producer focused on framing national issues, and in the latter year it was being tough on crime, resulting in the controversial "Willy Horton" ad. He worked with Lee Atwater, the architect of Bush's election victory, who later described Ailes as having "two speeds: attack and destroy."

Ailes was perfecting his skills and was credited with the "Orchestra Pit Theory," which he often demonstrated with the question: "If you have two guys on a stage and one guy says, 'I have a solution to the Middle East problem,' and the other guy falls in the orchestra pit, who do you think is going to be on the evening news?"

By the early nineties Roger Ailes was the executive producer of Rush Limbaugh's TV show, while at the same time Rupert Murdoch was building a media empire. During the 1950s and 1960s, Australian Murdoch acquired a number of newspapers in his own nation and New Zealand before 1969, when he expanded into the United Kingdom, buying the tabloid *News of the World*, later *The Sun*, and eventually *The Times*. Meanwhile, Murdoch had set his sights on the United States and in 1974 moved to New York City. He began the naturalization process because citizenship was a requirement to own television networks, and he aimed to increase his properties in News Corp, his holding company for his media outlets. In 1985 News Corp acquired the movie giant Twentieth Century Fox, a few years later the book publisher HarperCollins, and in 1990 the British broadcaster BSkyB, or Sky, while that same decade the company expanded into Asian networks and South American television. By the end of the decade Murdoch's News Corporation owned over eight hundred companies in more than fifty countries.

Murdoch understood business and changing technology. Within thirty years he was the first mogul to create and control a global media empire, the first to understand the opportunities offered by new technology such as computers, satellites, and wireless communications. He used them to create an international press, a television domain, a publishing empire, and movie studios. To help do that he had to make political allies, and while an advocate of free enterprise, he generally played both sides of the aisle in Australia, Britain, and the United States. As he told his biographer, he saw himself pretty much as a libertarian: "What does libertarian mean? As much individual responsibility as possible, as little government as possible, as few rules as possible. But I'm not saying it should be taken to the absolute limit."

Through a series of deal-making Murdoch bought out a half dozen television stations in America. He had tried to buy CNN, but Ted Turner was not interested, and in 1986 Murdoch established Fox Broadcasting Company. The network expanded and had financial success with programs such as *The Simpsons* and *The X-Files*. In a bold and brilliant move, in 1993 Fox Network took over exclusive

Rupert Murdoch, background, announced in 1996 that Roger Ailes would be chairman and CEO of Fox News. AP Photo/Richard Drew.

coverage of the National Football League, pushing out CBS and greatly boosting Fox Sports. Since 1980, Ted Turner's CNN had dominated cable news service, and in 1996 Murdoch entered the market with the Fox News Channel.

Murdoch hired Ailes as CEO of Fox News. "Fair and balanced" was Ailes's defining phrase for Fox News, along with another slogan: "We report. You decide." Liberals lambasted the slogans and the Republican-slanted coverage, often labeling it Fox Noise, Fixed News, Faux News, or the Republican Propaganda Network. Ailes punched back: "If we look conservative, it's because the other guys are so far to the left." To Ailes, CNN stood for Clinton News Network and CBS for Communist Broadcasting System. What Fox News did, he said, was apply a necessary corrective. "I don't ignore anything," Ailes later declared. "Somebody gets in my face, I get in their face."

Within a year Ailes was in liberals' faces with evening primetime shows featuring Bill O'Reilly and Sean Hannity, and within six years Fox News surprised the media industry by having more viewers than CNN. Many of their commentators had similarities with talk radio stars Limbaugh and Savage. They hurled opinions and vented resentments. They played the defense against the "liberal media." These hyperaggressive conservatives always made it seem to their listeners that they were under attack. Their plan was simple, and proven. They told their listeners that "liberals"—intellectuals, professors, elites, gays, feminists, George Soros, or whoever was in the mainstream media that week—were tearing down the nation, and they were standing up for America. These angry white male talk show hosts articulated just what their angry white male listeners believed—and wanted to hear.

What was true, what was real? "Reality," joked Stephen Colbert, "has a well-known liberal bias."

Moreover, these talk show stars usually peddled conspiracies. Naturally, those theories were out of the old playbook. They usually had a shred of plausibility, often involved a rich or famous person, and aimed to divide society: Them liberals versus Us angry white men.

This wasn't new for conspiracy theories—just amped up in the nineties on talk radio, and eventually on social media.

Toward the end of the nineties, another angry white man joined the choir of conspiracy theorists—Alex Jones. He grew up in Dallas and Austin, Texas, and was a typical teen who played football, but he also read a lot. A book that he later cited as very influential for him was a 1970s volume by Gary Allen, *None Dare Call It Conspiracy*, a book that described a global network of insiders who wielded the power over everyone in the coming New World Order, one quite different from that announced by President Bush. In this one, supposedly, international bankers financed the communist revolution in Russia, and then bankers enacted a global government with centralized monetary policies and social welfare programs that kept mankind dependent and subservient. While Jones was in high school an event supported his belief that there were evil forces at work in the nation—the federal siege of the Branch Davidian compound that ended in a tragic firestorm—and two years later those powers reappeared in the destruction of the Murrah building in Oklahoma City.

After dropping out of a community college, Jones hosted a call-in show on Austin's public access television, where he sharpened his bombastic style, and in 1996 he moved to Austin's KJFK-FM to host a show called *The Final Edition*. After he made incredible claims his audience grew, and in 1999 he began broadcasting from his house via Infowars.com. Genesis Communications syndicated him nationally, and soon he was on a hundred stations telling his followers that at Mount Carmel the FBI had "machine-gunned men, women, and children as they tried to exit" and that the Oklahoma City bombing "was an inside job—a false flag operation" coordinated by the Clintons. In fact, he said, he had interviewed people who had seen Timothy McVeigh planting explosives with a military escort and cops and that they held a bomb drill that fateful morning. After 9/11, he claimed, the WTC did not crumble because of airplanes flying into them but because someone held "controlled demolitions."

Eventually, Jones would concoct conspiracies about the moon landing, JFK's assassination, the Sandy Hook school massacre, and the Boston Marathon bombing. In an interview he said that he was proud to be known as a "thought criminal against Big Brother." He continued, "Basically, we as a nation have consumed poison . . . and if we don't vomit it up very quick, we as a country will expire like Nazi Germany."

Jones made kooky claims: that acts of terrorism were faked by the government; that the CEO of Chobani yogurt company was importing "migrant rapists" to work at its factory; that Hillary Clinton was a demon who lives in Hell and "personally murdered and chopped up and raped" little children; and that "They're turning the freaking frogs gay!"

Time out, said David Letterman. "America is the only country where a significant proportion of the population believes that professional wrestling is real, but the moon landing was faked."

The federal government helped such ideas spread across the nation. As stated, the Federal Communications Commission ended the Fairness Doctrine, and that allowed "anything goes" speech on the airways. Furthermore, Congress passed another form of deregulation with the Telecommunications Act of 1996. It was the first time that the internet was included in the broadcasting and spectrum allotment, and it also allowed companies to own more radio stations. Before, radio stations were usually owned by local community businessmen, but by the end of the decade more than 25 percent of American radio stations had been sold, as the nation witnessed the rise of conglomerates such as Clear Channel Communications. By 2010 Clear Channel owned some eight hundred radio stations across the nation, and its largest contract was with Rush Limbaugh.

With the termination of the Fairness Doctrine conservative radio took off, and liberal radio sputtered with small audiences. Why? Liberals were "genetically engineered to not offend anybody," said the manager of a talk station in Chicago. "People who go on the air afraid of offending are not inherently entertaining." The most notable liberal hosts in the mid-1990s were New Yorker Mario Cuomo and Texan Jim Hightower. "It's hard for the donkeys to win the race," Hightower declared, "if they're going to carry the elephants on their backs."

The big money, of course, was spent on television, and the liberals wanted to compete with Fox News. The same year Murdoch created his network, 1996, Microsoft and General Electric's NBC unit created MSNBC. The first few years were bumpy. The network originally wanted to appeal to tech-savvy young audiences by demonstrating the merging of the internet and television, but it suffered many changes in management and had many internal squabbles over its future direction and politics. In its first seven years the network hired such diverse anchors as Mike Savage, Joe Scarborough, Chris Matthews, and Jesse Ventura. In 1999, MSNBC began a partnership with the *Washington Post* that boosted its ratings, and the same increases were witnessed during the impeachment of Bill Clinton. Yet, the biggest boost to MSNBC's viewership came in March 2003, when President George W. Bush invaded Iraq and MSNBC hired Keith Olbermann to host his show, *Countdown*. Olbermann mixed the news with liberal opinions, many of them scathing, on the Bush administration, and many in direct contradiction of what Bill O'Reilly was stating on Fox News. This began a newsworthy feud between *Countdown* and *The O'Reilly Factor*.

Thus, the mid-1990s witnessed the creation of the 24-hour news cycle. CNN, Fox News, and MSNBC all competed to capture the audience market for their never-ending news, entertainment, and talk shows. While the Old Media of big city newspapers, national magazines, and the Big Three networks plus PBS tried to keep some vestige of objectivity and balance, the New Media paired with the internet threw open the floodgates. At any time of the day or night one could flip on the TV and see a "wide assortment of pundits, commentators, experts, hacks, and hucksters," wrote media journalist Howard Kurtz, "some of them cloaked in the thinnest journalistic garb. They analyze,

interpret, elucidate, expound, pontificate, and predict, an unprecedented barrage of blather and bluster that has dramatically ratcheted
up the noise level of political debate."

The Old Media tried to fight back and hold on to its declining
share of the market. On America Online the *Chicago Tribune* launched
its digital edition in May 1992, but most mainstream papers waited
until after Netscape appeared in fall 1995. Then in the first six months
of 1996 came the onslaught. The *New York Times* went online, followed
by the *Los Angeles Times*, the *Wall Street Journal*, and the *Washington Post*.

All the while Americans continued tuning in to talk shows. Those
programs gave people with similar views a sense of connection, and
before the 1994 elections Republicans realized that polls demonstrated that about 45 percent of Americans named talk radio as their
chief source of political information. They were just the type of audience Republicans wanted at the polls—white, male, conservative. Talk
radio captured 15 percent of the audience in the mid-1990s, second
only to country music as the nation's most pervasive format. Ten years
earlier there were about two hundred talk stations: by the mid-1990s
some one thousand. According to *Talkers Magazine*, about half of all
American adults listened to the format at least once a week for at least
an hour.

The explosion of talk shows created a new form of populism and
demagoguery. The middle ground became too dull, not as profitable,
so extremism in pursuit of ratings became the mainstay. The national
dialogue was weakened. Balanced views supported by facts were dismissed. Anyone could say anything with little fear that they would be
censored. Talk was cheap. Armchair warriors could defuse any crisis,
solve any national problem, resolve any sexual problem, all before
the commercial break. "The whole point of the talk show business,"
Kurtz explained, "is not so much to persuade as to posture, to slam-
dunk opponents and to build audience share." Thus, Kurtz continued,
talk shows reveled in their "one-sided pugnacity, spreading wild theories, delicious gossip, and angry denunciations with gleeful abandon-
ment. . . . It is raw, it is real, and it is immensely popular."

The 24-hour news cycle and the talk shows had an impact. "America is awash in talk. Loud talk. Angry talk. Conspiratorial talk. Raunchy talk, smug talk, self-serving talk, funny talk, rumor-mongering talk," Kurtz concluded. "A cacophony of chat fills the airwaves from coast to coast, from dawn to dusk and beyond, all talk all the time."

The talk was too loud not to notice. In 1995 one of the nation's most astute observers, commentator Russell Baker, gave a commencement speech. His topic was the national mood:

> I have never seen a time when there were so many Americans so angry or so mean-spirited or so sour about the country as there are today. Anger has become the national habit. . . . It pours out of the radio. Washington television hams snarl and shout at each other on television. . . . Rudeness has become an acceptable way of announcing you are sick and tired of it all and are not going to take it anymore.

Why? Baker asked, when the economy was good and the nation was at peace: "I suspect it's the famous American ignorance of history. People who know nothing of even the most recent past are easily gulled by slick operators who prosper by exploiting the ignorant."[5]

Indeed, all that appeared daily. The talk shows amplified the uneasy feelings of many Americans at mid-decade, what *Newsweek* labeled "The Nervous Nineties."

3

The Nervous Nineties

In 1995 *Newsweek* labeled the era "The Nervous Nineties." Journalist Joe Klein wrote an article that appeared after the Oklahoma City bombing. "The effect of explosives upon human flesh is too implausible to be easily assimilated. . . . What happened to the children of Oklahoma City is unimaginable." What was happening to the nation? "This is America," one severely injured child's father lamented. "We shouldn't have to run scared. We shouldn't be afraid to take a 2- or 3-year-old to the day-care center." Klein continued, "And yet, we are; even on normal days, even on the best of days. This is America. . . . These are the Nervous Nineties. Life—by any rational standard—is good. The economy is good. We are not at war. But we are not quite at peace, either. We are beset by amorphous threats."

There seemed to be many threats, many exaggerated by talk show hosts. A *Washington Post* poll taken after the Oklahoma City bombing found that 58 percent agreed that some hosts "spread hateful ideas and give the impression that violence is acceptable." Some 40 percent of those asked felt that what is said on radio should be restricted, a chilling thought for advocates of the First Amendment.

Restrictions, of course, would not happen, while another reason for citizens to worry was that HIV/AIDS was ravishing the nation. "Doctors in New York and California have diagnosed among homosexual men 41 cases of a rare and often rapidly fatal form of cancer," wrote the *New York Times* in July 1981. "Eight of the victims died less than 24 months after the diagnosis was made. . . . The cause of the outbreak is unknown." The virus spread rapidly, especially hitting gays and intravenous drug users. By 1985 it had killed more than 12,500 Americans and had become a world pandemic, spreading to more than fifty countries. President Reagan didn't discuss or confront the deadly disease, but his speechwriter Patrick Buchanan wrote an opinion piece to the *Washington Post*, concluding, "The poor homosexuals; they have declared war upon nature, and now nature is exacting an awful retribution." As the death toll mounted, the administration did little; as *San Francisco Chronicle* journalist Randy Shilts wrote, *And the Band Played On.*

Government inaction prompted gay playwright Larry Kramer into action. He noticed that a number of his friends in New York City were falling ill. Concerned, in 1983 he wrote an essay. "1,112 and Counting," which appeared in a gay newspaper. Kramer bluntly condemned gays who would not take action, along with researchers at the Center for Disease Control and the National Institutes of Health, even local doctors and Mayor Ed Koch, for not addressing the epidemic. Kramer was the catalyst in 1987 in establishing a direct-action protest organization, AIDS Coalition to Unleash Power (ACT UP), that targeted government agencies and corporations to publicize lack of treatment and funding for people with AIDS.

ACT UP had an impact as thousands died from HIV/AIDS. Finally, in his last months in office Reagan signed the HOPE Act, which supplied the first federal funds to combat the virus, and by that time the director of the National Institute of Allergy and Infectious Diseases, Dr. Anthony Fauci, also led the new Office of AIDS Research. President Bush did more. During the second month of his administration First Lady Barbara posed with an AIDS baby. The new president rarely mentioned the topic, but he did sign the first significant legislation on the virus, the Americans with Disabilities Act, which protected ill people, and the Ryan White CARE Act, which was federal funding for AIDS patients. Clinton responded aggressively, massively increasing funding for research prevention and treatment, which eventually had a major impact.

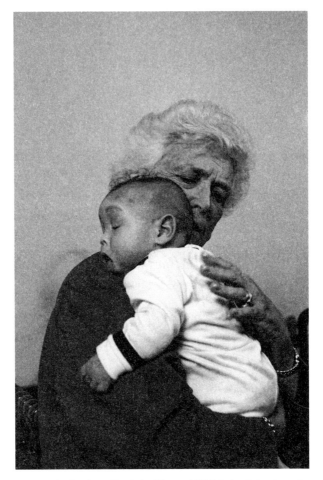

First Lady Barbara Bush holds an AIDS baby, March 1989,
demonstrating that federal neglect of the killer virus was
over. AP Photo/Dennis Cook.

AIDS took America by storm, creating anxiety throughout the
nation. In 1985, Ryan White, a thirteen-year-old hemophiliac with
AIDS, was barred from school in Indiana and later died, and so did
movie star Rock Hudson. That shocked Americans, for few knew that
the handsome film idol, who starred with many glamorous women,
was gay. Also shocking were his last photos, revealing the emaciated
star. Over the next years AIDS killed pianist Liberace, tennis great

Arthur Ashe, dancer Rudolf Nureyev, front man for Queen Freddie Mercury, and journalist Randy Shilts.

In 1992 *Time* ran a story, "Invincible AIDS," declaring that in the mid-1980s researchers announced that a vaccine could be ready in two years, but "Suddenly, the AIDS outlook has become bleaker: more heterosexual transmission, more cases among women and a rising death toll well into the next century." The World Health Organization said some thirty million people around the world could be infected by the year 2000, while other experts thought the number could reach over one hundred million. By 1995 AIDS had become the leading cause of death among all Americans ages twenty-five to forty-four. That year the CDC reported that since 1981 more than 513,000 citizens had been infected, and some 320,000 had died. "Humanity," the magazine's cover blared, was "LOSING THE BATTLE."

That prompted more action. In April 1993 some 300,000 gays, lesbians, and supporters marched on the Mall from the Washington Monument to the Capitol. The demonstrators came with a broad civil rights agenda that included many demands, including acceptance, equality, fighting AIDS, and ending the ban on military service; when gay Vietnam vets appeared, they received thunderous applause. A "sea of marchers, rainbow flags, banners, signs, red ribbons, and pink triangles," wrote the *New York Times*. "Chants welled up: 'Act Up! Fight Back! Fight AIDS.'"

By the early nineties it wasn't just gays and intravenous drug users who were contracting AIDS. For Arthur Ashe and Ryan White it was blood transfusions, and some tourists to hotspots like Africa began carrying their own pints of blood. "Doctors and AIDS," *Newsweek* proclaimed, and the article noted that scores of patients were getting the virus from their doctors, dentists, and health care workers, and that set off an "explosive national controversy over AIDS-infected healthcare workers."

For many other men and women, the cause was unprotected sex. At the beginning of the 1991 basketball season, Los Angeles Lakers star

Magic Johnson stunned the sports world. He was thirty-two, a veteran of twelve seasons in the NBA in which his team had won five championships. Recently, he had sat out some games, and it was rumored that he had the flu. With team members and the press in front of him, Magic declared that he was positive for HIV. He said that he would become a national spokesman about HIV, that "safe sex is the way to go. We sometimes think only gay people can get it, that it's not going to happen to me. . . . And here I am saying that it can happen to anybody, even me, Magic Johnson."

The disease had crept into the heterosexual world. Although married, Magic soon admitted that he had had numerous affairs with many women, who also were vulnerable to the virus. Between 1991 and 1995 AIDS was the fourth leading cause of death among women ages twenty-five to forty-four years in the United States, while the incidence of the virus was increasing more rapidly among women than men and represented about 15 percent of the new cases. In 1994 the FDA approved a female condom for sale in the United States.

Indeed, by the mid-1990s HIV/AIDS was putting not only America on edge, but people in most countries. Worldwide, more than fifty-five countries reported AIDS cases, all continents except Antarctica; some twenty-two million were infected and six million had died.[1]

Another worry to many Americans was Japan. During the 1980s many wrote about the "rise of the Asian tigers," or the "Asian Miracle" led by Japan and its surging economy. By the end of that decade Japan had the second-largest economy in the world, behind only the United States, and there were scores of articles about how the "Rising Sun" would eclipse the American economy in the nineties. For many years the Japanese yen had been trading at about 350 to one dollar, but by 1990 it had rocketed up in strength to about 100 to a dollar. Japan's per capita income was just below America's, industrial production in many areas was superior, and in the last five years of the 1980s the Nikkei average had tripled on the Tokyo Stock Market. The combined value of stock in Tokyo exceeded the value of the entire New York Stock Exchange.

Why? After the oil embargoes of the 1970s, Americans had been buying millions of fuel-efficient Nissans, Mitsubishis, Mazdas, Hondas, and Toyotas, while at the same time purchasing boat loads of electronics and cameras by Canon, Casio, Citizen, Fujitsu, Hitachi, JVC, Konica, Minolta, NEC, Nikon, Olympus, Panasonic, Pioneer, Ricoh, Seiko, Sharp, and of course Sony. The saying was, Japan sent ships to America loaded with cars and electronics and we sent vessels back loaded with dollars. The US trade deficit with Japan was soaring, from about $40 billion in 1990 to $65 billion in 1994 to over $80 billion by the end of the decade.

US politicians fought back. St. Louis congressman Richard Gephardt ran for the 1988 Democratic nomination for president, and one of his main appeals was to blame Germany and Asia for America's trade deficit and call on those nations to curb exports or face tariffs.

His opponents called foul, "Japan-Bashing," and the *New York Times* editorialized, "The Gephardt proposal sounds good—finally striking back at Japan." But the newspaper continued that in the long run the nation would face "higher prices and fewer jobs. Those are pretty bleak campaign promises."

The Japanese had bucks to spend, and with cheap capital, a strong yen, and loose lending standards, they were buying up prime real estate in the United States, including some of the most famous office buildings and hotels in California, New York, and Hawaii. Japanese interests bought CBS Records, Rockefeller Center, the Pebble Beach golf course and resort, and the Biltmore Hotel in Los Angeles, a city in which their investors own about 45 percent of the premium downtown office space.

Many wondered, as Professor Norman Glickman addressed, "Are the Japanese Taking Over the American Economy?" He declared that "Americans are confused and angry about our economic loss, and more than any other nation, Japan is seen as the villain, the country most likely to take away our economic birthright."

Japan was the topic for books and movies. Two authors published *The Coming War with Japan*, in which they claimed that both nations were in "a downward spiral from trade friction to protectionism to armed showdown over markets and raw materials." The last chapter was titled "Collision Course." Michael Crichton, already famous with his novels turned into movies *The Andromeda Strain* and *Jurassic Park*, wrote the 1992 best-seller *Rising Sun*. The novel was a murder mystery that questioned the idea that Japanese investment in American high-technology sectors benefited the United States. One scholar published *The Endangered American Dream*, partly subtitled *How to Stop the United States from Becoming a Third-World Country*, which included a chapter titled "Our Japan Problem." With the demise of the Soviet Union, the author contended, "any careful student of the American media can see how Japan has gradually been turned into the new Chief Enemy."

Another worry was money, more specifically income disparity. At the end of World War II no one would have suspected the booming American economy of the next twenty-five years. That all began to fall apart in the 1970s with oil embargoes and stagflation that helped elect a man who promised to get the economy rolling again. Ronald Reagan did that with tax cuts and greatly expanded budgets, but also with rising federal debt and income inequality. From 1981 to 1990, Pew Research reported, the change in mean family income ranged from a small loss for families in the lowest 20 percent of earners to a gain of 2 percent annually for families in the top 20 percent. The top 5 percent of families saw their income increase at over 3 percent annually during the Reagan years. Thus by the early nineties Americans were witnessing the long and steady rise in income inequality. Then came the 1990–91 recession, layoffs and downsizing, and most of the middle class felt squeezed. Although two salaries were the norm by then, pollster Daniel Yankelovich found the average household had "a lot more stress than people ever imagined."

Those stressed the most were members of Gen X, the children of the baby boomers, born between 1965 and 1980 The economic climate of the early nineties left a mark on the Xers. One poll showed that over 60 percent of them "worry about the future . . . a major source of stress." That percentage was far more than their boomer parents, and about 75 percent said, "No matter what I plan for the future, when I finally get there, it's always something different."

One Gen Xer, Chuck Klosterman, felt he and his companions had "a knee-jerk distaste for Boomer ideology and a fear of invisible market forces that infiltrated everything. These amorphous oppressors were bemoaned at length." Nevertheless, he thought it was absurd to define his generation, but if he had to, he wrote "with conviction: among the generations that have yet to go extinct, Generation X remains the least annoying."

What was annoying to many was the growing income gap. While the economy was on a roll, the second half of the decade income and wealth levels among African Americans, Hispanics, and whites remained vastly different. The *New York Times* reported, "the typical white family earned about $47,000 in 1996, almost twice that of blacks. Worse, the typical black household had a net worth of only about $4,500, a tenth of the white figure." And while the stock market was soaring, 95 percent of Blacks owned no stocks or pension funds. The Urban Institute reported in 1995 that the total wealth (income, savings, home, retirement) of the nation's white families averaged a little under $400,000, $96,000 for Latinos, and $70,000 for African Americans. Put another way, white wealth was seven times greater than that of Blacks and five times greater than for Hispanics.

The rich continued to get richer, as the income gap expanded. "My sense is that few people are aware of just how much the gap between the very rich and the rest has widened over a relatively short period of time," wrote economist and columnist Paul Krugman. Between 1979 and 1997, the after-tax incomes of the top 1 percent of families rose 157 percent, compared with only a 10 percent gain for families near the middle of the income distribution. Moreover, from 1970 to 1998 the average annual salaries of corporate CEOs had risen from over $1 million to over $37 million, or in other words, from about forty to over a thousand times the average earnings of their workers. Recalling the era of the robber barons like Carnegie, Vanderbilt, and

J. P. Morgan, Krugman declared that the United States had entered a "New Gilded Age." "John Kennedy was wrong." A "rising tide doesn't necessarily lift all boats. Right now, it seems to be lifting only yachts. The disparity in incomes is growing. That's cause for a lot of anxiety."[2]

The mid-1990s also were nervous for President Clinton. Whitewater would not go away. On January 5, 1994, the *Washington Post* editorialized that while no one had found that the Clintons had done anything wrong in the land deal, perhaps it was time for a special prosecutor to investigate. CNN amplified the message on its nightly news, anchor Lou Dobbs declaring, "storm clouds continue to gather around the president for his connection with the Arkansas Whitewater project. Late today, the Clinton administration announced that it would begin turning the president's Whitewater records over to the Justice Department under subpoena. There is mounting pressure for the appointment of an independent counsel."

Indeed, it was a pressure cooker. By March only a third of Americans surveyed in a Time/CNN poll thought they could trust the president, more than half thought "the Clintons are hiding something about Whitewater, and a third think they broke the law."

What to do? The president consulted his staff, and a majority of them thought he should "lance the boil" and hold the investigation. Clinton was convinced that since he and his wife had done "nothing wrong" they would quickly be exonerated, and they could move on to the nation's business. Clinton told Attorney General Janet Reno to appoint a special prosecutor to investigate himself and Whitewater, which he later called "the worst presidential decision I ever made."

Janet Reno appointed Robert Fiske Jr. as the independent counsel in charge of investigating financial irregularities at Whitewater Development Corporation, and by summer the House and Senate Banking Committees began hearings on Whitewater. They subpoenaed almost thirty administration officials to testify at congressional hearings, clearing the Clintons of any misconduct.

Yet in August a panel of judges concluded that Fiske should not have been appointed by the Clinton administration, and they replaced him with Kenneth W. Starr, a minister's son who became a corporate lawyer and a former federal appeals court judge and US solicitor who worked in the Reagan and Bush administrations. Starr had never prosecuted a case during his career before he set out to investigate the president of the United States.

Meanwhile, in January 1995, the Republicans took control of Congress. By summer they established the Senate Special Whitewater Committee, chaired by New York Republican Alfonse D'Amato, who began hearings not only on Whitewater but also on Vince Foster's suicide in 1993. The hearings kept Whitewater and the suicide in the news for the next year. By October the Senate Whitewater Committee had issued almost fifty subpoenas to federal agencies and others they claim were involved in the affair.

Of interest were Hillary Clinton's billing records from her employer Rose Law Firm during the 1980s when she did legal work for Madison Guaranty Savings and Loan. Those documents were located in August 1995 and showed that she performed sixty hours of legal work for Madison in 1985 and 1986.

That was well known, and she had told the public that years earlier, but conservatives pounced. *New York Times* conservative columnist William Safire indicted her in print with his commentary "Blizzard of Lies." Wrote Safire, "Americans of all political persuasions are coming to the sad realization that our first lady—a woman of undoubted talents who was a role model for many in her generation—is a congenital liar." He continued that Rose Law Firm records had been kept in Foster's White House office, and they were "spirited out in the dead of night and hidden from the law for two years—in Hillary's closet. . . . She had good reasons to lie; she's in the longtime habit of lying."

When White House press secretary Michael McCurry was asked what the president thought of Safire's invective, McCurry declared that if Clinton were not president, he "would have delivered a more forceful response to that on the bridge of Mr. Safire's nose."

Eventually in 1996, Kenneth Starr interviewed both the president and the first lady, and no charges were filed. Nevertheless, the seed had been planted. Issues about possible cover-ups involving Whitewater and Vince Foster damaged Hillary's credibility.

Speaking of credibility, earlier in January 1994 investigative reporter David Brock published an article in the conservative *American Spectator* about Bill Clinton's sex life. Brock said that he interviewed many Arkansas state troopers, and some of them told of how during the 1980s Governor Clinton used troopers to facilitate his extramarital sexual activities, which in the post-Nixon era soon became known as Troopergate. According to Brock, in addition to Gennifer Flowers, Clinton had sex with a "staffer in Clinton's office; an Arkansas lawyer Clinton appointed to a judgeship; the wife of a prominent judge; a local reporter; an employee at Arkansas Power and Light . . . and a cosmetic salesclerk at a Little Rock department store." But that's not all:

> Clinton also had a series of brief affairs and one-time encounters from 1987 through early 1993 of which the troopers had direct knowledge. He often met women at social functions in Little Rock or on the road. Sometimes he would even use troopers as intermediaries, sending them off with messages and outright propositions to women to retire to back rooms, hotel rooms, or offices with him. . . . One of the troopers told the story of how Clinton had eyed a woman at a reception at the Excelsior Hotel in downtown Little Rock. . . . Clinton asked him to approach the woman, whom the trooper remembered only as Paula, tell her how attractive the governor thought she was, and take her to a room in the hotel where Clinton would be waiting. . . . As the trooper stood by in the hall, the trooper said Paula told him she was available to be Clinton's regular girlfriend if he so desired.

Her name was Paula Jones, and that's not how she remembered it. She claimed that on May 8, 1991, she was excited to get invited to meet the governor. When she went to the room Clinton approached her and exposed himself and propositioned her. Embarrassed, she left as quickly as possible as he said, "Let's keep this between ourselves."

Keeping that between themselves lasted three years, for in May 1994 Paula went public, making statements to the press and filing a lawsuit against the president seeking $700,000 in damages for "willful, out-rageous and malicious conduct" at the Excelsior Hotel. She accused Clinton of "sexually harassing and assaulting" her, then defaming her with denials. In August Clinton surprised many, filing a motion to dismiss the suit on grounds of "presidential immunity." His lawyers argued that a president couldn't be sued for previous behavior before he moved into the White House.

The suit was *Jones v. Clinton*. In December US District Judge Susan Webber Wright ruled that a sitting president could not be sued and deferred the case until the conclusion of his term, prompting an appeal. In January 1995, Jones asked the 8th US Circuit Court of Appeals to reverse the decision postponing a trial, and in September 1995 a three-judge appeals court panel heard Clinton's lawyers argue that allowing Jones's case to proceed while the president is in office would distract him from more important matters. Jones's lawyers argue she should have the same rights as anyone else bringing a lawsuit. In January 1996, the federal court of appeals ruled that the president, like all other government officials and citizens, was subject to the same laws. Clinton then appealed to the US Supreme Court. The evolving court case kept the Paula issue on the nightly news for years.[3]

O. J. Simpson had other anxieties in the nervous nineties, and the media labeled it "The Trial of the Century."

During the night of June 12, 1994, a person quietly broke into the back entrance of an upscale condominium in the Brentwood area of Los Angeles. The intruder attacked and slashed the neck of Nicole Brown Simpson, almost severing it from her head, then stabbed her guest, Ronald Goldman, almost thirty times, killing both. Nicole was thirty-five, the divorced wife of O.J., and she was a friend of Ron, who was a twenty-five-year-old waiter at the restaurant where the Brown family had eaten that evening. Some surmised that the two were going to have a romantic interlude, while others stated that Goldman was returning a pair of glasses left at the restaurant. After the intruder escaped, Nicole's dog began howling, and a neighbor came over and found the two bloody bodies.

Orenthal James Simpson grew up in the tough Potrero Hill district of San Francisco. His mother and father divorced when he was young, and by the time he was a teen he joined gangs, getting arrested for petty crimes. Willie Mays, the great center fielder for the San Francisco Giants, met the teenaged troublemaker and convinced him to get involved in sports, and Simpson became a superb running back on his high school team. His poor grades prevented him from receiving a university scholarship, so he attended City College of San Francisco, where he excelled on the gridiron and was named to the Junior College All-American team. He broke all records and was offered numerous scholarships by powerhouse college football programs, accepting the one from the University of Southern California. At USC he led the nation in rushing for two years and in 1968 won the Heisman Trophy. For the next decade he played for the Buffalo Bills and the San Francisco 49ers, and in 1973 he became the first NFL player to rush for more than 2,000 yards in a season. After his retirement he was inducted into the College Football Hall of Fame and the Pro Football Hall of Fame.

O.J., or the "Juice," began careers in acting and football broadcasting in the 1970s before he retired from sports. He was famous on television ads for Hertz Car Rental, running through airports, hurtling over gates for the car lot as onlookers yelled, "Go, O.J., go!" He had roles in dramatic motion pictures such as *The Klansman* and *The Towering Inferno*, and in the 1980s continued starring in films and was a commentator for *Monday Night Football*. By the end of the decade and until 1994 the Juice was surprisingly funny as Detective Nordberg, the lackey sidekick to Detective Frank Drebin (Leslie Nielsen) in three hilarious *Naked Gun* spoofs. He felt so comfortable in the Hollywood scene, so homogenized in America, that he used to say to his friends, "I'm not black. I'm O.J."

O.J. met Nicole when she was eighteen and working as a waitress, and although Simpson was twenty-two years older and married, they began an affair. O.J. divorced his first wife in 1985 and at forty-eight married Nicole, twenty-six. They had two children, but the marriage was troubled; Nicole claimed O.J. abused her, and in 1992 she filed for divorce.

Five days after Nicole and Goldman were slain, police issued warrants for Simpson. Charge: murder. When he failed to turn himself in, as he had promised, police began the hunt for his car, a white Bronco, while his lawyer read a letter to the police. Written in the past tense, it sounded like a suicide note. "I've had a great life," it declared. "Please think of the real O.J. and not this lost person."

Police and TV helicopters found the white Bronco driving on a Los Angeles freeway. A friend and former teammate was driving the Bronco, and it was reported that O.J. was armed in the back seat, supposedly with a gun to his head. Was he going to commit suicide? Soon a battalion of cruisers, red lights flashing, had joined twelve helicopters, and all followed the vehicle for a procession of more than fifty miles that lasted two hours until the Bronco pulled into O.J.'s home and he surrendered. Sportscasters declared it was "O.J.'s last end-run home."

Television stations and talk radio shows cut out of their usual programming, beamed live coverage of the chase of the white Bronco. People left their shops, offices, homes and lined the highway, many of them yelling, "Go, O.J., go!" As the show went on, a rising crescendo of voices filled the airwaves. One woman summarized, "You watch this, and you go, 'What's going on? What's going on with our whole society?'"

Media experts estimated that almost one hundred million Americans saw at least parts of the pursuit of the Juice. Phenomenal numbers, for up to that time the only events that had gained that many viewers were the Kennedy assassination and funeral and the landing and walk on the moon. Commentators quipped that O.J.'s ride was the most famous one since Paul Revere's.

The nationally televised trial began in January 1995 and dragged on and on, day after day for nine long months. O.J. certainly was the most famous person prosecuted for murder in the era, if not in modern American history. The multimillionaire hired nine high-profile lawyers, led by the "Dream Team" of Robert Shapiro, Johnnie Cochran Jr., and F. Lee Bailey. O.J. had hired Shapiro immediately after his arrest; the well-known Los Angeles attorney basically thought that the large amount of physical evidence at the house and in the Bronco—Simpson's blood—demonstrated that O.J. was guilty, and that the only way out was to play the race card. To do that, he had Simpson hire Cochran, who had become the foremost African American attorney in Los Angeles by winning brutality cases against the LAPD. Bailey was perhaps the most prominent defense attorney in the nation and was extraordinary in the courtroom.

The jury selected was composed of eight Black and two white women, which surprised many, another Black man, and a Latino. Thus, a jury of nine out of twelve were African Americans. The Dream

O.J. hired a Dream Team of lawyers, including Johnnie Cochran Jr. and Robert Shapiro. Notice the 1995 computer. AP Photo/Reed Saxon.

Team got a Dream Jury, which made many in very multiracial L.A. wonder about the competence of the prosecuting attorneys.

Reporters rushed to Los Angeles. Some two thousand from all over the world, especially from tabloid nation USA. The press room on the twelfth floor of the courtroom contained the space for nineteen television and eight radio stations, along with twenty-three newspapers and magazines. A nearby parking lot was dubbed "Camp O.J.," with trailers, toilets, dumpsters, and 650 telephones.

Judge Lance Ito allowed the trial to be televised live, and what developed was two trials—one in the courtroom and the other on the media. Both sides called more than seventy witnesses. One reported that Nicole was a self-described party animal, that she drove a $90,000 Ferrari convertible, and, like her husband, was promiscuous. She often met Goldman at a trendy fitness center in Brentwood, and on the night of the murder, police found a blood-soaked brown leather glove near his body. But the prosecution produced no murder weapon, and the glove found at the townhouse did not fit O.J.'s hand.

Approximately two hours after the murders, O.J. boarded a plane to Chicago for a business appointment; he returned the next day to a media circus. Prosecutors demonstrated that O.J. had a history of battering his wife, that she had called the police many times, and that he had once pleaded no contest to assaulting her and was placed on two years' probation. The prosecution played a tape in which Nicole with a black eye called 911 and yelled into the phone, "He's going to kill me!"

Sex, violence, celebrities, power, privilege, money—what more could Americans want? Before the trial was over jurors were selling their stories to tabloids. *Saturday Night Live* regularly staged the satirical "Dancing Itos" in a mockery of the trial. The *National Enquirer* paid Nicole's father $100,000 for her diary and featured the trial on more than twenty covers; he also sold a home video of the wedding for over $160,000. One of Nicole's girlfriends received a $3 million book contract, and it was reported that Simpson's lead attorney and the lead prosecutor received book advances totaling about $7 million. The drama exposed many unflattering aspects of American culture and society, wrote the historian James T. Patterson, "the powerful role of money in the criminal justice system, the extraordinary allure of celebrity culture, the seductive appeal . . . of stories about sex and violence, and the saturation coverage by TV of sensational events." Celebrity reporter Dominick Dunne simply called the trial "a great trash novel come to life."

Television networks gave more coverage to this one trial than the combined attention they gave to all three other significant events that were going on at about the same time—bloodshed in Bosnia, the Oklahoma City bombing, and the next year's presidential election. Opinion polls showed that about 70 percent of whites thought O.J. was guilty; about 70 percent of Blacks thought he was innocent.

On October 2, after 266 days, finally it was time for the jury to deliberate. After only three hours they had come to a verdict, but Judge Ito deferred unsealing it until the next day at 10 a.m. Everyone gathered around televisions, in offices, at stock markets, airports, and colleges, as drivers tuned in their radios. The nation almost came to a standstill. More than 150 million viewers, 57 percent of the country, watched the live broadcast of the verdict—not guilty.

Most whites scratched their heads, and some were angry, labeling the defendant "The Butcher of Brentwood." Most Blacks cheered, "The Juice is loose." Just two years after the South Central riots, the verdict again demonstrated the great divide between races in America. "Payback for Rodney King!" declared one African American, and Black journalist Michael Wilbon wrote, "It was as if acquitting O.J. Simpson made up for Rodney King and Emmett Till. . . . A lot of black people . . . simply see this as payback, even if the score is still about 1 million to one. They feel the chickens might have come home to roost yesterday for all of our relatives and ancestors who've been beaten and raped and lynched and murdered by whites without any consequence whatsoever. . . . The bigger issue here, of course, is race. It's always race."

The long courtroom drama turned into a soap opera on steroids, and it stimulated the nation to talk about "domestic violence" and "spousal abuse," which since have become part of the American lexicon. "Domestic violence is an unacknowledged epidemic in our society," said Health and Human Services secretary Donna Shalala. "Just as women's groups used the Anita Hill–Clarence Thomas hearings as a springboard to educate the public about sexual harassment," wrote *Time*, "they are now capitalizing on the Simpson controversy to further their campaign against domestic violence." Lawmakers listened. States were passing laws, many of them mandating arrest for any person committing domestic violence, as the federal government was implementing the 1994 Violence Against Women Act.

The trial also had an evidentiary breakthrough—DNA. Deoxyribonucleic acid, the individual's distinctive genetic material found in blood, hair, saliva, skin, and semen, had been used by police earlier, but O.J.'s blood and DNA found at the scene and in his car greatly enhanced the use of forensic DNA analysis in criminal trials. As a *New York Times* editorial noted, "There is only a 1-in-170-million chance that someone other than Mr. Simpson matched a particular blood spot on the walkway" of the Brentwood townhouse, and as for "Mr. Simpson's bloody sock, only one in nearly seven billion people supposedly match Nicole Simpson's blood type found there." In the long run, the newspaper concluded, the trial's lasting importance "might be as a demonstration of the power—and complexities—of DNA technology."

Importantly, O.J.'s defense team did not question the science of the DNA evidence. Instead, they claimed that the evidence had been tainted by the way the police collected, stored, and processed the DNA. The defense thus claimed that the DNA evidence was contaminated.

That version apparently won over the jury, for with such overwhelming DNA evidence, and then the innocent verdict, the trial deepened public cynicism, and it provoked the news media to focus even more on spectacle and scandals. News as spectacle. Established news magazines like *Time* and *Newsweek* continued shifting gears from covering traditional topics like politics, international relations, the economy, race, and other issues of national significance to celebrity profiles, entertainment, exposés, and scandals—which was reflected on their covers.

The televised marathon boosted the merger of information and entertainment shows, "infotainment," in the nineties. The next decade led to a full agenda of "reality shows," from *The Survivor* to *The Bachelor* to *American Idol* to *The Apprentice*. As journalist James Fallows wrote after the trial, "People will pay attention to public affairs only if politics can be made as interesting as the other entertainment options available to them, from celebrity scandals to the human melodramas featured on daytime talk programs."

The trial also had an impact on Talk Show Nation, which expanded as armchair warriors expressed their opinions, and on the mainstream media. "News" became Tabloid TV. Early in 1995 opinion polls found that only half of citizens could identify Newt Gingrich, but two-thirds knew that Lance Ito was the judge in the O.J. trial. An important witness, Kato Kaelin, was recognized by 75 percent of respondents, but only 25 percent could identify Vice President Al Gore. Smelling profits, conventional media jumped in with an endless parade of interviews with relatives, friends, fans, lawyers of Nicole and O.J.

It was a trial that would not go away, for the Brown and Goldman families sued Simpson in a civil case for wrongful death of their children. In 1997 the trial concluded. O.J. was found guilty and was ordered to pay the families over $33 million in damages, of which he paid only a fraction and moved to Florida. "This time," a *New York Times* article said about the civil trial, "almost no one erupted in ecstatic cheers or gasped in stunned dismay. This time, almost no one seemed surprised."[4]

Yet people were surprised when in September the *Washington Post* published the Unabomber Manifesto. For seventeen years someone had mailed or delivered a number of bombs that injured two dozen and killed three Americans. The first bomb was at a university in Chicago, and subsequent ones kept citizens on edge, especially after he threatened to blow up airliners. The FBI investigated, labeling it the "UNABOM" case, named for the UNiversity and Airline BOMbing. Teams of agents searched recovered bomb components, but the Unabomber wisely left no forensic evidence, making his weapons from scrap materials commonly available. Nor were the victims in any sort of pattern, and that made citizens more nervous.

Finally, the Unabomber made his mistake—he sent his manifesto to the *New York Times* and *Washington Post*. If one of the papers did not publish it, he threatened, he would send another bomb "with intent to kill" apparently in a public place. The Attorney General and the FBI director met and recommended publication, so on September 22, 1995, the *Post* printed the enormous 35,000-word manifesto as an eight-page supplement, "Industrial Society and Its Future." It was a rather articulate attack, usually using "we" instead of "I" and claiming, "The Industrial Revolution and its consequences have been a disaster for the human race."

The manifesto gave clues about the author, and hundreds of citizens contacted the FBI. One of those was David Kaczynski, who described his troubled brother Ted, who had grown up in Chicago, earned a PhD in mathematics, and had taught at the University of California at Berkeley—before leaving and moving to a primitive small cabin in Montana. David had helped his brother build that cabin and, significantly, had saved letters from Ted, which he supplied to the FBI and which linguistic analysis determined matched the brother to the manifesto. FBI agents got a search warrant and seven months later arrested Ted at his cabin, where they found bomb components, descriptions of his crimes, and one bomb ready for mailing. The Unabomber pleaded guilty, received life, and was retired to a federal prison in Colorado.

Americans momentarily sighed relief, but not Europeans, who were shocked by Serbian behavior in Bosnia: genocide.

Begun by the Butcher of Bosnia, Ratko Mladić, and his Serbian troops in spring 1992, the siege of Sarajevo and killing continued on and on, eventually becoming one of the longest sieges in history, longer than the Battle of Stalingrad and the siege of Leningrad in World War II. In February 1994 Serbian forces unleashed an intense artillery bombardment against the Markale marketplace, which killed sixty-eight and wounded some two hundred civilians. The massacre prompted the UN Secretary-General to request that NATO immediately conduct airstrikes to destroy Serbian Army gun emplacements, and shortly thereafter American, British, and French jets began destroying artillery positions around Sarajevo.

Eighty miles east, Serb forces assaulted the Muslim Bosniak town of Srebrenica and local villages. For over two years Serb soldiers and paramilitaries surrounded Muslim hamlets, demanded that they surrender weapons, and then began attacking, expelling, or killing the people. Survivors and journalists talked about "ethnic cleansing." This indiscriminate slaughter resulted in casualties and massive numbers of people forced from their homes and villages, and it also triggered a UN response. In April 1993 the organization declared besieged Srebrenica a "safe area," but the UN did not have the military strength to enforce its declaration and both sides continued the deadly skirmishes, claimed atrocities, and advocated revenge.

The revenge reached its crescendo in July 1995—Srebrenica's fall and massacre. Ratko Mladić commanded the Bosnian Serb Army and some allies to move into the city. The troops rounded up at least eight thousand men and boys and separated them from their wives, mothers, and sisters, chased them into the woods, and massacred them. It became known as the Srebrenica "genocide."

One of those young men was engaged to then twenty-one-year-old Devia Ajsic. "The things they did to me," she sobbed, "they tied me to a desk, my neck and chest were blue from bruises, I was sprawled naked on that table," and Serb soldiers sexually assaulted her.

"So base were the emotions, so dark the actions, that at times you had to wonder which century we were in," wrote a journalist for the

Philadelphia Inquirer. "Was it 1995 or 1395? . . . At least there is one dif-ference between now and 600 years ago. The killing's become more efficient."

The Srebrenica massacre also prompted criticism at home of Clinton's nonintervention policy. The president would be "remem-bered in history as a man who feared, flinched and failed," wrote conservative commentator William Safire, as a national leader who "turned a superpower to a subpower." The fall of Srebrenica "is a devastating humiliation of the United Nations," wrote liberal colum-nist Anthony Lewis. "It calls into question the future of the North Atlantic alliance. But most of all it points to the vacuum of leadership in the White House." Even Clinton's advisers took aim. "We agree that Srebrenica is an absolute disaster," said Assistant Secretary of State Richard Holbrooke. The situation in Bosnia was the "worst mess we have seen in Europe since the end of World War II. It is . . . the greatest collective failure of the West since the 1930s."

Srebrenica provoked the West into action. In August NATO warned the Serbs against attacking, but to no avail. They attacked Sarajevo. One shell hit an open-air market and killed thirty-seven civilians. US warplanes under NATO responded with a savage attack on all Serbian installations, depots, camps, and communication towers, one of the most extensive strikes in Europe since World War II. That aided the Bosniak and Croat alliance to take the initiative and reclaim much of western Bosnia. After a siege of Sarajevo that lasted forty-one months, the Serbs agreed to a cease fire and to peace talks. Finally, after four years of bloody war, resulting in some 200,000 deaths and two million refugees, it was time to talk peace.

Clinton appointed Holbrooke to commence the talks at Wright-Patterson Air Force Base in Dayton, Ohio. The talks began in November, and after twenty-one days of isolation negotiators signed the Dayton Accords. It set borders and required NATO forces as peacekeepers. Everyone knew that if those troops were not sent then ethnic tensions would again erupt into war. The agreement needed congressional support and funding, since the administration agreed to send about twenty thousand US troops alongside similar contingencies of British and French soldiers. They all deployed, and peace came to the blood-smitten land.

The Bosnian war was brutal, and it contributed to popularize terms such as ethnic cleansing and genocide. The Central Intelligence Agency claimed that Bosnian Serb forces were responsible for 90 percent of the ethnic cleansing committed mostly against Bosnian Muslims. Serb troops also raped Muslim women and girls. No one knows how many, but estimates ran between 10,000 and 50,000, boosting usage of another term, "mass rape."

Serbian behavior resulted in calls for war crime trials, and the UN formed the International Criminal Tribunal for the former Yugoslavia located in The Hague, Netherlands. During the next dozen years that court convicted forty-five Serbs, twelve Croats, and four Bosniaks of war crimes. Serbian president Slobodan Milošević was charged but died in 2006 during the trial. Bosnian Serb president Radovan Karadžić was found guilty of genocide and war crimes and sentenced to life imprisonment, and so was the "Butcher of Bosnia" General Ratko Mladić of the Sarajevo siege and Srebrenica massacre. The prosecutor said Mladić "ranks among the most notorious war criminals in modern history. His name should be consigned to the list of history's most depraved and barbarous figures."

Just a week after negotiators signed the Dayton Accords in November 1995, Clinton landed in London to continue the peace process for Northern Ireland.

During World War I, Ireland revolted for independence from Great Britain. The revolt was over in 1921, and the Emerald Isle was divided. The Republic of Ireland was made up of the twenty-three southern counties while six northern counties remained part of Britain as Northern Ireland. An important issue was the status of Northern Ireland. Unionists, who were mostly Protestants, wanted Northern Ireland to remain within the United Kingdom. Irish nationalists, who were mostly Catholics, wanted Northern Ireland to leave the UK and join a united Ireland.

In Northern Ireland the majority Protestants discriminated against minority Catholics in land rights, public jobs and housing, business, and in voting by gerrymandering, creating friction and resentment. Teaching Irish history and language was banned in northern schools, and so was Sinn Féin, the leftist party of Irish republicanism. Generally, Catholics identified as Irish and Protestants felt they were British, and they did not want to lose their heritage and privileges.

Changes began to come to Northern Ireland during the 1960s. The civil rights movement in America, along with Prague Spring and May 1968 events in France, infused Catholics with a desire for more equality in Northern Ireland. Irish activists formed the Northern Ireland Civil Rights Association and began marches in 1968, but often were confronted by counter-marchers and the Northern Ireland police, the Royal Ulster Constabulary (RUC). Meanwhile, Sinn Féin and its military wing, the Irish Republican Army (IRA), began a political and military revolt against the North Ireland government. London responded by sending the British Army. The Belfast authorities began to intern, or imprison, hundreds of suspects during the next few years, some going on hunger strikes, resulting in more marches and demonstrations against the government. In January 1972, one march in Derry turned violent. British troopers fired over a hundred live rounds on the young protesters, even shooting them in the back as they ran away. All of the protesters were unarmed. Fourteen died in what became known as Bloody Sunday.

Bloody Sunday created a spike in IRA recruitment, and Northern Ireland buckled into what the Irish called The Troubles, which continued for the next generation, scarring Ireland. The IRA conducted sabotage and bombings, and both sides formed numerous paramilitary militias. The antagonists blocked off roads and erected walls to separate Catholic and Protestant neighborhoods. Police and paramilitaries checked for car bombs. Tension ran high and peaceful marches usually turned violent. IRA splinter groups adopted guerrilla warfare tactics against the RUC and British Army, much of it financed by Irish Americans, with many arms coming from Libya and the Middle

East. The IRA attacked police stations, army bases, and shops using mortars, grenades, and rockets. They set off bombs in London, in Belfast, and throughout Northern Ireland, killing thousands of British citizens. An IRA bomb attack on the Conservative Party Conference in Brighton, England, in 1984, took five lives and threatened Prime Minister Margaret Thatcher. Between 1968 and 1998 more than 3,500 people were killed during The Troubles.

At the beginning of The Troubles, Bill Clinton was a graduate student at Oxford University in England. He was interested in the conflict, and years later, while campaigning for the presidency, he spoke at an Irish candidate's forum night and surprised the crowd by promising a visa to the United States for Sinn Féin leader Gerry Adams. The Irish were delighted; the British were outraged. By meeting Adams, whose IRA was conducting a campaign of terror, Clinton was jeopardizing the long-standing British–American "special relationship." After the election the new president's advisers were split over the visa, but eventually Clinton was convinced that Adams could play a useful role in the peace process. Both the Irish and British had signed an agreement committing Northern Ireland to democracy, and since the northern counties were about 10 percent more Protestant than Catholic, Northern Ireland was going to remain part of the UK. "Adams understood that," Clinton later wrote, "but he also knew that terror couldn't bring victory and he seemed genuine when he said he wanted the IRA to give it up in return for an end to discrimination" against Catholics.

The Brits lashed out. One headline read: "Slimy Snake Adams Spits Venom at Yanks." British media lambasted Clinton, calling the visa the greatest insult ever given to a British government. For days British prime minister John Major refused phone calls from the president.

Gerry Adams arrived in New York at the end of January 1994. He spoke at the Waldorf Astoria Hotel at an event hosted by Irish American businessmen, and he went on *Larry King Live*, forcing British authorities to ban the show in Britain. He promised to be more cooperative, which calmed the wary British. Seven months later the IRA declared a cease fire. It was the beginning of the end of The Troubles.

"The visa decision had worked," wrote Clinton. "It was the beginning of my deep engagement in the long, emotional, complicated search for peace in Northern Ireland."

In late November 1995 Clinton landed in London. He met with Prime Minister John Major, gave a talk to Parliament, and thanked Britain for help in Bosnia. The next day he became the first president to visit Northern Ireland, where 50,000 were waiting and children were waving American flags. He and Hillary stood by Catholic and Protestant leaders, and he read a letter from an Irish girl: "Both sides have been hurt. Both sides must forgive." And then the American president pledged, "We will stand with you as you take risks for peace." The next day he flew to Dublin, where even a larger crowd waited, and after he met with the Irish president and prime minister, Bill and Hillary went to Trinity College Green. While 100,000 waved American and Irish flags, he again called for peace. He then met with Bono of the band U2 and went to Cassidy's Pub, where he shared some brews with his distant Irish relatives. "On their first visit to Ireland," wrote Irish journalist Niall O'Dowd, "they were feted and celebrated in Belfast, Derry, and Dublin like no one since JFK." The visit, Clinton later wrote, was "two of the best days of my presidency."

While the Irish and British negotiated the end of The Troubles, Clinton brought an end to the policy of nonrecognition to Vietnam. With the collapse of our ally South Vietnam, and the creation of a new nation, the Socialist Republic of Vietnam, in 1975, the American government did not extend diplomatic relations to Hanoi. President Carter attempted to normalize relations, but that was prevented by a series of events in Southeast Asia. The next two Republican presidents were not interested in our former enemy, but Clinton was, and in 1994 he was considering lifting our trade embargo against Vietnam.

Republican senator John McCain and Democratic senator John Kerry met with and pressed Clinton. Both senators were decorated war veterans who served on the Senate Select Committee on POW/

MIA Affairs, and they had traveled to Vietnam to get the Hanoi government to cooperate on those issues. Hanoi agreed and allowed Americans into their country to search crash sites and battlegrounds, which improved relations.

Clinton, as mentioned, had avoided military service in Vietnam and had written his draft board that he "opposed and despised" the conflict. But since he had McCain and Kerry supporting normalization, he could ask for a Senate resolution to end the boycott. Some veteran groups and Republican senators opposed, stating that Vietnam was stalling on the MIA issue. Others stated that ending the embargo was an insult to the memories of those who fought and died during the Vietnam War. Kerry proposed the Senate resolution, and the American Legion declared that it was "disappointed and concerned. . . . Vietnam has not cooperated by a long shot." After an emotionally charged debate about Vietnam, the war, and the boycott, the Senate easily passed the resolution, and Kerry said it was time "to put the war behind us." Amen.

Clinton ended the embargo. More Vietnam vets stepped forward, and in 1995 with the support of McCain, Kerry, Bob Kerrey, Chuck Robb, and Pete Peterson, Clinton granted diplomatic relations to Vietnam. The president named former POW Peterson as the first American ambassador to Hanoi. Trade soared, and during his last year in office Clinton became the first president to visit our former enemy. "The history we leave behind is painful and hard," the president said in Vietnam. "We must not forget it, but we must not be controlled by it."[5]

Back in Washington, DC, in 1995, Newt Gingrich was trying to force Clinton to accept his Republican budget. During that spring, fresh off his victory lap from the 1994 congressional triumph, and after becoming Speaker of the House, Gingrich began hinting that if the Democratic president didn't accept the Republican budget, then he'd shut down the federal government.

For the first two hundred years of the Republic, politicians had shied away from shutting down the government and always worked out compromises. But in 1976 President Gerald Ford vetoed a spending bill during a dispute over the budget, and the subsequent quarrel with the Democratic Congress resulted in the first partial shutdown. Still, shutdowns remained short, without much public interest. There were five during Carter's one term and eight during Reagan's two terms, but all along both sides kept negotiating, kept searching for a compromise, and kept the shutdowns to a day or two. Many agreed with Reagan, who called shutdowns "un-American."

Gingrich demanded that Clinton sign on to his congressional budget, one that he said would balance the budget in seven years while it would decrease taxes for the wealthy, diminish environmental regulations and social programs, even cut Medicaid and Medicare. Republicans aimed to shrink government and sent through their budget declaring it was "the largest domestic decision since 1933." Gingrich called the measure "central" to Republicans. "It will decide for a generation who we are," he said. "This is not a game of political chicken . . . this is not a bunch of juveniles," the speaker said. "This is a serious, historic debate and a serious, historic power struggle."

Clinton vetoed it. That shut down the government for six days in November, and a few days later Newt held a breakfast press conference. When asked about his standoff with Clinton, the speaker surprised journalists and complained that the president had not talked to him on Air Force One. Earlier that month Clinton led a large delegation of American officials to Israel to attend the funeral for assassinated Israeli prime minister Yitzhak Rabin. Gingrich also complained that he had to exit from the back of the plane.

The *New York Daily News* jumped on that comment. The paper ran a cover picture of pudgy little Newt with a baby bottle, and headline: "CRY BABY Newt's Tantrum: He Closed Down the Government Because Clinton Made Him Sit at Back of Plane." A congresswoman brought a poster to Congress with the picture on it, and holding an

Academy Award, declared the speaker had "sewn up the category of best performance by a child actor this year."

Senate Democratic Minority Leader Tom Daschle, who also was on the Israel trip, demanded that Gingrich "quit the whining—let's get on with the real business here."

When funding ran out in December, Gingrich triggered another shutdown. Large portions of the government, all "non-essential" offices, shut down, as did all national parks and monuments. Almost 800,000 federal workers were sent home (but like during all shutdowns, were still paid). It dragged on for twenty-one days, the longest up to that time.

Gingrich and most of the GOP felt that the public would back them. A year earlier they had won Congress in a landslide, and for eight years citizens had supported Reagan, who had stated many times that "government is the problem." But as the shutdown continued polls demonstrated that the people wanted the government to operate. It was December, the holiday and tourist season, and all parks, museums, and other facilities were closed, which was bad for vacations and for business. The public blamed Gingrich and the GOP, which soon cracked the Republican solidarity on the issue. Congress held a rare session on New Year's Eve, and Senate Majority Leader Bob Dole signaled that the fight was over. "We ought to end this," Dole said on the floor. "I mean, it's gotten to the point where it's a little ridiculous as far as this senator is concerned."

Gingrich resisted, saying that the Republicans would prevail. "We're on the right side of history," he declared, "we're on the right side of this culture." Newt was wrong on both counts. He had come to believe his own worldview, which was at odds with the public. When the shutdown began, half of Americans blamed the Republicans and a third blamed Clinton; those percentages continued to grow against the GOP. About 75 percent agreed with the president that shutdowns should not be used to negotiate a budget, and over 60 percent of citizens viewed the Republicans more negatively after the shutdown. The Republicans took a beating.

Another issue making many citizens nervous was affirmative action, and that topic sprang back on center stage after the November 1994 Republican victory.

In the wake of the election the new chairman of the Senate Judiciary Committee, Orrin Hatch, said that he would review the administration's civil rights agenda and would require Assistant Attorney General Deval Patrick to testify at hearings. "Senator Hatch," Patrick joked, "I haven't even had a chance to congratulate you on your appointment before I read in the paper that you are coming after me." Hatch stated that the administration's policies seemed to be moving in the direction of quotas. Asked about that, Patrick fumed, "There are no quotas. I don't know how many times I have to say that."

After the Republicans took their seats in Congress, they announced they would study if it was time to repeal all federal affirmative action policies. In the House, Representative Charles Canady of Florida announced hearings to demonstrate that the administration's civil rights policies exceeded the original intent of the 1964 Civil Rights Act. In the Senate, Majority Leader Dole wondered if affirmative action discriminated unfairly against white men, if they should "have to pay" for discrimination practiced by generations "before they were born." "Has it worked?" Dole asked on NBC's *Meet the Press*. "Sometimes the best qualified person does not get the job because he or she may be one color. And I'm beginning to believe that may not be the way it should be in America."

Those were the first shots at affirmative action, and the barrage continued during the winter and spring of 1995. Ward Connerly, an African American member of the University of California Board of Regents, declared that the college admission offices had gone too far with affirmative action. "What we're doing is inequitable," he said. "We are relying on race and ethnicity . . . as the dominate factor to the exclusion of all others." Wrote the *New York Times*, "For supporters of affirmative action, these are nervous days."

Many moderate and conservative Democrats realized that. Connecticut senator Joseph Lieberman declared "preferential policies

... patently unfair" as concern mounted at the White House. Liberals began advocating recasting the affirmative action debate from helping minorities to aiding all those based on need, the "class based" alternative, which had more popular support. Vice President Gore met with civil rights leaders while the president called House Democrats to the White House. "We have to outsmart the Republicans," Clinton declared. "We have to help those who deserve help. . . . But we should also be prepared to recommend modifications where there are problems. We cannot walk away from this fight." He ordered an "intense, urgent review" of all federal affirmative action programs.

The Republicans intensified their attack, especially those who declared their candidacy to lead their party in the 1996 presidential election. Texas senator Phil Gramm joined the race, pledging that if he was elected his first executive order would be to abolish racial and sexual "quotas, preferences and set-asides." Former Tennessee governor Lamar Alexander declared he would do the same thing, and so did California governor Pete Wilson, who also announced his presidential intentions, declaring that he had a duty to seek the White House in the name of "fairness." He pledged that he would abolish "unfair" racial and gender preferences.

"Race and Rage," declared *Newsweek*, was the mood of the nation during spring 1995. The magazine noted that in the 1970s the hot political issue was busing, in 1988 it was crime, in 1994 it was welfare reform. "But the most profound fight—the one tapping deepest into the emotions of everyday American life—is over affirmative action. It's setting the lights blinking on studio consoles, igniting angry rhetoric in state legislatures and focusing new attention on the word 'fairness.' When does fairness become 'reverse discrimination'? When is it fair to discriminate on the basis of race or gender? Louder than before, Americans seem to be saying, 'Never.'"

A reason more Americans were saying never was because of the problems that had appeared with affirmative action during the first half of the nineties, problems that were attracting ample media attention.

The first concerned set-asides. The policy began as a response to the urban riots in the mid-1960s, when federal bureaucrats had stapled together a program to aid "economically or culturally disadvantaged individuals" establish businesses, often in slums. The Small Business Administration defined disadvantaged not only as people of African, but also of Hispanic, Asian, and Native American descent. Later, Carter signed an act that established a minority set-aside program for "Negroes, Spanish-speaking, Orientals, Indians, Eskimos, and Aleuts."

By 1995 the set-aside program was riddled with problems. Many of the participants were recent immigrants, some not US citizens, when the program was established first for women and African Americans. There was fraud, and there were rich immigrants with green cards that were benefiting from the program.

"The Set-Aside Charade," declared *Forbes*, as the administration and others examined the program. In Washington, DC, for example, a lawsuit revealed that between 1986 and 1990 there were more than five hundred firms certified in the set-aside program, but 80 percent of the city's road and sewer contracts were given to just four companies. The largest of those firms was owned by Jose Rodriguez, an immigrant, and another of the four companies was owned by his brother; together the wealthy immigrants received about two-thirds of the city's road and sewer contracts. Set-asides, the *Tampa Tribune* headlined, had become "A Fast Track for Minority Millionaires."

The unintended result was hostility. "It is hardly surprising that unfavored Americans are increasingly resentful," wrote a white commentator, "the American experience still concerns fairness."

In July 1995, Bill Clinton finally addressed the nation on affirmative action at an appropriate venue, the National Archives. For the first time a president stood before the American people and devoted an entire speech to examine and explain the policy. "Let me be clear about what affirmative action must not mean and what I won't allow it to be. It does not mean—and I don't favor—the unjustified preference of the unqualified over the qualified of any race or gender. It doesn't mean—and I don't favor—numerical quotas. It doesn't mean—and I don't favor—rejection or selection of any employee or student solely on the basis of race or gender without regard to merit." He stated that the federal government received "more than 90,000 complaints of employment discrimination based on race, ethnicity or gender; less than 3 percent were for reverse discrimination." He admitted problems, hoped that the day would come when the policy is not needed, but the "job of ending discrimination in this country is not over.... We should reaffirm the principle of affirmative action and fix the practice. We should have a simple slogan: Mend it, but don't end it."

Like affirmative action itself, the speech received mixed reviews. Liberals responded warmly. "Mr. Clinton took the high road," declared the *New York Times*. He promised "reform that would improve, not undercut, the crusade for fairness." The speech seemed to have an impact on popular opinion. A Time/CNN poll found that 65 percent wanted to mend affirmative action, while only 24 percent wanted to end it. Some conservatives had different views. "The real issue here isn't preferences for the unqualified, which virtually every American opposes," said Senator Dole, "but preferences for the 'less qualified' versus those who are 'more qualified.'" California Republican governor Pete Wilson added, "He should have said end it. You can't mend it," and Pat Buchanan proclaimed, "Affirmative action belongs in the same graveyard as Jim Crow."

The 1996 election focused on many issues, including affirmative action, and perhaps the largest conservative victory was in the unlikely state of California. Citizens there passed Proposition 209, the California Civil Rights Initiative, which amended the state constitution to prohibit the government from considering race, sex, or ethnicity in public employment, contracting, and education. But 1996 would be the last presidential election concerned about the policy. In the long run most citizens accepted the idea that minorities and women had been left behind white men, and by the end of the decade and into the next millennium most universities—and businesses—had recognized affirmative action, or at least diversity, as part of the American social fabric.

But that was not true for gay marriage. Just two years after the Stonewall riot in New York City, which stimulated the gay liberation movement, in 1971 two Minneapolis men applied for a marriage license; it was issued, and a state judge ruled the marriage valid. While that case remained in legal limbo, Maryland in 1973 became the first state to ban gay marriage, and most of the other states followed for the next two decades into the mid-1990s; meanwhile, such unions were becoming legal in Scandinavia.

Social conservatives for years had been interested in passing a federal law that declared marriage was reserved only for a man and a woman. That idea had been boosted when the AIDS epidemic introduced the topics of inheritance and death benefits to same-sex couples. In 1989 Denmark allowed them most of the rights associated with marriage, the New York Supreme Court ruled that two gay men qualified as a family, the State Bar Association of California urged recognition of gay marriages.

Same-sex marriages emerged as an issue in the nervous nineties, and in summer 1996 social conservatives fought back. Republican representative from Georgia Bob Barr and Senator Don Nickles of Oklahoma introduced the Defense of Marriage Act. To Barr and many conservatives, same-sex marriage threatened straight marriage and American society. The "flames of hedonism, the flames of narcissism, the flames of self-centered morality," Barr declared in Congress, "are licking at the very foundations of our society, the family unit."

The House passed DOMA, and only one of the sixty-seven House members voting against it was a Republican, Steve Gunderson of Wisconsin. In a demonstration of how vicious debate on gay topics could become, two years earlier in the House another Republican, Robert Dornan of California, outed Gunderson, saying that his Republican colleague gives talks to "homosexual groups" and "has a revolving door on his closet. He's in, he's out, he's in, he's out."

Clinton was out on DOMA, declaring the proposal "divisive and unnecessary" because there were many state laws banning same-sex marriage. But the Senate's vote demonstrated that Congress had a veto-proof margin. It allowed states not to recognize same-sex marriages from other states, and it established a legal definition of marriage as "a union between one man and one woman." Embarrassed by the act but determined not to be overridden on this popular bill just two months before the November election, Clinton said nothing about the bill. Then, late one night he signed it into law with no fanfare—and later did not even mention DOMA in his memoirs.

There were two other bills that Clinton signed before the presidential election that would have a lasting impact on America—HIPAA, the Health Insurance Portability and Accountability Act, and the Personal Responsibility and Work Opportunity Reconciliation Act. The portability part of HIPAA ensured that people would be able to maintain their health insurance between jobs, and the accountability part guaranteed the security and confidentiality of patient information—which was becoming very important as scientists were involved in the Human Genome Project, mapping the human genetic code. Many people were worried that employers might bar certain workers from employment based on possible predisposition to various diseases. This bill prevented that, and it also mandated uniform standards for electronic data transmission of administrative and financial data relating to patient health information.

The Personal Responsibility Act divided Democrats, and the Clinton cabinet, for it "ended welfare as we know it," one of the New Democrat's 1992 campaign promises. Since the New Deal the federal government had guaranteed a fixed monthly benefit to those who qualified for welfare payments, often unemployed single mothers with children. The new aim was to get people off welfare and back to work, which had been proposed a generation earlier by President Richard Nixon. This bill mandated work requirements for recipients, placed a five-year lifetime limit on welfare benefits, and cut funding for food stamps. The law also restricted eligibility of legal noncitizen immigrants for food stamps and Medicaid. Most Republicans cheered, stating that the government for years had been subsidizing "out-of-wedlock pregnancies," and this bill would end the cycle of "welfare as a way of life." Most Democrats were outraged. Senator Daniel Patrick Moynihan called the bill "the most brutal act of social policy since Reconstruction," and liberal columnist E. J. Dionne declared, "The bill's premise is that if we kick poor people and their kids around a little more, maybe they'll go to work. Then again, maybe they won't. We have no idea. But, hey, maybe the savings from this bill can pay for a little election-year tax cut."

The New Democratic president signed it, two of his cabinet secretaries resigned in protest, and a large number of unemployed mothers grew anxious as they began looking for work. By 1998, the government declared, the number of people on welfare dropped below ten million for the first time, and the percentage was the smallest since 1970.

While politicians were wrangling over welfare, researchers at a conference in Vancouver announced a breakthrough on the AIDS virus that had killed almost six million people, including about 350,000 Americans. "Scientists are heralding a 'new chapter' in the history of the AIDS pandemic, with the advent of a potent drug cocktail that may drastically reduce the level of HIV in the blood, and even stop the virus from replicating."

The study included a dozen gay men in their thirties who all had tested positive for the virus. They were given a cocktail consisting of AZT, the first drug licensed to treat AIDS, and a new class of inhibitors called 3TC. Scientists said that the protease inhibitors blocked an enzyme crucial to the multiplication of HIV. Up to nine months after treatment began, HIV levels in nine of the men had fallen to below the level of detection, and their white blood cell counts had increased. Dr. Martin Markowitz, who presented the study at the summer 1995 conference, said: "If you think of HIV as a raging fire . . . we put out the fire. Cure is a dangerous word. What this means is that we have turned off viral replication."

That was the beginning of the demise of the killer virus. Dr. David Ho and his team focused on the nature of HIV replication in the infected, which led them to support a combination antiretroviral therapy, including the use of protease inhibitors; that changed the fatal disease into a treatable chronic one. He used this cocktail on many, including Magic Johnson, who surprisingly announced his virus was under control. In 1996 *Time* named Dr. Ho "Man of the Year," for he and his team had changed what it meant to be an HIV patient. "Not so long ago, Magic was the poster boy for how to avoid AIDS," wrote the magazine. "Now he is The Man to show people how to deal with it."[6]

The summer of 1996 increased tensions in the nervous nineties with two bombings—one in Saudi Arabia and another in Atlanta. Since the bombing of the World Trade Center, federal security expert Richard Clarke had been wondering who was so intent on attacking America. The eventual answer was "a group that the FBI and CIA had not yet heard of: al Qaeda."

Osama bin Laden had formed al Qaeda ("the base") around 1990, and the CIA discovered that the blind sheik Rahman had spent time at bin Laden's guest house in Peshawar, Pakistan. But at that time, it was difficult to tell which group was responsible for the WTC bombing; al Qaeda did not take responsibility for the act, and there were numerous terrorist organizations with evil designs against the West. During the nineties the State Department listed about forty groups worldwide; all of them hated Israel and Western troops in Saudi Arabia, and they or their associates conducted numerous assaults against Americans. In 1995 terrorists bombed the Riyadh headquarters of the US military training mission in Saudi Arabia, killing five Americans. Within days the Saudis had arrested four men, obtained confessions, and beheaded them—all before Americans could interview them.

After the Oklahoma City bombing the federal government began to address terrorism. In June 1995 Clinton signed Presidential Decision

Directive 39, "U.S. Policy on Counterterrorism." It probably was the first policy document that addressed the threat of "asymmetric warfare," and it delineated the jobs of the different agencies in "consequence management," or which agencies had what responsibilities after a terrorist attack. PDD-39 also instructed the CIA to conduct an "aggressive program" of foreign intelligence gathering and covert action and to capture terrorist suspects "by force . . . without the cooperation of the host government." The next January the CIA's Counterterrorism Center established "Alec Station," a separate unit with the sole mission of collecting intelligence on bin Laden and al Qaeda.

Five months later, in June 1996, terrorists drove a truck bomb up to the fence of Khobar towers in Saudi Arabia. That building housed US Air Force pilots who were enforcing the no-fly zone in Iraq. They parked the truck at night about seventy feet from the barracks and got into another car and left. About four minutes later the truck exploded, with an enormous blast equal to over 20,000 pounds of TNT, so strong that all of the windows in a two-mile radius were blown out and it was felt twenty miles away in the Persian Gulf island state of Bahrain. The explosion killed nineteen airmen and injured more than 350 service members and civilians.

In both cases, it appeared that the culprit was Iran's Qods Force and their front, Saudi Hezbollah. "I've got little pieces of that truck in me still," said a US sergeant in a military hospital bed a week later to the visiting US secretary of state. "If you can catch the people who did this, you really should punish them bad," he told the secretary. The Saudi ambassador to the United States assured the sergeant: "We'll catch the guys who did this, and I promise you it won't be an O.J. Simpson trial."

The next month in Atlanta, the *New York Times* reported, "A pipe bomb spiked with nails and screws shattered the Summer Olympic Games today, transforming an international celebration of sport and fellowship into a symbol of the dark side of modern life."

During a night rock concert in the Olympic Park an agent noticed an unattended knapsack under a tree. Concerned, he called the bomb squad and had started to hustle people out of the area when the bomb exploded. "We had a lot of people on the ground, screaming, and a lot of people in pain and severely injured," said the agent. The pipe bomb killed one and wounded 111. Clinton, who attended the Games in the first week, denounced the bombing as "an evil act of terror" and vowed that those responsible would be punished. "I'm heartbroken," said Atlanta's mayor. "Clearly it has cast a long shadow over this wonderful joy that we've been experiencing for the last two weeks in our city."

Security was tight at the Games. Agents were concerned about domestic and international terrorists, and three months before the Games federal agents arrested two Georgia men about eighty miles south of Atlanta and charged them with possessing bomb-making materials; the men were linked to a right-wing paramilitary group. Moreover, a man posing as a security guard entered the opening ceremonies armed with a loaded weapon before agents intercepted him, seized the gun, and arrested him.

The director general of the International Olympic Committee said the Games would go on, but he continued, "This is the sort of incident which can, unfortunately in our society today, happen anywhere at any time." Just like the Oklahoma City bombing the previous year, there seemed to be no public space in America where one could be safe during the nervous nineties.

The FBI did a massive manhunt for the suspect, which became a media circus, and after numerous missteps landed Eric Robert Rudolph, but not until 2003. He was an antiabortion and antigay survivalist who evaded officials in the wilds of North Carolina and became an FBI Top Ten Most Wanted Fugitive. After the Olympic bombing he continued bombing abortion clinics and gay establishments in the South for two years, killing three people and injuring 150 others. He plea bargained for a life sentence without parole.

That same summer, 1996, citizens became immersed in the presidential campaign. Clinton hit the trail, declaring that terror was "an equal opportunity destroyer with no respect for borders" and "the enemy of our generation."

The Republicans held their convention in San Diego and nominated Senate Majority Leader Bob Dole; for his running mate he picked former Buffalo Bills quarterback and New York congressman Jack Kemp. Both were relatively moderate Republicans. Dole's acceptance speech stressed his service during World War II and that he would be the last of that generation to run for the presidency in a battle of generations. "Let me be the bridge to a time of tranquility," he said, "faith and confidence in action," that won a war and brought about American world leadership. The Republican derided the baby boomer president as an "elite who never grew up, never did anything real, never sacrificed, never suffered, and never learned."

But it would be an uphill battle for the Dole–Kemp ticket. The Economy, Stupid, but this time it had rebounded and was soaring with unemployment down to only 5 percent and the GNP surging with low inflation. This translated into the president's approval rate hovering around 60 percent and a heathy lead in the election polls. Furthermore, Clinton had no challengers for the Democratic nomination. He spent his time campaigning across the country speaking on his accomplishments and pairing Dole with unpopular Newt Gingrich, while declaring that the seventy-three-year-old Republican wanted to "build a bridge to the past" while the fifty-year-old president wanted to "build a bridge to the 21st century."

To complicate matters, H. Ross Perot joined the campaign in October. This time, and unlike in 1992, he was too late to qualify for the presidential debates but not to attack the president as a "draft dodger" who would be "totally occupied for the next two years in staying out of jail."

As in 1992, the voters were not interested the draft status of young Clinton or the allegations about the president's behavior; that would come later. Thus, the November election was an easy victory for Clinton, with 49 percent of the vote to Dole's 41 and almost 9 for

Perot. The New Democrat won the election, according to one pollster, because "on every issue that the Republicans hoped to dominate—balancing the budget, welfare, crime, immigration, and taxes—Clinton staked out a centrist position early on." He put the Republicans on the defensive, and he won the woman and minority vote, split that of white males, and surprisingly carried thirteen of the seventeen most affluent congressional districts in America. Clinton won over twice the electoral vote as Dole, including all the West and New England, again splitting the South, and all the Midwest except Indiana. It was a surprising revival from 1994 for the president, the Comeback Kid, but not for Congress, which remained Republican. Clinton was the first Democrat to be elected to a second term since Franklin D. Roosevelt in 1936, which few in the nation remembered, except Bob Dole.

A few nights later the Republican appeared on *Late Night with David Letterman*. "Bob, what have you been doing lately?" Letterman asked with a grin, and Dole retorted, "Apparently not enough."

Twenty-five years later, in 2021, Bob Dole died at age ninety-eight. Looking back at Dole and his time in the sun, the *Washington Post* editorialized that the paper didn't always agree with his political positions, but he "led to get things done" in the Senate. The paper quoted a liberal Democrat and a Senate colleague, Bill Bradley of New Jersey. When the Republican Senate Majority Leader left that body in June 1996, the Democrat said, Dole, "knew how to use power because he understood how to make things happen in the center of this institution. And that is ultimately built on a couple of personal facts. . . . He always kept his word. He listened very carefully. He never held a grudge."

The *Washington Post* concluded, Bradley's statement was "barely 25 years ago. Kind of makes you wish there really was a bridge to the past."[7]

4

Revolutions That Changed the World (Wide Web)

"Tminus 10 seconds and counting," was the announcement on April 24, 1990, at the Kennedy Space Center in Florida. NASA was about to launch Mission STS-31. Space Shuttle *Discovery* was carrying five astronauts—and the Hubble Space Telescope.

Astronomer Edwin Powell Hubble was born in Missouri in 1889, attended Oxford University as a Rhodes scholar, and received a law degree. He practiced law for only a year before he decided to become an astronomer, and he went off to the University of Chicago to earn his PhD. Mount Wilson Observatory in Pasadena hired him, and he was the first to discover that there were other galaxies outside the Milky Way. He later found that these distant galaxies were moving away from the Milky Way, or in other words, he developed the concept of the expanding universe, which has been called "the most spectacular astronomical discovery of the 20th century."

During the space race NASA scientists and others were interested in developing a large space telescope that would be above the Earth's atmosphere orbiting the globe. Congress allotted the funding in 1977, and in the next decade the construction and training began, as the telescope was renamed in honor of Hubble.

The Space Shuttle *Discovery* was on the launch pad that beautiful bright April 1990 morning. The countdown was continued, and at a little after 8:30 a.m., engines ignited, and the enormous triple rocket lifted *Discovery* up toward space. The astronauts deployed the Hubble at 380 miles above the surface, and it circumnavigated earth every ninety minutes.

Yet the Hubble had problems. Its 7-foot, 10-inch mirror had been ground incorrectly, and that compromised the telescope's capabilities. Hubble was the only telescope to be serviced in space, and so in 1993, and five additional times, astronauts flew up to correct the mirror and replace parts.

The results have been stunning. Hubble has measured the expansion and age of the universe, about 13.7 billion years, discovered black holes in the center of nearby galaxies, and dwarf planets in the far edges of the solar system. It also has allowed astronomers to "watch" a super-nova explosion that took place some 10 billion years ago, determine the size of our Milky Way, and discover oxygen in the atmosphere of Jupiter's moon and numerous planets like Earth orbiting around other suns. By 1996 Hubble had taken 100,000 pictures, including the world-famous image the Pillars of Creation, which showed newborn stars emerging from dense pockets of interstellar gas. Every year the telescope photographs a "weather report for the outer planets," and its crystal-clear images focus on areas such as the Great Red Spot of Jupiter, a cyclone bigger than Earth that has been swirling for more than 150 years at speeds of some 400 miles per hour.

Hubble is expected to last until about 2030, and its successor was launched in December 2021, the James Webb Space Telescope, which is about three times larger. Webb was designed also to see infrared or "heat" radiation rather than visible wavelengths and thus can see through the clouds and hazes on planets. As long as both telescopes are up above, astronomers have two complementary ways of under-standing what is going on in our solar system—and beyond.

Helping in that task was the International Space Station. In 1984 President Reagan directed NASA to start building the ISS, and Russia and America sent components into space in 1998. Two years later US astronaut Bill Shepherd and Russian cosmonauts Yuri Gidzenko and

Sergei Krikalev become the first crew to reside onboard the station, performing the necessary tasks to prepare for permanent occupants. The station orbited 250 miles above Earth and traveled at 17,500 miles per hour, eventually becoming the size of a football field. By 2020 some 230 astronauts from 100 countries would perform experiments that would try to answer the original question for the ISS: "What if we built a bridge, between and above all nations, to jointly discover the galaxy's great unknowns?"

The ISS and Hubble truly were visualizing the *Star Trek* motto: To Boldly Go Where No Man Has Gone Before.

And so was Bill McKibben, for as mentioned, one year before Hubble was launched, McKibben wrote what many consider the first book on global warming, *The End of Nature*. In 1992 Al Gore published another alarm bell, *Earth in the Balance*, writing that humans were having "an increasingly powerful influence over the whole of nature," like winds and tides, and that people were "threatening to push the earth out of balance."

Most Americans were not listening, but many international scientists were paying attention. The United Nations developed their Framework Convention on Climate Change, and it went into force in March 1994. Shortly thereafter almost all countries ratified it, aiming at preventing "dangerous" human interference with the climate system. Three years later the Kyoto Protocol committed industrialized nations who were most responsible for high emissions to begin limiting their greenhouse gases. In response, the US Senate unanimously adopted a resolution *opposing* the protocol, but nevertheless the long process to confront what Bill McKibben and Al Gore had warned about, global warming, was under way.

There already was a sea change under way concerning human genetics. In 1990 the National Institutes of Health and the US Department of Energy launched the Human Genome Project, labeling it "one of the great feats of exploration in history." Declared the mission's website, "Rather than an outward exploration of the planet or the cosmos, the HGP was an inward voyage of discovery led by an international team of researchers looking to sequence and map all of the genes—together known as the genome—of members of our species, Homo sapiens."

Of course, scientists had been interested in the role of genetics on disease for some time. On the morning of America's bicentennial, July 4, 1976, medical student Robert Cook-Deegan woke in a ranch house on the Oklahoma panhandle and peered into the brilliant sunlight. He had had a distressful sleep, for he was at the home of a man just fifty years old, a man inflicted with Alzheimer's. The family had survived the Dust Bowl, "weathered the Depression only to succumb to another catastrophe," Cook-Deegan later wrote, noting that ten of the man's thirteen siblings also developed Alzheimer's, along with a half-dozen cousins. The "toll of disease left the family reeling, attempting to deal with a remorseless foe they could not see, whose advance they could not stop."

The young medical student wondered along with others if Alzheimer's was inherited and eventually thought that genetic research of the disease was necessary. His idea was to isolate a gene associated with the disease and to trace it through a large family that had a higher percentage of inflicted siblings to see if there was a pattern suggesting inheritance of a single gene. Genes are fragments of deoxyribonucleic acid (DNA) that contain the instructions to make a biological molecule, and humans contain about six feet of DNA packed into about a trillion cells in their bodies.

Cook-Deegan completed medical school, became a genetic researcher, and fifteen years later returned when his Alzheimer's patient died, age sixty-five. He cut into the cranium and lifted out the diminished and ravished brain, which had become "a pound of gelid mush." He sent the tissue off to the National Institutes of Health, where he and others discovered that the brain was "riddled with microscopic plaques, craters left by the bombs in his genes." In 1987, two groups of scientists linked the inheritance of Alzheimer's to an area of chromosome 21, but other inflicted individuals had it in the zone of chromosome 19, and early onset of the disease often was in part of chromosome 14. Of course, he wrote, it was, and still is, "unclear how many cases of Alzheimer's disease are genetic in origin, as opposed to other unknown causes" such as head trauma, viruses, environmental toxins, and other agents. But finding even an approximate chromosomal address for a gene causing the disease encouraged other scientists interested in constructing a genetic map of human chromosomes and the molecular detail of the DNA each one contained. That was in the mid-1980s. In 1990 the US government began the Human Genome Project; shortly thereafter scientists joined from Britain, France, Germany, Canada, Japan, and China.

Scientists and advocates of the HGP compared it with the Manhattan Project to build the atomic bomb, a task so complex and so extensive that only the government had the funding and research labs to complete the task. Once completed, some promised, scientists would have access to the "book of life," wrote *Time*, "the precise biochemical code for each of the 100,000 or so genes that largely determine every physical characteristic in the human body. Once researchers knew that they'd be able to figure out exactly how each gene functions—and, more important, malfunctions to trigger deadly illnesses from heart disease to cancer."

Government and some university scientists went to work during the nineties. The HGP was making slow progress, and they hoped to complete the gene sequence by 2005.

Enter Craig Venter. This maverick scientist had grown up in California, been a US Navy medic in Vietnam, and attended the University of California in San Diego, where he earned a BS in biochemistry and a PhD in physiology and pharmacology. After being a professor at the State University of New York at Buffalo, he joined the National Institutes of Health. There he worked on the HGP but became frustrated with the approach and slow progress. He believed that researchers did not have to identify all parts of a cell's genome, just focus on the RNA, ribonucleic acid, which is present in all living cells. RNA usually acts as a messenger carrying instructions from DNA. Venter switched his attention from the DNA blueprint to the

RNA templates the cell makes from those blueprints, which simplified the task and resulted in producing gene sequences at faster speeds.

Other scientists criticized Venter's approach, so he met with Wallace C. Steinberg, the chairman of the Healthcare Investment Corporation. The two men agreed on funding, and Venter started his own lab, Celera Genomics Corporation, a name he picked because Celera was derived from the word celerity, or swiftness. He hired a team and went to work.

Then in 1998 he stunned the scientific world by declaring that he would complete the gene sequence in just three years. "It was as if private industry had announced it would land a man on the moon before NASA," wrote the *New York Times*. "As if an upstart company intended to build the first atomic bomb."

Some scoffed, but many others listened, because Venter's labs had quickly decoded more genes than anyone else in the world, and he was first to sequence the genome of an entire living organism. In fact, when he made his announcement almost half the genomes decoded had been in his lab.

The competition was on. Soon thereafter, HGP announced that they would produce a "working draft" of the genome in 2001, followed by a final draft two years early, in 2003.

As the scientist worked, law enforcement was discovering another use for DNA. If a suspect or criminal left blood, skin, or virtually any biological evidence, officers could extract the DNA and compare it with a database. Soon states were passing laws that all suspects had to give DNA samples, and that could convict or clear suspects, including those already incarcerated. In 1995, for example, the Florida Department of Law Enforcement linked evidence found on a rape-homicide victim to a convicted rapist's DNA profile just eight days before he was scheduled for parole, which was canceled. In another case four years later in New York City, authorities linked a man through DNA evidence to seventeen sexual assaults. "It's just something that unless you find DNA evidence or catch them in the act," said the police commissioner, "it's very difficult to solve because they are loners primarily."

Meanwhile, interest in DNA soared when in February 1997 Dr. Ian Wilmut, a scientist at the Roslin Institute in Edinburgh, introduced the world to Dolly the Sheep. "Scientists in Scotland have announced the birth of the world's first successfully cloned mammal," the BBC announced. "The sheep's birth has been heralded as one of the most significant scientific breakthroughs of the decade," which was accomplished "by inserting DNA from a single sheep cell into an egg and implanting it in a surrogate mother." Dolly was an exact genetic duplicate of the animal from which the single cell was taken. As for her name, Wilmut explained, "Dolly is derived from a mammary gland cell, and we couldn't think of a more impressive pair of glands than Dolly Parton's."

Before Dolly, many scientists thought that cloning was biologically impossible, but Dolly proved them wrong and ushered in an era in which cloning was seen as a possible cure for many diseases. Shortly thereafter, the cloning race was on. The Roslin Institute with their commercial partner PPL Therapeutics created the first cloned pigs, and during the six years after Dolly. scientists at Texas A&M University College of Veterinary Medicine became the first academic institution to clone numerous species in six years: cattle, boar, goats, pigs, horses, CC the Cat, and Dewey the Deer. And in the next decade, the country that eats more pork than any other, China, was cloning pigs on an industrial scale, with the idea: "If it tastes good you should sequence it."

Naturally, cloning and genetic testing raised many moral questions. If a genetic test is done on a fetus and the results are negative or ambiguous, should the potential mom have an abortion? If a person has a genetic test, should blood relatives be warned of genetic flaws, since there are some four thousand inherited diseases genes may predispose people toward? If scientists can identify the genetic basis for height or intelligence, could parents be able to specify their children's height or intelligence, or can parents "choose" their child? Can new forms of life be created? The United States and many other governments passed laws to ban human cloning and prevent employers from discriminating against applicants because of genetic information.

By 1999, molecular biologists could identify specific disease genes, and that created new genetic centers that offered DNA tests for commonly inherited disorders such as cystic fibrosis, Huntington's disease, some types of breast cancer, muscular dystrophy, degeneration of the brainstem and spinal cord, and Alzheimer's. "We'll soon be governed by a new paradigm—genomic medicine," said the director of the DNA diagnostic lab at the UCLA Medical Center, "with tests and ultimately treatment for every disease linked to the human genome."

The competition worked, spurring on both government scientists and Craig Venter leading the private sector. In June 2000, President Clinton and British prime minister Tony Blair announced that "the international Human Genome Project and Celera Genomics Corporation have both completed an initial sequencing of the human genome—the genetic blueprint for human beings." Clinton congratulated the scientists working on "this landmark achievement, which promises to bring new ways to prevent, diagnose, treat and cure disease."

Scientists agreed at the end of the nineties that once the gene sequence was completed, they would inspect how genes vary in people with the hope of identifying genes and sets of genes that push people toward a particular disease. That will be "our most powerful tool," said Francis Collins, director of the National Human Genome Research Institute. "Finding these weak-susceptibility genes will be moderately useful for predicting risk, but they will be far more useful in allowing us to see the real molecular basis of diseases—all diseases—whether it's multiple sclerosis or brain tumors or diabetes." Of course, at the end of the nineties, no one could predict possible breakthroughs from the decoding of the human genome. "It's like it was before electricity," Venter said in 1999. "No one could have envisioned personal computers back then."[1]

Indeed, no one at the beginning of the nineties could have envisioned the cyberspace revolution and its results by the end of the decade and century. "The two most profoundly influential technologies of our times," declared Cook-Deegan, "are computing and genetics. The 1990s have been the decade when these two technologies converged in a powerful way."

As writer Kurt Andersen recalled, "The digital age . . . got fully underway in the '90s. At the beginning of the decade almost none of us had heard of the web, and we didn't have browsers, search engines, digital cell phone networks, fully 3-D games or affordable and powerful laptops. By the end of the decade we had them all."

In 1990 most people listened to music on compact discs (CDs), watched videos on their home VCRs, and to be mobile they listened to cassette tapes on their boomboxes or Sony Walkmans. That same year Microsoft launched Windows 3.0, which began the corporation's dominance in operating systems; Dycam, which became Logitech, introduced the first consumer digital camera, its Model 1; and Apple Mac released Photoshop 1.0, which became indispensable in photography, advertising, and publishing.

Those were the harbingers for the digital future, but for the rest of us? We only had desktop computers, and the best-seller then was the IBM PC loaded with Microsoft Windows, while Apple Corporation's Macs came with their own operating system, Classic Mac OS. Most owners used their machines as word processors and to send the new emails, and they could use the mouse to point and click. As for the internet, it was being used only by those who knew and understood Unix, a complicated operating system that was developed in the 1970s and used mostly on university research computers.

That all changed on August 9, 1995. On that day a sixteen-month-old Silicon Valley start-up company—Netscape—held its initial public offering (IPO) on the New York Stock Exchange. The company never had made a profit, and it was giving away its new product—the web browser Navigator. The cofounders' initial idea was to offer their stock at $14 so they could generate about $13 million to run and expand their young company, but before the opening bell there was so much interest and demand that they doubled the price to $28. Then the bell—and within an hour the stock had soared to $71 a share; by the end of the day it cooled back down to $58. That meant, as one writer claimed, that this newcomer was worth as much as established corporations Bethlehem Steel and Owens-Corning. By the end of the year "its market capitalization would exceed those of United Airlines, Apple Computer, Marriott International, and Tyson Foods." The *Wall Street Journal* declared, "It took General Dynamics Corp. 43 years to become a corporation worth $2.7 billion. . . . It took Netscape Communications Corp. about a minute."

Why were investors so excited about Netscape? Others already had created browsers for the World Wide Web (WWW), which were software applications that allowed the customer to navigate and view the web. There was the Line Mode Browser, the Lynx browser, and the ViolaWWW, but in 1993 the most popular was Mosaic. At that time, most users had to dial up on their telephone line to get on the web. Browsers were slow, and they would not display a page until all graphics on it had been loaded over the network connection, meaning that a user could stare at a blank page for many frustrating minutes.

Netscape accelerated the process. People using dial-up connections clicked on a web address and within seconds could begin reading the text of a web page as the graphics finished downloading. This made the web much more attractive, for Netscape permitted every user to view text—and pictures—as they surfed the internet. Moreover, Netscape was very innovative, setting the standard for years to come. It developed JavaScript, a programming language that became a core technology of the World Wide Web, and SSL, or Secure Sockets

Layer, which encrypted messages and orders and eventually allowed ecommerce.

Both Mosaic and Netscape had been developed by professors and graduate students at the University of Illinois's National Center for Supercomputing Applications (NCSA). The center was a leading research institution in computing and had been building computers since the 1950s. The center also was flush with money, since in 1991 Senator Al Gore sponsored the High-Performance Computing Act, or the Gore Bill, that pumped dollars into research institutions and funded scores of graduate students. An "essential prerequisite to sustainable development for all members of the human family," Gore later said, "is the creation of this network of networks." He continued that the infrastructure "will circle the globe with information superhighways on which all people can travel."

The hunt for a usable browser was on. Hundreds of computer geeks all over the world were developing browsers and other options so the average person could use the internet more easily.

There were a few dozen graduate students at NCSA working on this problem, and one of them was Marc Andreessen. He was a big midwesterner who was filled with energy and ideas. He wanted to make the web easy to use, and he envisioned an internet with graphics, newspapers, business, even videos. He enlisted Eric Bina, who worked for NCSA, and they got to work; Bina wrote most of the original code, and in January 1993 they released X Mosaic, which was designed to work with computers installed with Microsoft's operating system X Windows. Success: Mosaic users immediately shot up to three million, adding 600,000 every month, meaning that most people who began surfing the internet were using Mosaic. "The software is transforming the Internet into a workable web," penned *Fortune* at the end of 1994, "instead of an intimidating domain of nerds." The NCSA director added, "Mosaic is the first window into cyberspace."

Meanwhile, Andreessen graduated and headed west to Silicon Valley. Once there he met with entrepreneur Tim Clark, who began raising capital, and soon some of his former graduate student colleagues were joining the team. They thought of creating a new browser that would work with the newest, most powerful Microsoft Windows and be another platform for the internet, one that supported innovation and would be employed by millions so it would become the standard. And it would be easy to use, free—and secure with encrypting technology.

That was the beginning. As technology writer Brian McCullough wrote about August 9, 1995, "the Netscape IPO was the big bang that started the Internet Era." By 1996 users had downloaded forty-five million copies of Navigator, a remarkable 80 percent of the browser market. America—and the world—had entered the Internet Age.[2]

The computer age began during the late 1930s with engineers in Europe and America, including John Mauchly and J. Presper Eckert. World War II hastened interest in machines that could accelerate calculations, especially for weapon systems and breaking enemy codes, which the British had been doing since 1942 to the German Enigma cypher. But humans were too slow to keep up with the flood of German-encrypted messages to their navy and Wehrmacht. Thus, British mathematicians and computer visionaries at Bletchley Park created the Colossus, the world's first electronic computer. The Colossus reduced the time from weeks to hours and provided the Allies with German military intentions. This was especially helpful concerning enemy submarine attacks. At night subs would surface and receive orders for their next assault on Allied shipping. The Brits would inform the Royal and the US navies, and with such information the Allies had sunk virtually all Hitler's subs by 1943. That opened Atlantic shipping lanes for massive amounts of supplies to the Allies from the Arsenal of Democracy.

Moreover, and before D-Day in June 1944, Colossus broke the message that Hitler was not ordering extra troops to Normandy. Allied messages had tricked Der Fuhrer into believing that the invasion of Fortress Europe would be 150 miles northeast of Normandy at Pas de Calais, directly across the Strait of Dover.

In the United States, Mauchly and Eckert started work on their computer in 1943, but it was not completed until after the war in November 1945, the Electronic Numerical Integrator and Computer, ENIAC. It was designed to calculate artillery firing ballistics, and it was fast; better yet it could be programmed to do different tasks. ENIAC was over 1,000 times faster than previous computers. It also was enormous, occupying more than 1,000 square feet, using 18,000 vacuum tubes, and weighing in at 30 tons. Over its use in the next ten years scientists believed that ENIAC had done more calculation than had all of humanity up to the mid-1950s.

In the years after the war British and American universities and companies continued research in computer systems. In the early 1950s Mauchly and Eckert developed, and Remington Rand produced, one of the first commercial computers, the Univac 1. IBM got into the game in mid-decade by producing its 701 computer, and toward the end of the era RCA created the 501. Meanwhile, the US military introduced the first large computer communications network, SAGE. Used for defense, it connected over twenty computer sites in the United States and Canada to detect and prevent incoming Soviet bombers.

At the same time, scientists were creating software, the interface between computer systems and human users that gives programming instructions and data telling the computer how to execute tasks. Computer scientist Tom Kilburn wrote the first piece of software in 1948, and in 1957 John Backus at IBM developed and published FORTRAN (Formula Translation), which was and remains a programming language that is especially suited to numeric, scientific, and high-performance computing. During the next decades computer scientists developed other programming languages: Cobol, Pascal, and BASIC.

While computer scientists were developing software, companies were switching away from vacuum tubes. Those tubes were expensive and consumed a lot of power. The "true birth of the digital age," wrote historian Walter Isaacson, "the era in which electronic devices became embedded in every aspect of our lives," occurred at Bell Labs in Murray Hill, New Jersey, in December 1947—the invention of the transistor.

Every once in a while, innovators create something that changes how people live—electricity, steam and gas engines, airplanes, automobiles, radio, television, and the transistor. A transistor is a semiconductor device used to amplify or switch electronic signals and electrical power and is one of the basic building blocks of modern electronics. Transistors can be used to create an integrated circuit, which is a tiny collection of electronic circuits and components that has been implanted onto the surface of a single crystal, or chip, of semiconducting material such as silicon. Integrated circuits in silicon chips became the principal components of almost all electronic devices, since they were inexpensive, small, fast, used little power, and were very reliable.

During the late 1960s and 1970s other visionaries were creating the internet, what eventually became known as the "information superhighway." The US Department of Defense funded the research that created the first workable internet, the creation of ARPANET, the Advanced Research Projects Agency Network. The aim was to connect military installations and some American universities. ARPANET used efficient "packet switching" to allow multiple computers to communicate on a single network. During the 1970s, Vinton Cerf and Bob Kahn, who eventually became known as the "Fathers of the Internet," developed the TCP/IP, Transmission Control Protocol/Internet Protocol. TCP/IP set standards for transferring data between many networks, meaning that any computer and network could now talk to each other despite the type of computer or the software they used on their own individual system. ARPANET adopted protocol on January 1, 1983, and researchers then began to assemble the "network of networks" that became the modern internet.

While companies were working on faster supercomputers, others were considering "personal computers." The idea that individuals could have their own electronic device—at home instead of a business or university computer—had been popularized in the mid-1950s when Texas Instruments mass produced cheap transistors and then introduced the Regency TR-1 transistor radio for $49.95. During the Cold War the company promoted its invention partly as a security item as the Soviet Union built atomic bombs and intercontinental missiles. "In event of an enemy attack," the owner's manual declared, "your Regency TR-1 will become one of your most valued possessions."

Teenagers, however, had a more exciting use for a portable radio—rock and roll. Within a year the Regency had become one of the most popular new products ever, selling 100,000 copies. So popular, in fact, that Texas Instruments could not keep up with demand, and that gave an opening to a young Japanese company that helped fill the demand: Sony.

In July 1974 *Radio-Electronics* magazine ran a cover story declaring, "Build The Mark 8. Your Personal Minicomputer." Hobbyists could buy plans for the build-it-yourself computer for $5; blank circuit boards sold for $50. Six months later, January 1975, rival *Popular Electronics* featured a cover story "PROJECT BREAKTHROUGH," and it featured another computer kit: MITS' Altair 8800. The next month customers ordered a thousand plans—two of those were Bill Gates and Paul Allen.

Gates and Allen and other visionaries had been working to establish an operating system for personal computers since 1975 when they founded Microsoft. Originally, they established the company to develop and sell BASIC software to run the Altair 8800 computer. They located their company in Albuquerque because that was where MITS produced the Altair 8800. By the end of 1978, Microsoft's sales topped more than $1 million, and in 1979 the business moved its headquarters to Bellevue, Washington, near the original homes of Gates and Allen.

The next Altair version employed the new Intel 8080 Central Processing Unit, or CPU, which ran at the "blistering" speed of 2 MHz. Intel was founded by American engineers Robert Noyce and Gordon Moore, with the business side of the company run by Andrew Grove. Unlike many of the young computer geeks who developed the computer culture and its machines, these were middle-aged men who had worked in the technology industry for years. They were instrumental in changing Intel from focusing on memory chips that worked on one problem at a time to developing a single general-purpose chip that could perform almost all tasks—the microprocessor. In 1971 the company presented its Intel 4004, announcing "a new era of integrated electronics—a micro-programmable computer on a chip!" In a prophetic statement, Noyce proclaimed, "This is going to change the world. It's going to revolutionize your home. In your own house, you'll all have computers. You will have access to all sorts of information."

The Altair 8080 was the machine that ignited the personal computer revolution. It became the first commercially successful PC, and during the late 1970s it soon was followed by many others. Tandy Radio Shack's TRS-80 quickly sold 10,000 units; it was fully assembled and priced at about $600. Tandy recruited Gates and Allen to write software, and the company also provided an understandable manual and assumed that buyers knew almost nothing about PCs. Xerox's Alto used icons and menus, and the computer worked together with other Altos over a local area network. It shared files and printed documents on a Xerox laser printer, and the computer had an impact on two young men who visited the Xerox PARC laboratory in Palo Alto, California—Steve Wozniak and Steve Jobs.[3]

Jobs and Wozniak were high school friends in Cupertino, California, and they took an introductory electronics class together. Jobs went to Reed College, and his friend attended the University of California, Berkeley, but they both dropped out. "Woz," as he was known, got a job at Hewlett Packard and reunited with Jobs often at the Homebrew Computer Club. This San Francisco Bay Area group was focused on making their own personal computers, and they were fascinated with the new Altair 8800 kit. Woz worked as an engineering intern at Hewlett Packard, and he designed his own microcomputer in 1976, but the company was not interested in developing his design. Jobs showed enthusiasm for Wozniak's design, and they decided to work together, forming their own company, Apple Computer.

The two young men set up production in the Jobs family garage to build microcomputer circuit boards. Sales of the kit were promising, so they decided to produce a finished product, the Apple II. They introduced it to the market in 1977, and for about $1,300 it included a built-in keyboard and support for a monitor; most people used their television screen. The Apple II, which combined Wozniak's engineering with Jobs's aesthetic sense, was the first personal computer to appeal beyond hobbyist circles, and during the next fifteen years they sold millions of the PC.

During the early 1980s the race was on to produce the best desktop computer. Apple continued pumping out massive numbers of Apple II and in 1984 presented the Macintosh with ads on the Super Bowl. With a wonder woman running through an auditorium of cloned men, the ad declared, "On January 24th Apple Computer will introduce Macintosh," and referring to George Orwell's famous book. "And you'll see why 1984 won't be like *1984.*"

The popular ad not only enhanced sales of Apple, but of other existing PCs. Commodore introduced the VIC-20 in 1980, and it quickly sold a million machines. Texas Instruments TI 99/4 had their microprocessor running at 3 MHz, the fastest CPUs then available in a home computer. IBM PC was in the hunt, and with their huge marketing campaign they sold to individuals but perhaps more importantly to businesses and universities that were arming their workers and faculties with new desktops. In 1982 *Time* magazine selected the personal computer as its "Man of the Year."

During the 1980s the PC market was a battle between IBM and Apple, and in 1983 the PC sales surpassed the Apple II. The rivalry became a David and Goliath parable. "Apple is two guys in a garage undertaking the mission of bringing computing power, once reserved for big corporations, to ordinary individuals with ordinary budgets," wrote *Byte* magazine. "The company's growth from two guys to a billion-dollar corporation exemplifies the American Dream."

Meanwhile, Bill Gates was also demonstrating the American Dream. In 1982 he introduced MS-DOS, Microsoft Disk Operating System, and wisely entered an agreement with IBM to provide the operating system for their PC. Intel supplied the CPU for IBM's machine—all three companies struck gold. During the 1980s Intel emerged as the leading chip maker, IBM PC became the computer of choice, while Microsoft quickly became the leading vendor of PC operating systems.

Gates took the company public in 1986 and held the IPO on the New York Stock Exchange. One share sold for $21, and the next day it was about $28. The next year thirty-one-year-old Gates became the world's youngest billionaire. (According to the Motley Fool, if you had bought just one $21 share of Microsoft at the 1986 IPO, in 2020 after all the stock splits you would have 288 shares worth about $45,000.)

With IBM's incredible success, copies or clones soon appeared in the mid-1980s. Compaq Portable cashed in on being a cheaper machine that ran the same software as the IBM PC. The Compaq Deskpro 386 was the first computer to use Intel's new powerful 80386 chip which ran at an astonishing four million operations per second. The result was that Compaq stunned the business world with its sales its first year of over $100 million.

There was money to be made producing IBM PC clones, and that did not escape the imagination of a student at the University of Texas, Michael Dell. He established Dell Computer Corporation and used his dorm room in Austin as its headquarters until he dropped out of U.T. In 1985, the company produced its first computer, the Turbo PC. Dell advertised in electronics and computer newsletters and magazines, and then they assembled each computer according to the options the buyer purchased. Again, the business world was astonished to learn that the first year Dell grossed more than $73 million. By 1987 the company was expanding globally, and five years later Michael Dell was featured in *Fortune*. At age twenty-seven, Dell was the youngest CEO ever of a Fortune 500 company.

IBM struck back against the fast-selling clones. In 1987 it introduced its PS2, Personal System machines, which quickly sold more than one million units the first year. The PS2 also released a new operating system that allowed buyers to use a mouse, and importantly, users would now have a 3.5-inch floppy disk drive instead of larger floppy drives, making it easy and convenient to take their work with them and transfer files to other machines.

Other buyers were interested in taking not just a floppy disk with them but also their computers, leading to the rise of the laptop. The first "portable" computers were clunky, heavy, expensive machines. The Osborne 1 appeared in 1981, had a five-inch screen, weighed almost twenty-five pounds, and was advertised as the only computer that would fit underneath an airline seat. It cost about $2,000, so not many were sold, leaving the sales door open four years later for the Kaypro 2000. It had a brushed aluminum clamshell case, so it was similar in design to modern laptops, and that year Toshiba launched its T1100, which used longer-lasting lead-acid batteries.

The fight was on. IBM introduced its PC Convertible, weighing in at thirteen pounds, and in 1989 Apple introduced their first laptop, the Macintosh Portable. Computer geeks praised the machine for its high performance and matrix display but noted that the Mac "portable" weighed in at sixteen pounds. Also, it was expensive. When a user could buy Dell's desktop Turbo PC for $795, the Macintosh Portable would set someone back $6,500. At that price, sales were weak, but during the nineties businesses were producing more portable machines so users could have mobile devices to put in their briefcases or backpacks, such as Apple's PowerBooks, Sony Vaios, and IBM ThinkPads.

As PCs proliferated in the 1980s, two Pakistani brothers in 1986 invented the first known computer virus, at a time when another virus, HIV/AIDS, was ravishing the world. These brothers were not trying to destroy PCs but were curious. They wanted to see how far their invention would travel, and so they included their names, address, and telephone number, and named the virus after their computer shop, Brain. In no time their phone was ringing, for in a few months Brain had infected computers all over the globe—and that encouraged John McAfee.

McAfee had grown up in a troubled family in Virginia. John escaped, went to Roanoke College, earned a math degree, and was

working in California when he first read about Brain. The idea of
a computer virus terrified him, and within a year he had started
McAfee Associates in his house with the aim of creating the first
antivirus program. He advertised on electronic billboards, and it was
easy to convince users that they needed protection. In 1988 he was
on *The MacNeil/Lehrer News Hour* telling the country that viruses
were causing so much damage, some companies were "near collapse
from financial loss." Next year he published a book on the topic. "The
reality is so alarming that it would be very difficult to exaggerate,"
he wrote. "Even if no new viruses are ever created, there are already
enough circulating to cause a growing problem as they reproduce. A
major disaster seems inevitable."

That story line did it. By 1990, McAfee was making $5 million a
year selling his product, and in 1992 he told the media that the recently discovered Michelangelo virus was an enormous threat that
would destroy as many as five million computers around the world.
Sales of his software soared, and by the end of that year half of the
Fortune 100 companies were running McAfee virus protection and
paying the license fee. He later explained, "My business increased ten-
fold in the two months following the stories [about Michelangelo]
and six months later our revenues were 50 times greater, and we had
captured the lion's share of the anti-virus market."

Everyone was paranoid about computer viruses, and that made
McAfee a wealthy man. In October 1992 his company held its IPO,
and his shares were suddenly worth $80 million.[4]

As users fought off viruses in the late 1980s, the role of their PCs
began to change from glorified writing machines and email transmit-
ters: a scientist developed the World Wide Web.

After the destruction of World War II, a handful of European thinkers imagined creating an atomic physics laboratory. The idea was that
a laboratory would bring scientists together, and they would share the
costs of this new nuclear physics facility. At the end of 1951 numerous
governments held a UNESCO meeting in Paris, and the next year
they established the Conseil Européen pour la Recherche Nucléaire,

or CERN. A dozen member states began groundbreaking in a suburb of Geneva, Switzerland, and eventually built the largest particle physics laboratory in the world.

Scientists conducted most research on various aspects of atomic particles, but in 1989 British scientist Tim Berners-Lee invented the World Wide Web (WWW). Berners-Lee grew up in London. His parents were mathematicians who helped develop the computer at the University of Manchester, and Tim went to Oxford, where he would earn a degree in physics. By 1980 he was at CERN working as an independent contractor, and he proposed a project based on the concept of hypertext, a software system that links topics on the computer screen to related information and graphics. That, he thought, would facilitate sharing and updating information among researchers. During the next years numerous computer scientists were looking at hypertext and computer networks to see how they could combine them, or how they could marry hypertext to the internet. Berners-Lee married them in 1989 in creating the World Wide Web. "I pieced it together," he wrote. "I articulated the vision, wrote the first Web programs, and came out with the now pervasive acronyms URL, HTTP, HTML, and, of course, World Wide Web." URL is Uniform Resource Locators and serves as a universal online address system. HTTP is HyperText Transfer Protocol, and when followed by the domain name it creates a web address such as http://www.netscape.com.

Berners-Lee credited a number of theorists who came before him but added that his idea was that "computers could become much more powerful if they could be programmed to link otherwise unconnected information," like the human brain does all the time. "Suppose all the information stored on computers everywhere were linked," he thought. "Suppose I could program my computer to create a space in which anything could be linked to anything." Then he labeled that bit of information and told the computer to find the label to retrieve the information. By being able to reference and use the computer to get it, he could find items that seemed not to be related but in fact were, and that created a "web of information."

Berners-Lee's invention soon became the most common way to access the internet—the network of connected computers. The web was significant because it popularized the internet to the public. It served as a decisive step in developing the vast amount of information that users could access. When Berners-Lee announced the World Wide Web only a few computer geeks knew what he was talking about. By the end of the nineties virtually everybody knew, and most people were using, the WWW.

Part of the reason for that rapid transformation was the development of a browser, an easy way to access the web, retrieve and present information. Berners-Lee developed the first one, released it in 1991, but as mentioned the first popular one Andreessen and Clark launched in 1995—Netscape. It really was the "first web company," wrote Brian McCullough, "the first true dot.com." It quickly became the market standard, ten times faster than previous browsers, continually upgraded with new products, all of which made it very popular. In just a few months six million users downloaded Netscape, and by 1996 some forty-five million copies were in use, about 80 percent of the browser market. *Newsweek* labeled Andreessen "the uber-super-wunder whiz kid of cyberspace."

Andreessen and Clark decided to take the company public. They had expanded their business as fast as possible, adding engineers, scientists, technicians, secretaries, and they felt the time was right. On that sunny day in August 1995, Netscape went public at $28 a share; it soared. "By the end of the day," wrote *Time*, "the shares owned by chairman James Clark were worth $566 million. Netscape's technical whiz, Marc Andreessen, who is 24 years old, was suddenly worth $58 million." A few months later the stock price was $171. The 100,000 shares given to their recruits were worth about $17 million. "Netscape started the gold rush," wrote McCullough. "More than anything, the speed of Netscape's ascent shocked people. It had taken twelve years before you could begin to talk about millionaires Microsoft had minted. Netscape had done it in fifteen months."

Netscape helped create another piece of American nineties culture—the Silicon Valley image. Young computer visionaries created a useful new way to surf the web, or a new means to provide digital content, even a new computer, and then they took the company public. They become wealthy with the IPO, which attracted other entrepreneurs with new ideas, contributing to a booming American economy. "More capital was raised in IPOs by emerging high-tech firms in 1995—$8.4 billion—than in any other year in U.S. history," wrote *Time*. "And when an IPO is successful, the people who already hold shares in the company make out well. Sometimes very well. Sometimes unbelievably well." The magazine labeled them "High Stake Winners."

These winners moved into various parts of Silicon Valley. That basin had been orchards between San Francisco and San Jose, and it didn't get its name until the rise of the microprocessor with silicon chips in the 1970s. With Stanford University in Palo Alto, a powerhouse of innovation and education, it attracted its own students and others in the late 1970s and early 1980s to establish Cisco, Silicon Graphics, and Sun, which stood for Stanford University Network. Hewlett Packard already had been established, and by the nineties high-tech headquarters were established: Netscape, Apple, Google, Yahoo. Eventually the building facades in the former orchards read like a Who's Who of tech giants: Hewlett Packard, Intel, Microsoft, Oracle, Amazon, LinkedIn, Facebook, Netflix.

Those who moved into Silicon Valley usually were young, hardworking, hard-playing people who questioned authority, admired nonconformity, and nurtured creativity. While IBM workers would show up for their 8-to-5 day in white shirts and ties, the Silicon Valley people often had no fixed hours and no dress code; what they created was important, not how they looked. Many were soon making high wages with large stock options, meaning that rents and home prices were soaring in towns like Palo Alto and Portola Valley, Atherton and Los Altos Hills, or Woodside.

Another high-stakes winner was watching Netscape from Bellevue, Washington: Bill Gates. By 1995 Microsoft dominated the software industry; between 70 to 90 percent of all computers sold were pre-packaged with the MS Windows operating system. Yet Gates was slow to realize the potential of the World Wide Web until the appearance of Netscape. In May, Gates wrote a memorandum, "The Internet Tidal Wave," and sent it to his management, assigning the internet the "highest level" of importance. "I want to make clear that our focus on the Internet is crucial to every part of our business. . . . A new competitor 'born' on the Internet is Netscape. Their browser is dominant, with 70 percent usage share. . . . We have to match and beat their offerings."

It was a slugfest: Netscape versus Microsoft. "Netscape and Microsoft are competing not against each other so much as against their own obsolescence," wrote *Time*. "The victor will be not the company with the best browser but the team that can run the longest on this insanely fast product-development treadmill." Andy Grove, the Intel CEO, who led his microprocessor company through a series of battles a decade earlier, had condensed high-tech competition down to a single sentence: "Only the paranoid survive."

Gates's team went to work, and three months later they released Internet Explorer, which was as good as Netscape, free, and was bundled in their new Microsoft Windows 95. To promote 95, Gates went into warp speed, spending some $300 million on ads, including paying for the entire daily print run of the *Times* of London so for the first time in its 307-year history it was given away with Microsoft ads. In Toronto, Microsoft hung a 300-foot Windows 95 banner from the city's CN Tower, and in New York City for the first time the Empire State Building was illuminated by spotlights of Microsoft's colors. The billionaire also paid the Rolling Stones to use their song "Start Me Up."

"Windows 95 Launch Felt Around World," exclaimed the *Chronicle*.[5] "It is the computer retail event of the decade," said a CompUSA spokesman, which broadcasted Bill Gates giving a live demonstration to its eighty-six stores. Many computer retailers put up Windows 95 displays, and CompUSA, Future Shop, Office Depot, Computer City, and OfficeMax opened their doors at 12:01 a.m. for people who could not wait until morning to buy the program.

With that stiff competition, Netscape went into decline. It seemed that everyone wanted a copy of this new, improved operating system. Jay Leno joked, "To give you an idea of how powerful Windows 95 is, it is able to keep track of all of O.J.'s alibis at once."

"Year of the Internet," proclaimed *Newsweek* at the end of 1995. If you bought a computer in or after that year there was a 90 percent chance that you would take home a machine that had the Microsoft 95 operating system to run the computer and would come with Internet Explorer, which would allow the user to surf the internet. Bundled in that would be word processing with MS Word. You would be connected to the internet over a telephone line or cable with a service such as Prodigy, CompuServe, or America Online (AOL). You would send email or surf websites; now all that was needed was websites. In 1991 there were only ten on the internet, and they grew to almost three thousand by 1994. Then came Navigator and Internet Explorer, and websites ballooned. By the end of 1995 there were over 23,000, and that number increased to over a million in 1997, and seventeen million by the end of the decade.

"What do O.J. Simpson, the Louvre, an Australian guy called Wigs, prostitution, the Franklin Institute and a coffeepot in England all have in common?" asked a journalist in the *Philadelphia Inquirer* in 1995. "Maybe nothing, except that they are all on the Web—the World Wide Web—a multimedia digital universe probably appearing on a computer screen near you."

With the incredible expansion of websites, geeks thought of how they could sell advertisements, and the answer was a software called "cookies." Netscape developed cookies, and they appeared in the first edition of the Navigator browser with the intent of allowing a user to return to a website; cookies would remember the site and return the next log-in. Yet cookies also tracked a user's web surfing and could record online usage, sites visited; when users filled out online forms the cookies would remember names, gender, locations, favorite sites, or interests—all which advertisers could target. "The internet represented the first new advertising medium to come along since the advent of television," wrote Brian McCullough. Businesses quickly bought up various ways to advertise on the web and spent increasing amounts of capital. In 1995 about $50 million was spent on web advertising; two years later that amount had surpassed $1 billion, and by 2020 it was over $330 billion, more than companies spent on television ads.

With websites multiplying daily in the mid-1990s it became increasingly difficult to find what you were looking for, but in 1994 that was made easier by two Stanford University graduate students, Jerry Yang and David Filo. They had created a list of websites called "Jerry's Guide to the World Wide Web," which by word of mouth quickly became very popular. By September the men had compiled a directory of more than 2,000 sites, and it was getting 50,000 hits for searches a day. Late one night they realized that needed a new, more marketable name, and they realized that it would probably have to be an acronym. A favorite with Unix users was "Yet Another Compiler Compiler" (YACC), so they came up with "Yet Another Hierarchical Officious Oracle" (YAHOO). They thought that was fitting, since they were vulgar and uncouth and thought of themselves as yahoos. The appellation was born and in a year would become a household name. A new version of Netscape Navigator made Yahoo its default search engine, and by early 1995 it had expanded to 10,000 sites getting 100,000 visitors a day. In a sense it was the Yellow Pages for the internet. Investors called and in April 1995 supplied $1 million for a quarter of the new company. The number of sites on the search engine grew exponentially, and by 1999 that one-million-dollar investment was worth $8 billion.

Within a year other search engines appeared—Excite, Lycos, Ask Jeeves, MSN, Infoseek, AltaVista—and then in April 1996 Yahoo went public with their IPO. Its stock started the day at $24.50 and ended at $33, giving the stock a market value of $850 million and each of its founders about $130 million on paper. Yahoo started selling advertising space on their platform, and by 1997 an astonishing sixty-five million people a day were using Yahoo, making its advertising space prime territory for businesses. By the end of the year the company was valued at $4 billion—a corporation that never would have been necessary, or invented, without the World Wide Web.

And then two other Stanford University PhD students created BackRub/PageRank—which morphed into Google. Larry Page grew up in East Lansing, Michigan, and Sergey Brin was born in Moscow and brought to America as a child; both had academic parents, and both attended Montessori schools. They realized in the mid-1990s that conventional search engines ranked results by counting how many times the word or phrase appeared on the webpage. So if one asked AltaVista to find "automobile companies," Ford.com and General Motors.com would appear, but they might be on page 10, 30, or 60. Brin and Page understood that the web was built on links, one page linking to another, or one idea linked to another. At that time all search engines could link only forward, and they wondered: what if they could link forward and backward, and what if the links were graded as to which ones were most useful to the user's search and which was the most authoritative webpage? They decided to "rank" search results in the most meaningful way. When his academic adviser asked Page how much of the web he intended to map, he modestly replied, "the whole web."

Page and Brin at first then named the search engine BackRub, searching back, then PageRank, most important, and devised the appropriate algorithm, fine-tuned it, and searched for funding from the other search engine companies, with no luck. Thus, in 1997 they made their search engine available, and even without advertising they were receiving 10,000 inquiries a day by the end of 1998. They also renamed their product Google, a play on the word "googol," which is a 1 followed by 100 zeros, symbolizing that they were capturing everything on the web universe. By word of mouth in 1999 Google was becoming known as the fastest, most reliable, most comprehensive, indeed the best search engine in the world. Usage of the search engine was increasing some 50 percent a month. The *New Yorker* labeled it "the default search engine of the digital in-crowd," and Brin modestly declared that they were only "building a way to search human knowledge."

Indeed, Google changed the way people found knowledge, information, or the news; they no longer went to encyclopedias or newspaper indexes. Within a few years fans were using the noun as a verb; to google meant to search. They "googled" for information, and they were using Google Maps to find their date's apartment building and Google Books to read a library online. Google also changed the way people thought of services on the web. All of the company's services were free because Google also was presenting advertising that was relevant to someone's search queries. All the while Page, Brin, and the other stockholders were getting rich. Seven years after its founding in 1998 Google shares were worth an incredible $80 billion.

One of Google's early investors was Jeff Bezos, who also was finding a way to make money on the web. He was born in Albuquerque, moved to Houston, attended high school in Miami, and went to Princeton University, where he earned a degree in electrical engineering and computer science. Graduating with honors, he was offered many jobs in 1986 but eventually joined D. E. Shaw & Co., a Wall Street hedge fund with a strong emphasis on mathematical modeling; by 1992 he was senior vice president at age twenty-eight. One of his duties was to search out business possibilities on the new internet, and he began thinking about selling online—software, CDs—and he landed on books. There were three million titles in print then, and if he could figure out a way to sell one and ship it from the store or publisher: bingo. His team loaded his site with titles, a customer searched for a book, the company ordered the book, took quick delivery or simply had the stores send it direct, and they made money being a middleman. It was the oldest game in business, but new on the internet.

In spring 1994 Bezos and his wife, MacKenzie, left New York and drove west, eventually landing in Microsoft-land, Bellevue, Washington. Armed with recruited talent, he set up shop in the garage of his rented house, started selling books, and thought up a name for his company—Amazon. It would be first in the alphabet but also, "This is not only the largest river in the world, it's many times larger than the next biggest river," said Bezos. "It blows all the other rivers away."

Amazon was fortunate. As mentioned, Netscape that year had launched Secure Sockets Layer, SSL. Many buyers would call Amazon and give their credit card number because they did not trust giving that information over the internet. That was slow, but the system began to change with SSL. This encrypting technology made secure interactions possible, which of course allowed for the first electronic shopping—ecommerce—on the web. Moreover, Amazon introduced digital merchandise that made online shopping very easy, such as the "shopping cart," which allowed customers to keep products available until they either bought or deleted them. Then the company introduced product reviews. Traditionally retailers tried to remain neutral and let the customer decide what to purchase, but Amazon encouraged buyers to rate the quality of merchandise, which helped future customers decide which one to buy. Eventually, Amazon would use cookies to give buyers their browsing and buying history, along with other goods that they might like, again an entirely new way to purchase goods because of the invention of the WWW.

Amazon sales were slow the first year. The company lost over $50,000 in 1994, and more than $300,000 the next year. The internet users bought books on repairing antiques and musical instruments, sex guides, and computer manuals. The best-selling book that year was *How to Set Up and Maintain a World Wide Web Site: The Guide for Information Providers*.

The next year, in May 1996, Bezos got lucky—the *Wall Street Journal* ran an article under the headline "Wall Street Whiz Finds Niche Selling Books on the Internet." Bezos "fell under the spell of one of the iffiest business propositions of modern times: retailing on the Internet." The newspaper noted that "Amazon has caught fire" because Bezos had found a way to use internet technology. A customer could search through a name and subject database of over a million titles, five times more than the largest book superstore's inventory. Then after a buyer selected a book, Amazon was programmed to show other related titles. Once customers told Amazon their favorite authors and topics, the company emailed recommendations, even telling the buyer when the book appeared in paperback. "Amazon provides a singular case in which the frequently hyped Web is actually changing consumers' lives," declared the newspaper. "It also suggests how on-line retailing could change the way publishers market books." But not just publishers—all businesses.

Sales soared. In 1996 Amazon sales reached over $15 million and the next year up to ten times that amount. Amazon's ecommerce flourished. The company launched its music store in summer 1997 and its movie store that fall. By the end of the nineties Americans were buying about $15 billion worth of goods online, and for the 1999 holiday season some $5 billion, twice that of the previous season. People were buying products online that they never thought they would purchase anywhere but from a brick-and-mortar store—perfume, shoes, clothing, toys, mortgages, insurance, power tools, hotel rooms, concert and plane tickets—even books.

Time in 1999 named Jeff Bezos their Person of the Year, noting that at age thirty-five he was the "fourth youngest individual ever, preceded by 25-year-old Charles Lindbergh in 1927; Queen Elizabeth II, who made the list in 1952 at age 26; and Martin Luther King Jr., who was 34 when he was selected in 1963." The magazine gushed that he was a pioneer and royalty, the "king of cybercommerce."[6]

Soon there appeared other royalties of cybercommerce, and one was Jeff Taylor. In 1994 Taylor and associates created the Monster Board for employment classifieds, later Monster.com. Monster was the first job search website on the internet, it was the first public resume database, and the first to have job search agents or job alerts. From then on someone looking for work could browse the site and find potential employers, who also were looking for talented employees. By 1996 the company was issuing press releases to gain popularity, and by the end of the decade they were making enough money to run remarkable ads, "When I Grow Up," during the Super Bowl and Olympics.

Another royalty included Gary Kremen of San Francisco. During autumn 1994 Kremen was working on launching the first dating site online, Match.com. He realized that a prime business opportunity could be connecting millions of online lonely hearts, including his own. "I started the company because I decided it was the best way, maybe the only way, to find the best woman in the world," he said. "I was tired of eating and drinking alone."

No one had created an internet dating service, so he decided to collect information about customers, based on his instinct and own dating, and then try to match them with others with similar interests. He started by creating categories with headings—everything from education and occupation to active role in social or political movements to gender equality, and finally to sex. Kremen and his colleagues created some seventy-five categories of questions. Yet the more he studied how to attract customers the more he realized that he was not the customer—neither were men. In order to get men to subscribe, and entice advertisers, he had to appeal to women, for as Kremen declared, "every woman would bring a hundred geeky guys."

Attracting women at that time was difficult, because at the beginning of 1995 only about 10 percent of users online were female. Yet there was hope; at the same time the typical computer user was an unmarried male who spent hours a week online.

Kremen asked women to read and critique his categories and questions, and then he asked Fran Maier, a former Stanford classmate, to help him bring classifieds to the internet. She would take charge of gender-based marketing for Match. She quickly discarded questions about sex, weight, real names, and online pictures and developed queries about individual characteristics and values, education, work, leisure interests, and desires for mates.

In April 1995, Kremen launched Match.com. The thirty-one-year-old bragged, "Match.com will bring more love to the planet than anything since Jesus Christ." It was a free service, supported by ads, with the idea to eventually charge for subscriptions. He started the company with a $2,500 credit card loan and was fortunate that *Wired* wrote a profile of the company. Membership soared, so by 2004 Guinness World Records recognized it as the Largest Dating Site in the World, since more than forty-two million people had signed up for Match.com. Kremen changed the way people met, dated, even married, eventually declaring, "I am responsible for over 1,000,000 babies!"

Kremen also was partly responsible for the rapid and massive spread of pornography on the web. "For those interested in pornography, there's plenty of it on the Internet," *Time* declared. "It comes in all forms: hot chat, erotic stories, explicit pictures, even XXX-rated film clips. Every night brings a fresh crop, and the newsgroups that carry it . . . are among the top four or five most popular."

Time's cover story continued in June 1995 with a story titled "Cyberporn," while at the same time Kremen was developing sex. com, which he registered with a .com domain registrar, Network Solutions. Unfortunately, he was too busy with matching to pursue his pornography site, so felon Stephen Cohen filed for the rights to the sex.com domain, and an employee at Network Solutions mistakenly gave him the domain, prompting a legal battle between Kremen and Cohen that lasted until the end of the nineties.

After all, sex.com was very lucrative. People interested in porn would begin their searches there, so Cohen's new site was receiving twenty-five million hits a day and advertisers would pay $1 million a month to promote their locations. While the legal war was ensuing, Cohen reportedly was making up to $500,000 a month, quickly becoming a multimillionaire. "Let me make it real simple for you," Cohen told *Wired*. "Our audience is not America. It's the whole world. There's only one word in the whole world that everyone understands—sex. You type the word 'sex,' you come to Sex.com."

The last half of the nineties became the Wild West days of internet porn. People no longer had to go to sex shops to buy magazines or videos, then walk out hoping nobody saw them; now they could just stay home and turn on their computer. Internet sex websites rocketed, and it soon totaled about 35 percent of all web traffic. By the end of the nineties online porn was a $1.4 billion business, accounting for almost 70 percent of all ecommerce.

Another internet royalty quickly appeared, a French Iranian immigrant—Pierre Omidyar. He had been interested in ecommerce in the early nineties and the issue of classified ads in newspapers, which he thought were cumbersome and inefficient. If you wanted to sell something you owned, antique to zoot suit, you placed an ad in the local paper with a firm price. A potential buyer would call, come over to your house, and either buy it or start haggling to get a better price. That was advertising to a limited number of people in your community, time consuming, and often frustrating and unsuccessful. Omidyar thought that if you sold something online then the customer base could be unlimited, worldwide, and the process would be in real time and interactive: an online auction. The seller would post the item, with information and a picture, and then potential buyers would bid on the price—AuctionWeb, which morphed into eBay.

Omidyar knew that he had an intriguing idea when he listed his broken laser printer on his site. He told the audience that it did not work even with new batteries, so he listed it for $1. He was surprised when a bidding war started and eventually someone bought it for $14.

The question was: how would Omidyar make money from an online auction service? He decided to have the seller pay a nominal fee for listing an item (10 cents) and a percentage of the final sale price, and he trusted clients to pay the fee after the sale. They did, and then he decided to have the buyer rate the seller on a Feedback Forum and provided a Discussion Board. Soon, a community of patrons were posting ideas on how to use eBay, how to present an item, how much it was worth, what should be the starting bid. Within a year Omidyar had hired a friend with business acumen, Jeff Skoll, and a marketing expert as CEO, Meg Whitman, along with a growing staff who created a platform that was the first of its kind—a virtual marketplace. Unlike Amazon.com, eBay did not store or ship goods, it just facilitated the exchange. Again, an entirely new way to buy because of the invention of the WWW.

eBay took off. In fall 1996 the website hosted fewer than 30,000 auctions a month, but by January 1997 that number soared to 200,000, and those numbers continued to double almost every month. As one of their managers said, "It was like holding back a hurricane."

By February 1998 eBay had 500,000 registered users, by June it had one million, and Omidyar and his expanding staff decided to take the company public in September. Its stock rocketed from $18 to $53 before dropping back to $47, an increase of 160 percent. By the end of the day more than 60 percent of the staff, about seventy-five people, became millionaires on paper, and by the next year *Time* listed Whitman's worth at about $1 billion, Skoll's at $3 billion, and Omidyar's at $5 billion.

Naturally, this racetrack had speed bumps. Many people—single moms, retirees, collectors—decided to make a living by selling junk from their attics. Sometimes it worked; sometimes not, especially if the person quit a full-time day job in order to strike it rich in the auction room. Late night talk show hosts roasted eBay on many occasions, such as when a joker put a kidney up for sale. The bidding was up to $5.7 million before eBay stopped the purchase, and then there were those who tried to sell military equipment such as bazookas, or the seventeen-year-old boy who tried to raffle off his virginity.

Nevertheless, eBay was a hit because it became the global garage sale with fluctuating prices. Fixed prices had been around for a century; Sears, Roebuck and Montgomery Ward sent out catalogues along the railroads to towns and villages in the Great Plains. Farmers and ranchers would buy an item, and it would take weeks to receive the skirt or shovel in the mail. But now eBay bidders could change the price in a second and buy it with a click of the mouse. "Speed kills," wrote a journalist. "It kills old economics, it kills old companies and it kills old rules."

eBay was the first one on the auction ebusiness and it was making its own rules, which completely changed the way that people—and many companies—did business. A survey found that the average Amazon.com buyer viewed that site for about thirteen minutes a month, but for eBay that figure was one hour and forty-five minutes. It especially helped antique shops and small businesses expand. An antiques store in Maine advertised an old calculator for $100. Within a week, calculator collectors had bid the price up to $6,500. The internet economic system changed the way sellers set prices: it found the appropriate price. A rancher went up to an eBay marketing executive and said, "I'm in the bull-semen business, and eBay's completely changed the access I have to bull semen."

Other internet royalties appeared in 1996, revolutionizing email. By then almost all computer users had electronic mail, a form of communication that had been around for three decades. Massachusetts Institute of Technology in 1965 had a system known as MAILBOX. The problem was that everyone who used email had to connect to the same mainframe computer. As computers evolved in the 1970s, so did email. To make sure that a message got to the right user, Ray Tomlinson in 1972 invented the @ symbol to send a message from one computer to another, and others developed the appropriate software. During the 1980s businesses, universities, government, and organizations began supplying computers for employees, and they also assigned email addresses. Thus, a person's name would be followed by @ and the name of the company, college, agency, or organization followed by com, edu, gov, org. Moreover, until the mid-1990s almost all personal internet access was through dial-up services over the telephone line using an Internet Service Provider (ISP) at a company such as AT&T, Comcast, AOL, or others that provided access. People logged on to their email by subscribing to a provider and installing their program; they were only able to access messages from a specific computer.

Then two other internet royalties stepped forward—Sabeer Bhatia and Jack Smith. They were working at Apple when they thought of allowing people to access their email with their own personal computer, instead of only through their employer, university, or agency. It was such a good idea—and so obvious—that when Smith called Bhatia to tell him of the concept, the latter replied, "Call me back on a secure line when you get to your house! We don't want anyone to overhear!"

The result: Hotmail. On July 4, 1996, Smith and Bhatia launched "HoTMaiL" which referred to HTML, the language of the World Wide Web. Launching on American Independence Day symbolized "freedom" from ISP-based email and the ability to access a user's inbox from anywhere in the world. From now on, users could access the Hotmail website from any browser, enter their credentials, and read and send emails. Every time a user sent an email the bottom read "Hotmail: Free, trusted and rich email service. Get it now." It was a brilliant idea, an ad on every email—and that spread the word and became commonplace on the internet. By the end of 1997 Hotmail had some twenty-five million users.

As usual, Bill Gates was watching. He ordered his team led by Marco DeMello to launch their own web-based email program, but it soon became obvious to DeMello that it would take too much time and that the only real option was to buy an existing service. This was not popular with Microsoft executives, because they adhered to the policy of "eating our own dog food."

Yet time was of the essence in the hyper speed cyberspace businesses. Thus, Gates simply outbid all others and bought Hotmail for about $450 million, a nice sum for Smith and Bhatia's two years of creativity and work. That buy was the largest internet startup purchase of its day, and Microsoft jumped into the emerging world of web-based email. Eventually Microsoft changed Hotmail into Outlook, as the number of users soared with free email accounts on Yahoo and Google. By 2020 there were about 4 billion people using email, half the world's population.

Yahoo also wanted Hotmail, but Gates beat them with the check, so David Filo and Jerry Yang decided to purchase a competitor, Rocket Mail, for a relatively cheap $94 million. They soon dropped the name and rebranded it Yahoo Mail.[7]

Other internet royalties of the late nineties included Max Levchin and Peter Thiel. Levchin was an online security expert, while Thiel was a hedge fund manager. The two met in 1998 when Levchin was searching for financial support for a company that would develop a system for transferring money using wireless devices. The two joined forces, obtained a few million dollars of support, moved to Silicon Valley, and created a digital wallet—PayPal. In 1999, with six employees and two computers, they launched the first version of their electronic payments system.

The beginning was slow, but the two partners realized that no means of electronic payment had been developed to handle the buying and selling that was surging on the internet. For example, users of eBay were sending checks and money orders by mail, a slow, outdated system in the digital era. Levchin and Thiel realized that electronic business lacked an easy and convenient payment system designed for the World Wide Web, a system that would enable a person or business to email and receive money.

Moreover, the founders desired to keep their payment system simple and based on internationally accepted institutions. While others were considering a new type of electronic currency, eventually cryptocurrencies like Bitcoin, the two partners mandated that the US dollar was the medium of exchange and email and established banks and credit cards were the standard for transfer. Users also could deposit funds, and it earned interest until depleted.

Soon, eBay users discovered PayPal—and both took off. In the first eight months of 2000 PayPal accounts swelled from a little over 10,000 to almost three million. Two years later PayPal went public. A share sold for $13, rose to over $21 that day, and the IPO generated over $60 million.

At the same time music lovers were wondering how to download their favorite tunes to their computers, many of them now equipped with high-speed chips and large hard drives. Earlier in the nineties Germans had developed a coding format for digital audio, MP3, and in 1997 nineteen-year-old Justin Frankel answered their prayers by releasing the software program Winamp. It quickly was downloaded by twenty-five million grateful MP3 devotees. Then Shawn Fanning joined in, and word spread all over the internet; the idea was "sharing media was superior to . . . going and buying an album." That way, Fanning continued, you could "have access to the entire universe of recorded music."

With help from a few others Napster was born, an entirely new way to disseminate music and other media. Individual users would upload digital copies of their CDs one song at a time to a shared network of other users. People visited the network, downloaded the song—not buying a CD at a record store—so the tune was free. It was not "stealing" music from record corporations and artists, users rationalized, it was "sharing" music. With that happy thought in mind, Brian McCullough wrote, "Napster was like a supernova that exploded across the tech, media and cultural landscape." Less than a year after it was launched Napster had ten million users, and by the end of 2000 around forty million, thanks mostly to university students who plugged into their broadband dorm room internet connections; by spring semester 2000 it was estimated that some 70 percent of college kids were regularly using Napster. It had become, according to *The Guinness Book of World Records*, the fastest-growing service of all time.

Yet that same year, Napster would have legal problems. Musicians and the record industry were losing millions in royalties each year, claimed copyright infringement, and sued the website. The court ruled in the musicians' favor and ordered the end of free transfer of copywritten music. Napster rebuilt their system and became the first legal song downloading program where songs were purchased for an amount that included royalties, meaning that all sites that offered music downloads charge and artists receive their share.

Steve Jobs was watching, and in 2001 he introduced Apple's iPod, proclaiming to eager music lovers, "You can take your whole music library with you." They did, buying a remarkable 150,000 iPods in the first three months; by 2007 the company was selling a remarkable fifty million a year.

After music went digital, others turned to films: Netflix. In the nineties the way one watched home movies was shifting from tapes on VHS (Video Home System) to DVDs (Digital Video Disc) on those players. One would go to a store such as Blockbuster and rent a tape or DVD, usually for two or three days, take it home and play it, plugged into and appearing on their television. Most rental companies charged late fees, and when Reed Hastings returned a copy of the excellent 1995 film *Apollo 13* he got slapped with a $40 late fee.

Outraged, Hastings paired up with Marc Randolph, and in April 1998 they launched Netflix. Aware of Amazon.com's ecommerce model, they decided that for a monthly fee a customer would be mailed three or four movies each month, watch and send them back—no late fees—and automatically get a new one in the mail. It was fast and cheap. While a Blockbuster store might have a couple thousand titles at their stores, Netflix carried thousands, eventually 100,000. Also, the company let customers form a "Queue" to line up future films and injected an algorithm that informed them of similar films that they might like. Netflix took off, and within a decade the company, and YouTube, were streaming videos while Blockbuster was filing for bankruptcy.

The travel industry was beginning to wonder why anyone needed a travel agent in the digital age. In the mid-1990s the airline reservation system SABRE combined with Worldview Systems and in 1995 launched the first website that allowed consumers to purchase travel tickets online without the help of an agent—Travelocity. Bill Gates was watching, of course, and in 1996 Microsoft launched Expedia, and soon others appeared, such as Booking.com and Agoda.

Others were thinking of creating an online encyclopedia, including Jimmy Wales and Larry Sanger. During the nineties a few people

considered the concept of Wiki, a hypertext publication collabora-
tively edited and managed by its own audience, not by a single author
or company. Computer programmer Howard Cunningham developed the first wiki, started coding the WikiWikiWeb in 1994, and the
next year coauthored a book, *The Wiki Way*. By that time some companies had begun to digitize their encyclopedias, leading to Microsoft
Encarta and Encyclopedia Britannica, but the Wiki way was that no
single source should be in control and that the size of the online
source could be basically infinite. Wales and Sanger agreed; the former
was an entrepreneur, and Sanger was a philosopher who studied
epistemology, the study of knowledge. Early in 2000 they launched
Nupedia, but the articles went through peer review, meaning that
few folks wanted to donate their time to get criticized by a so-called
expert; in the first six months only a handful of articles were on the
website. Thus, they changed the format in 2001 and called their new
venture Wikipedia. Google took notice and sent hundreds of its users
to the new website each day, and that same year the *New York Times*
wrote: "For all the human traffic that the Web attracts, most sites
remain fairly solitary destinations," but "some sites are looking for
ways to enable visitors not only to interact but even to collaborate to
change the sites themselves," such as Wikipedia, which is "involved
in a kind of virtual barn-raising." The idea took off, and twenty years
later Wikipedia had more than fifty-five million articles in more than
three hundred languages.

    All the while scientists were developing what eventually would be
called the cell phone, and they could do that because of the miniatur-
ization of transistors, new potent lithium-ion batteries, creative software that could run on a small silicone chip, and the development of
high-speed cellular wireless networks: 2G in 1991, which for the first
time encrypted calls, allowed picture and text messages (SMS); and
3G in 2001, which was four times faster and for the first time allowed
international roaming services.

    During World War II the US Army developed the "walkie talkie,"
which weighed twenty-five pounds and had a range of five miles. After

the war a few companies made heavy phone units that fit in automobile trunks, but by the 1980s Motorola took charge of the industry
with the introduction of DynaTAC. This cellular phone weighed just
two pounds but was very expensive, about $4,000 in 1981 ($11,500 in
2020), and it worked on North America's first 1G analog service. By
the end of the decade Motorola launched MicroTAC, which was the
first small-sized pocket phone with a flip phone design, and in 1992
the company introduced Motorola International 3200, which was the
first hand-sized digital mobile phone that used 2G digitally encrypted
technology.

IBM took over the game in August 1994 when it released what
many consider the first "smartphone," the IBM Simon. It was a mobile phone and pager that could send and receive faxes, emails, and
cellular pages. It came loaded with a touchscreen with a QWERTY
keyboard, the same as a typewriter. It also provided a calendar, address
book, clock, calculator, and notepad. It was expensive, at about $900,
bulky, and had an old nickel battery that only lasted about one hour.
IBM sold about 50,000 of them, but it set a superior standard since
it had several elements that became staples for all future smartphones.

Nokia challenged IBM and Motorola on the cell phone battlefield in 1997, when the Finnish corporation introduced their 9000
Communicator. It was more of a computer than the previous cell
phones, for it had all the previous features—plus access to the web—
with its CPU Intel 386 processor, LCD screen, and full QWERTY
keyboard. It was heavy at about 14 ounces, about twice the weight of
later cell phones, but it became very popular. In 1999, Nokia introduced its 3210 model, which quickly became one of the most popular
mobile phones in history, selling an astonishing 160 million.

Thus, during the late nineties smart cell phones captured America—
and the world, especially when actors used various portable devices
in films such as *Clueless*, *Wag the Dog*, *The Player*, *Scream*, *The Saint*,
Bad Company, and Arnold Schwarzenegger's *Terminator 3: Rise of the
Machines*. Customers lined up at vendors to see and buy the newest
device. During the next decade cell phone sales exploded, and many

Many films, including *Clueless*, 1995, helped to popularize cell phones. Photo by Paramount Pictures/Getty Images.

other corporations joined the battle—BlackBerry, Samsung, Ericsson, Sharp, Sanyo, and of course Apple (the iPhone).

These devices became so popular and so addictive that many referred to the BlackBerry as "CrackBerry." "It should be reported to the DEA," declared Intel's chairman, and another CEO declared, "It is the heroin of mobile computing. I'm serious. I had to stop. I'm now in BA: BlackBerry Anonymous."

Eventually, BlackBerry was superseded by Samsung, which became the largest cell phone producer in the world, as smartphones changed human behavior, from instant worldwide telephone calls, to encrypted texting, to watching videos and playing games, to driving with Google Maps. By 2020, about 90 percent of Americans, and about two-thirds of all people in the world, owned a smartphone.

Then in 1999, the Japanese electronics corporation Kyocera claimed to launch the first camera phone, or "Visual Phone" 210. CNN aired the story to a fascinated audience. The phone had a 0.1 megapixel camera and only could take twenty pictures before its limited storage was full. It sold for about $325 and had a stand so the users could take pictures of themselves, or "selfies."

Kyocera dominated the market for only a year, for the next summer Samsung introduced the SCH-V200. It could take up to twenty pictures at a resolution of 0.35MP, and you could see them on the phone's 1.5-inch screen. However, one could not use the phone to send the pictures to someone else directly. That happened at the end of the year when Sharp introduced their J-Phone, a cell that integrated the phone's hardware with the camera. With that the user could send the image directly from the phone to email—which proved incredibly popular. Next year, the Sanyo SCP-5300 hit the United States running, and *Time* labeled it the "Most Influential Gadget and Gizmo" of 2002, claiming that by 2010 the "total number of images captured on camera phones will reach 228 billion . . . exceeding the number of photos taken on digital still cameras and film cameras combined."

Next for the cell phone came applications—apps. In the 1980s Steve Jobs imagined a place, an "App Store," where software could be bought or obtained over a phone line, but his vision was off in the future. The future arrived in 1997 when the Nokia 6110 phone included a built-in version of the basic arcade game "Snake," which many consider the first mobile app. The first iPod would also come with built-in games: Solitaire and Brick.

Meanwhile, America Online was in many ways the company that began social networking. AOL created member communities with searchable "member profiles." Customers could list particular traits about themselves that other users could utilize to find similar people with similar interests. Engineer Randy Conrads saw the potential in this information. A child of a military family that moved a lot, he was frustrated finding old friends, so he decided to quit Boeing and in 1995 founded perhaps the first social networking site, Classmates. com. The idea was to allow members to find, and stay connected with, friends from school, college, work, and the military. The site proved quickly that finding old friends was popular, and in a few years the site had millions of members. Two years later, in 1997, AOL returned to the fold by launching Messenger, a chat program that allowed numerous members to talk to each other. Next came short-lived SixDegrees.com, one of the first to allow its users to create profiles, invite friends, organize groups, and surf other user profiles, and by the turn of the millennium social networking sites really caught on with AsianAvenue.com, BlackPlanet.com, MiGente.com, followed by Friendster, LinkedIn, MySpace, and of course Facebook and Twitter.

Internet networking caught on, and there were many who were interested, including feminists. That 1970s activism had produced numerous state Equal Rights Amendments and significantly decreased educational and workplace discrimination. As stated, the Clarence Thomas–Anita Hill testimony provoked some African Americans to emerge as a Third Wave of feminism. In 1992 women helped elect Clinton, and that year Marie Wilson cofounded "Take Our Daughters to Work Day," to encourage girls to strive for the professions. During the previous generation the women's movement grew by bounds but lost focus, and during the nineties, according to historian Lisa Levenstein, feminism had become "a movement without a center."

Enter the internet. In 1995 hundreds of international feminists attended the Fourth World Conference on Women in Beijing, and many of them set up a computer center with two hundred machines donated by Apple and Hewlett-Packard. That was the beginning of global "online feminism." What resulted, according to a reporter, was a "simultaneous 'virtual' women's conference in cyberspace," giving the Beijing conference a "far broader reach and more immediacy than any global gathering in history." One participant, Shana Penn, authored one of the first handbooks on digital organizing, *The Women's Guide to the Wired World*. Thousands of feminists began building virtual communities that extended their movement and brought in new multicultural voices, eventually resulting in new organizations such as Sister Song: Women of Color Reproductive Justice Collective and INCITE! Women of Color Against Violence. African American feminists used the internet to spread the word about the 1997 Million

Woman March in Philadelphia. Next year, Aliza Sherman published *Cybergirl: A Woman's Guide to the World Wide Web*, and her website was receiving about two million hits a month, reinvigorating feminism throughout the world.

Cyberspace, computer sales, and the dot.com revolution throughout the nineties helped to create a red-hot American economy, which already was growing strong because of lower oil prices, higher productivity, and Clinton's economic policies. In 1990, only a handful of technology pioneers were online and fewer than 20 percent of households had a computer; by the end of 1999 half of Americans were online and some 60 percent of households owned an IBM, Dell, Compaq, HP, Apple, Packard Bell, Gateway, or Toshiba. In 1995, the S&P 500 index returned more than 37 percent, and then in the next four years companies such as Yahoo, Amazon, eBay, and many more went public. The results were phenomenal, for both the overall markets and for the individual. In April 1991 the Dow crept above 3,000 for the first time. In November 1995 it inched above 5,000, as Netscape went public and ignited the dot.com craze. By the end of the nineties the Dow had screamed above 11,000. At the end of 1990 the stock market was valued at $3 trillion; at the end of 1999 it was appraised at $15 trillion. The bull market of the nineties had become the longest run in American history and only the second in growth, just behind the Roaring Twenties.

The dot.com economy had an impact on individual investors. Now, with the growth of online trading employed by E★TRADE, Ameritrade, Schwab, and others, investors no longer had to call their stockbroker and buy stock. Instead they could turn on their computers, go to the website, and make trades online. By 1999 nearly 40 percent of retail security trades were done online, and many of the stocks they were buying were digital firms. Those stocks were soaring. If investors bought $1,000 worth of stock at the time that Amazon or Yahoo went public, then by the end of 1998 their investment in the former had rocketed to over $30,000, and the latter was worth over $45,000! In twelve months of 1998, Yahoo stock returned over 580 percent, AOL was almost 600 percent, and Amazon screamed up 970 percent—an eBull Market.

This frenzy created what would be called the dot.com bubble, which like all stock market bubbles, eventually would burst. Nevertheless, US government data at the end of 1999 credited the internet with generating more than a third of America's economic growth between 1995 and 1998, the peak of the boom.

CEOs sensed the revolution. Companies employed the internet to email their customers for the first time, or to improve relations with their suppliers or trading partners, or to sell off perishable stocks of goods. New companies and business models emerged in as little as two years, in industries ranging from selling books to chemicals to bull semen, to bring buyers and sellers together in new electronic market-places. Senior managers by the end of the nineties no longer needed convincing, as a worldwide survey of five hundred major corporations found that more than 90 percent of leading managers believed the internet was transforming the global marketplace. In hyper speed ecommerce, traditional retailers would join the internet action or fall by the wayside. IBM's CEO described new dot.com companies in 1999 as "fireflies before the storm—all stirred up, throwing off sparks." He predicted, "The storm that's arriving . . . is when the thousands and thousands of institutions that exist today seize the power of this global computing and communications infrastructure and use it to transform themselves. That's the real revolution."

That year, the last one of the decade and century, the *Economist* wrote that the digital online elites were claiming that "the Internet is the most transforming invention in human history. It has the capacity to change everything—the way we work, the way we learn and play, even, maybe, the way we sleep or have sex. What is more, it is doing so at far greater speed than the other great disruptive technologies of the 20th century, such as electricity, the telephone and the car."

Humorist Dave Barry wasn't so sure, writing that we don't know what the future holds for the "Information Superhighway; we cannot predict where, ultimately, the Computer Revolution will take us. All we know for certain is that, when we finally get there, we won't have enough RAM."

At the end of the decade, century, and millennium, there appeared a glitch in the cyberspace revolution: Y2K.

Y2K had become shorthand for a problem stemming from the clash of the upcoming Year 2000 and the two-digit year format utilized by early mainframe computer programs to minimize use of its memory, which did not become readily available until the invention of larger hard drives in PCs in the nineties. If early computers interpreted the "00" in 2000 as 1900, this could mean headaches, and during the last year of the century rumors raged that when December 31, 1999, turned to January 1, 2000, all kinds of computer malfunctions would take place.

The entire notion was rather ridiculous, as cultural writer Chuck Klosterman noted. "Why did a computer chip need to know what year it was in order to work? If an Apple computer thought it was 1900, would it somehow believe it had not yet been invented?"

Many jumped on the bandwagon. Bill Gates denied that there would be massive problems, but survivalists, cults, and conspiracy theory buffs claimed that there would be large-scale urban blackouts and infrastructure damage and that now was the time to stock up on food, water, firearms, generators, and cash. The Reverend Jerry Falwell suggested that Y2K would be the confirmation of Christian prophecy, "God's instrument to shake this nation, to humble this nation." The crisis might incite a worldwide revival that would lead to "the rapture of the church." The more extreme evangelicals used Y2K to promote an agenda in which the downfall of the government was a desired outcome in order to usher in Christ's reign.

Banks started saving up dollars, fearing a rush. The federal government printed up more cash, increasing the supply by about a third by the end of the year. The Feds dispatched the new bills in armored cars and vaults across the country. A few days before the new year, British bank HSBC suffered a computer failure in which 20,000 credit card terminals stalled because of a computer glitch. A spokesperson for the bank said that the devices could not recognize 2000. Back in the United States, Chase, Citigroup, Wells Fargo, and Bank of America braced for the worst, while a vice president for Chase said, "We're all hoping this will be the biggest nonevent of the century."[8]

It was. Governments, businesses, programmers, all had prepared— and nothing happened. In the first days of the new millennium there was a collective sigh of relief. Bill Clinton beamed that the United States had won "the first challenge of the 21st century," and then Y2K became the joke: the KY Jelly company announced it was now Y2K compliant. Y2K? Because 1 K isn't enough.

5

Fin de Siècle @ Anything Goes America

At the beginning of the new millennium, commentator Frank Rich, one of the keenest observers of the nineties, wrote that Americans were waging a culture war in a time of declining norms of civility and decency. He continued in a related column that there were two big stories in 1998, one from Washington, DC, about a middle-aged president and his young female intern and the other from Hollywood about the record sales and rental of adult videos, over $4 billion, which that year surpassed the annual revenue amassed by the National Football League, the National Basketball League, or Major League Baseball. He wondered why voters weren't blushing about Bill Clinton's affair with Monica Lewinsky until he realized that a very "large percentage of Americans" was "routinely seeking out stories resembling that of the president and the intern—and raunchier ones—as daily entertainment fare."

What happened in the nineties? ABC interviewed high school students in 1996 about their interest in drugs and sex. They claimed that their attention was captured because of the continual bombardment of sensual images and drugs in magazines, television shows, and popular films. All the while pharmaceutical companies flooded media with countless ads about "medicines" and "mood enhancers," from Effexor to Zoloft.

The immense impact of television and films cannot be overstated in America's cultural battleground. Of course, the nation always has been in conflict, especially since the WASP decade of the 1950s was confronted, challenged, and changed by all those marching in the streets during the 1960s. Ever since there has been division over race, gender, religion, politics, foreign policy, war, sex, drugs, obscenity, and virtually anything else that would generate cultural carnage.

Trying to define American culture in any era is risky, but perhaps the most significant characteristic of the nineties was broadcast on the endless talk shows, television, and, in the second half of the era, on the internet: Anything Goes.

Anything Goes America emerged during sexual liberation of the 1970s and in music continued on in the 1980s, especially in rock and roll, where rock lyrics were breaking new barriers. One of the first songs to upset parents was released in 1984 by Prince, "Nikki," who was "a sex fiend/I met her in a hotel lobby/Masturbating with a magazine."

Tipper Gore, wife of Senator Al Gore, was outraged that their eleven-year-old daughter was listening to such lyrics, and the next year she and other politicians' wives established the Parents Music Resource Center. The PMRC aim was to increase consumer awareness of music with explicit lyrics, and they created a list of fifteen songs that they labeled objectionable because of sex or violence in the lyrics. The "Filthy Fifteen" included songs by many artists, including AC/DC, "Let Me Put My Love Into You"; Judas Priest, "Eat Me Alive"; Madonna, "Dress You Up"; Mötley Crüe, "Bastard"; and Twisted Sister, "We're Not Gonna Take It."

Later in 1985 the US Senate actually held hearings, the so-called porn-rock investigations, with musicians Frank Zappa, John Denver, and Dee Snider of Twisted Sister. Asked how something as insignificant as rating music lyrics could merit a Senate inquiry, Zappa simply remarked, "A couple of blowjobs here and there and Bingo!—you get a hearing."

Tipper Gore and her colleagues knew that the First Amendment would not allow banning such lyrics, but eventually they got the music industry to place a warning sticker on records and CDs: Parental Advisory Explicit Content.

Such warnings appeared on many records, including one that cultural critics often state began the nineties, Nirvana's *Nevermind*. Actually, that Seattle grunge band emerged in the 1980s, and it helped to popularize Alt rock, or indie rock, which began in the 1970s with artists like Lou Reed, Patti Smith, and, by the 1980s, the Dead Kennedys, 10,000 Maniacs, and R.E.M. Nirvana, with front man Kurt Cobain, drummer Dave Grohl, and bassist Krist Novoselic, released *Nevermind* in 1991, "the most far-reaching work of the grunge genre," and it included "Smells Like Teen Spirit." The five-minute video played endlessly on MTV was a "controlled riot" inside a high school gym, with the only authority figure an elderly janitor dancing with a mop. It is complete with slapstick cheerleaders, the lighting is bad, and the band wails, "I'm worse at what I do best/And for this gift I feel blessed." Cobain strikes a Gen X theme when he sings, "Oh well, whatever, never mind." The old was being ushered out, the new era in, as cultural commentator Chuck Klosterman wrote, "The hedonistic, euphoric, high-gloss 1980s are over. It took five minutes to killdoze an entire decade."

And to start a new one, which, at the beginning, was the subject of a *Time* cover story, "DIRTY WORDS, America's Foul-Mouthed Pop Culture." The magazine asked, "So are the '90s destined to be the Filth Decade? What has happened to comedy, not to mention the English language?" The article noted that "words and ideas formerly on the extremes have engulfed the cultural mainstream. But have they polluted it? Many people think so."

During the nineties, Anything Goes America went Full Monty. The TV action-drama *Baywatch* was on the entire decade, with Pamela Anderson and other bikini-clad lifeguards pictured in slow motion running bouncing along the beach. By the end of the decade the show was syndicated to almost 150 countries, drawing an incredible billion viewers a week. In 1991 Michael Jackson produced his "Black and White" video, in which he grabbed his crotch, played with his zipper. The next year Madonna published her picture book *Sex*, which showed her naked with other nude celebrities. It sold for about $50. and during its first week it grossed $25 million. In a 1993 episode of the police show *NYPD Blue* a character broke new ground in primetime by referring to another as "a pissy little bitch" and used four-letter words on network TV. By the late nineties three of the four attractive professional women in HBO's sitcom *Sex and the City* appeared topless during sex scenes. One episode of *Seinfeld*, the most popular sitcom of the era, revolved around the question of which of the four characters could hold off the longest from masturbating. In one of the most honest answers in TV history, Jerry Seinfeld was asked about the significance of his show. He answered, "It was about nothing, and it didn't matter."

Yada, yada, yada, and a lot of shows were about nothing except entertainment. At the beginning of the nineties the most popular was *Cheers*, a bar in Boston where "everyone knows your name." After work every day a group of friends appeared to discuss, well, everything. Its series finale in May 1993 was watched by almost 40 percent of the US population.

Another very popular show was the animated series that began airing regularly in 1990 on Fox Broadcasting—*The Simpsons*. Created by cartoonist Matt Groening, the program was about the Simpson family, and it was controversial from its beginning. The rebellious lead character, Bart, was ten years old and the eldest child and only son of Homer and Marge; Bart also had sisters, Lisa and Maggie. Bart was mischievous, rebellious, and disrespectful; he often misbehaved and usually did not receive any punishment, which irritated parents raising kids. This smart aleck quickly had a mass following, "Bartmania," and he became one of the most popular characters on television. In the early nineties kids bought millions of T-shirts featuring Bart, and some of the most famous captions were "I'm Bart

Simpson. Who the hell are you?" and "Underachiever ('And proud of it, man!')." In the season two opening episode "Bart Gets an 'F'," he proudly fails four history exams in a row. Several public schools in the nation banned the T-shirts. Nevertheless, they sold like hotcakes, and First Lady Barbara Bush made the series political when she declared that *The Simpsons* was "the dumbest thing" she had ever seen, and her husband, running for reelection in 1992, declared on the campaign trail, "We are going to keep on trying to strengthen the American family, to make American families a lot more like the Waltons and a lot less like the Simpsons."

Groening, his staff, and his writers laughed all the way to the bank. *Time* named Bart one of the 100 most important people of the twentieth century, and *Entertainment Weekly* in 1990 named him "entertainer of the year." At the end of the decade the Simpson family was awarded a star on the Hollywood Walk of Fame.

Other popular shows of the nineties were *60 Minutes*, *ER*, and *Murphy Brown*, which discussed fiery topics such as alcoholism, breast cancer, and even then-Vice President Dan Quayle. He criticized the main character for having a baby out of wedlock; it was a no-win for the VP, since thirty-eight million tuned into the show to watch Murphy's delivery. *Law & Order* set the stage for other popular similar shows that earned strong ratings, *CSI* and *NCIS*. *Sex and the City* depicted four attractive single professional working women while focusing on their sex lives; the theme was that men come and go but women can have supportive female soul mates. Perhaps more significant was *Ellen*. The series in 1997 took on lesbian love in "The Puppy Episode." Star Ellen DeGeneres's character, Ellen Morgan, develops a crush on a woman, which was startling television at the time, and later DeGeneres admits, "I am gay." So was Will, in the first show that featured a sexually active gay man as the central character, *Will and Grace*.

The nineties also witnessed a new genre, reality television. Inspired by the earlier PBS documentary series *An American Family*, MTV premiered *The Real World* in 1992; it became one of the longest-running television series, lasting an astonishing three decades. Each week a narrator began the show with: "This is the true story . . . of seven strangers . . . picked to live in a house . . . (work together) and have their lives taped . . . to find out what happens . . . when people stop being polite . . . and start getting real . . . The Real World." The producers picked new young people every season and moved them to new cities across the nation, starting in New York, then another thirty cities, and the last season in Atlanta. Critics at first hailed the series because it graphically discussed issues of young adults that appealed to Gen X—prejudice, religion, abortion, illness, sexuality, politics, substance abuse, sex, and AIDS. But later in the series critics panned it because it degenerated to episodes portraying immature behavior such as the one in which one housemate urinated on another's tooth-brush. Nevertheless, the initial success generated other reality television series in the nineties, *Cops*, *Road Rules*, and *The Challenge*, and by the beginning of the new millennium viewers would be hooked on the genre as they turned on *Survivor* and *The Amazing Race*, *The Bachelor*, and scores of others, including *The Apprentice*.

All these programs discussed one topic like never before—sex—which ran hot and heavy on television. In 1998 the director of the center for Media and Public Affairs was right on when he declared: "People used to think that television was aimed at the mind of a 12-year-old. Now it seems aimed at the hormones of a 14-year-old."

The same was true for the emergence and boosting of tabloid talk shows that included many hosts, including Maury Povich, Sally Jessy Raphael, Morton Downey Jr., Montel Williams, and perhaps the one that had the most impact, Jerry Springer. The *Jerry Springer Show* went national in 1991 and was not very successful discussing politics until the mid-1990s when it changed its format to have "ordinary people" discussing controversial topics such as adultery, incest, and anything outlandish: "mother-daughter dominatrixes, people who had self-amputated various body parts, a man who married a horse." Unlike the *Oprah Show*, which became popular by appealing to mainstream values, Springer invited guests who seemed delighted embarrassing themselves on emerging trash television by bragging about bestiality,

shouting profanity, and even throwing punches. Friendships, engagements, and marriages dissolved as ratings soared. By the end of the
era *TV Guide* rated it "The Worst TV Show Ever," and even Springer
commented that his show was so outrageous that it "ruined the
culture."

The *Jerry Springer Show* "threw the studio doors open," wrote television critic James Poniewozik, "and all hell broke through. The show
"didn't so much create reality TV as it rose on the same heated cur-
rents: It was a product of the same era that gave us 'The Real World'
and 'Cops.'" Springer was "one of the most talented accelerants, and
he steered lustily into the nosedive. After him came the reality-TV
deluge. . . . America became unshockable."

Not far behind were two other popular hosts—Don Imus and
Howard Stern. The Imus morning show was a potpourri of talk and
parody and was syndicated in twenty-three cities. He claimed that
Gingrich earned his college degree from the "Close Cover Before
Striking University of Armpit, Georgia." To Imus the news was "entertainment," a "device designed to revel in the agony of others."
Stern presented "shock talk." As one critic declared, the show was "for
12-year-olds who get excited when they hear the word penis." By the
late nineties Stern aired in sixty markets and attracted twenty million
listeners, often talking about genitalia, "bitches," and declaring "kiss
my ass." Consequently, the Federal Communications Commission
began issuing citations for his obscene talk, and eventually he earned
the honor of becoming the most fined radio host in history, some
$2.5 million. He didn't care; talking dirty was earning him about $20
million a year.

"We have become a talk show nation," observed media journalist
Howard Kurtz, "pulsating with opinions that are channeled through
hosts and reverberated through the vast echo chamber of the airwaves."
The old media of newspapers, magazines, nightly news, still tried to
present some balance, some checks and verification of their reporting
to the public, but in the nineties anyone could say anything—gossip,
speculations, conspiracies, no matter. "The gatekeepers of the elite

media have been cast aside," Kurtz continued, "and the floodgates thrown open."

They certainly were, as Anything Goes America broke another barrier: the F-word. That word had been a no-no forever, but one could tell that the media was inching closer in 1993 when animated characters *Beavis and Butthead* premiered on MTV and repeated over and over, "This sucks." Later in the decade on *South Park*, a profane satire about four boys in Colorado, there was no problem singing "Kyle's mom is a big fat bitch." And of course, proclaimed writer Kurt Andersen in 1998, "The word 'fuck' recently appeared in a piece of fiction excerpted on the Web site of the *New York Times*—the *New York Times*! . . . What is the appropriate response to the epidemic of stark obviousness, high-concept literalism, rude candor? Is it thumbs up or thumbs down? Neither. Some of it is refreshing; some of it is appalling; a lot of it is amusing; most of it is just the American way. By definition, therefore, it doesn't totally suck."[1]

"Sex is everywhere these days," wrote *Time*, "in books, magazines, films, television, music videos and bus-stop perfume ads." In just 1997 alone the trade magazine *Adult Video News* reported that porn producers released some eight thousand films, and they appeared in hotels and fashion. Popular hotel chains installed pay-for-view "adult-TV" in some rooms and soon noticed that they were selling those quarters at a much higher rate than normal ones. In 1994 Wonderbra introduced its push-up bra in Europe and America. It plunged at the front center and pulled the breasts together to create an elevated cleavage line. "I've got a couple of those . . . Wonderbras," said slender supermodel Kate Moss. "They are so brilliant . . . even I get cleavage with them." The company quickly achieved fast sales after they displayed a model in a Wonderbra from roadside billboards gazing down at her breasts with the caption "Hello Boys." Allegedly, a number of male drivers had rear-end automobile accidents.

Sex quickly appeared on the internet in the form of sex.com and numerous other sites. The *Time* article cited one of the first large "stud[ies] of online porn—what's available, who is downloading it, what turns them on." The Carnegie Mellon University study found that online porn was "immensely popular . . . one of the largest (if not the largest) recreational applications of users of computer networks."

Like music in the 1980s, in the nineties such findings were disturbing to parents and politicians, of course, and some attempted to pass legislation to try to ban porn from cyberspace. Democratic senator Jim Exon brought a binder to the Senate floor filled with "perverted pornography" that he declared was online "just a few clicks away." He continued, "I want to keep the information superhighway from resembling a red light district." Republican senator Dan Coats added, "We face a unique, disturbing and urgent circumstance because it is children who are the computer experts in our nation's families." He and others tried to pass the Communications Decency Act, but it got stiff resistance. "It's a frontal assault on the First Amendment," said Harvard law professor Laurence Tribe, and a veteran prosecutor declared, "It won't pass scrutiny even in misdemeanor court." Nevertheless, Congress overwhelmingly passed and Clinton signed the CDA in 1996, prohibiting individuals from transmitting "obscene or indecent" online messages to recipients under the age of eighteen. As Exon said, "If nothing is done now, the pornographers may become the primary beneficiary of the information revolution."

Yet Tribe and other civil libertarians were right. Six months later a federal judge panel declared most of the CDA unconstitutional, except for the unenforceable eighteen-year-old age limit, and that was later affirmed by the US Supreme Court.

There was no end to the topic, and pornography continued to grow on the internet while at the same time many thought it was growing on stage—rappers and gangsta rappers were grabbing their crotch. Rap is a form of rhythmic speaking in rhyme, while hip-hop refers to the music and culture for rap. While rap evolved out of 1970s hip-hop, according to music critics, "the '90s really were a golden age for rap. In the early part of the decade, the genre was ushering in its platinum era. By the end of the decade, it was a full-on commercial monster, a dominant force—the dominant force—in pop music."

Many decades are associated with a certain type of music. The 1920s was labeled the Jazz Age, the 1940s the big band swing era, the first rock appeared in the 1950s, followed in the next generation by the golden age of various types of rock 'n' roll. "And how will we remember the last days of the '90s?" asked *Time*. "Most likely, to the rough-hewn beat of rap." In 1998, for the first time ever, rap out-sold what previously had been America's top-selling format, country music, more than eighty-one million rap CDs, tapes, and albums, nine million more than country. "Hip-hop is the rebellious voice of the youth," Jay-Z boasted. "It's what people want to hear."

America became unshockable. Hip-hop was flooding the nation. Artists like Jay-Z, Ice Cube, The Notorious B.I.G., Public Enemy, Snoop Dogg, Scarface, 2Pac or Tupac Shakur, and a legion of others like Dr. Dre, Eminem, 50 Cent, and the "Queen of Hip-Hop Soul" Mary J. Blige, were shaping youth culture worldwide. It appeared in films, such as Will Smith's movies, and in Tommy Hilfiger and FUBU fashion. While at the beginning of the nineties Blacks mostly bought hip-hop, by the end of the decade whites purchased over 70 percent of these albums. As one white twenty-two-year-old working gal in New York City said, "You do develop a sense of self through it. You listen and you say, 'Yeah, that's right.'"

"Hip-hop," wrote author and fan Bakari Kitwana, was "arguably the single most significant achievement of our generation," one that paralleled the mostly white labeled Generation X. And those stars had an impact. Ask any Black American in the Hip-hop Generation "where they were on September 13, 1996, and most can tell you," Kitwana continued. "Ask them where they were six months later on March 9, 1997, and you'll get recollections as crystal clear as a baby boomer" recalling the Kennedy or King assassinations: the deaths of Tupac Shakur and of Notorious B.I.G.

In 1999 the cover of *Time* declared, "HIP-HOP NATION." These musicians were mostly young Black men rapping about their lives and the lives of others. As mass incarceration rates soared, especially with

Black men, their brothers rapped many tunes, including Ice T "The Tower," 2Pac "16 on Deathrow," and Snoop Doggy Dogg "Murder Was the Case." Music critic Toure later wrote, "For inner-city black audiences, rap seemed like a realistic depiction of their world, and they appreciated the no-holds-barred look at their streets." Rappers also took a slap at the mostly white-dominated society "Elvis was a hero to most/But he never meant shit to me," rapped Public Enemy in "Fight the Power." "Mother f– him and John Wayne."

Naturally, as more and more hip-hop hit the top 20 charts and was played over the airways there were many detractors, for rap's unsavory message often was violence, vulgarity, misogyny, and materialism. In 1995 the Boston Chapter of the National Coalition of 100 Black Women sponsored a forum on rap music. The mostly female audience was denouncing the male rappers use of "nigga," "bitch," "hos," when a young woman took the mic and declared, "Some women act like that and deserve to be checked. I know I'm not a bitch or a ho, so I don't care 'cause I know they ain't talking to me."

The argument never would be settled, and the male rappers maintained that a similar message, with different terms, appeared daily from white rockers on MTV. Kitwana said that when the music became mainstream many recognized that it was "debilitating and dehumanizing. I don't ever accept that the n-word has been divorced from its historical roots, no matter how many times people use it. People who believe [it's OK] are deceiving themselves. . . . When I hear young kids on the playground refer to young girls as bitches and know that they got it from listening to this music, that's inexcusable to me," and he continued that rap too often was "Blacks selling Black self-hatred as entertainment."

There was a lot of inexcusable behavior in Anything Goes America, and it was spread by the internet, of course, and in many electronic forms at the local video arcade. During the decade, developers produced several controversial videos and games: *Splatterhouse*, a "violent, excessively gory brawler," and *Mortal Kombat*, with blood and brutality, the first big-budget game to raise the issue of violence in videos. *Grand Theft Auto* included ample sexual themes, drug use, racism, language, drunk driving, and violence against civilians and law enforcement, the first to be rated "adult only," and *Postal*, which included all of the above, even animal cruelty, so it eventually was banned in Australia and New Zealand. Parents were increasingly alarmed when their teens played these games. When a reporter questioned a sixteen-year-old in Los Angeles playing *Primal Rage*, a game in which dinosaurs tear one another to pieces, he said, "Sure, the violence influences kids. . . . But nobody can do anything about it."

Some tried, to little avail. Recall that during the 1992 campaign Clinton castigated rap singer Sister Souljah for saying that Blacks have killed one another long enough, that it was time for them to start killing whites. That had no impact on rap music sales. *Time* wrote at mid-decade, "When you glamorize murder, as *Natural Born Killers* does; or glorify violence against women, as does 2 Live Crew; when lyrics are anti-Semitic, as Public Enemy's are, or advocate hatred of gays and immigrants, as those of Guns N' Roses do, it's not just conservatives who know something has gone wrong; any thinking liberal does too."

And thinking conservatives, such as Bob Dole. At the beginning of his presidential run, Dole took the fight to Los Angeles. He castigated the entertainment industry, even Disney, for making huge profits off smut, and the Republican accused the executives behind US movies, music, and television of flooding the country with "nightmares of depravity."

Speaking of Bob Dole, two years after he lost the presidential election the seventy-four-year-old surprised many by becoming the pitch man for Viagra. "Courage, something shared by countless Americans," Dole said in a one-minute ad for the Pfizer medicine. He told about his prostate cancer treatment and then said that it left him with "E.D., erectile dysfunction." "You know, it's a little embarrassing to talk about E.D.," Dole continued. "But it's so important to millions of men and their partners."

The Viagra ads hit home, literally, during the 1998 football season, when families were gathered around the dinner table or sitting on the living room sofa snacking. A couple dancing, holding hands, touching, and then the low voice talks about side effects—possible headaches, and "In the rare event of an erection lasting more than four hours, seek immediate medical help."

"Football is family time," wrote author David Friend. "So talk of uncontrollable erections elicited not groans but an icy hush . . . . Here was talk of sexual congress—out in the open, over chips and guac and wings."

Men across the nation, and world, began searching for and buying the little blue pill as Pfizer produced many other ads. Middle-aged men dancing down a street to the Queen song, "We Are the Champions"; an older band playing, "I can't wait to go home," with the recurring verse "viva Viagra." "We're doing it like bunnies," states a guy while his exhausted wife sarcastically says, "Thanks Viagra. Thanks a lot." When a husband romantically calls, "Honey," his wife flushes his Viagra down a toilet. When asked about his own ad, Dole quipped, "I wish I'd have bought stock earlier."

Or he should have bought stock in the networks as they cashed in on salacious stories during and after the O.J. trial. ABC's *Prime Time Live* interviewed Marla Maples, the mistress of millionaire Donald Trump, and she discussed her love life, while another episode on the show interviewed Paula Jones. Not to be outdone, CNN interviewed Gennifer Flowers, while NBC interviewed John Bobbitt. He apparently abused his wife, Lorena, and in a fit of rage while he was asleep, she cut off his penis, drove away from home, and threw it out the car window. ABC's *20/20* interviewed her, as late-night hosts had a banquet:"I just watched a *20/20* special about John and Lorena Bobbitt. It was good, but I got tired and had to cut it off." . . . "Why was Lorena Bobbitt found not guilty? Because the evidence wouldn't stand up in court."

Anything Goes America continued spreading by other new technologies; during the nineties viewers shifted to cable and satellite television. In the early nineties about 60 percent of homes had access to cable, and by the end of the decade that increased to 80 percent that had access to cable or to satellite connections. In mid-decade satellite DIRECTV and the Dish Network began operations. The result was phenomenal, the soaring of the number of channels dedicated to well, anything goes—news, sports, movies, shopping, music—along with the Food Network, Nick at Nite, Turner Classic Movies, Comedy Central, Discovery Channel, Animal Planet, Game Show Network, Cartoon Network, and a banquet for sports fans—the Tennis Channel, the Golf Channel, and eventually conference channels such as the Big Ten, Pac-12, SEC, and ACC.

Anything Goes America, of course, was boosted by the O.J. trial. As stated, the courtroom drama turned into a soap opera on steroids. It stimulated the nation to blab about "domestic violence" and "spousal abuse," but also devalued public discourse, increased public cynicism, and set media on a frenzy for huge profits for focusing their cameras on sex, scandal, and celebrities. News became "infotainment."

Simpson's trial encouraged publishers to cut mainstream news and replace it with the rich, beautiful, and powerful. This had begun in 1974 with the introduction of *People*, which quickly became the most popular magazine in America. O.J. appeared on the cover of *People* once in the 1970s, another time in the 1980s, but then the trial and he probably set the annual world record—he or his family that year were pasted on the cover five times. Subscriptions soared, and that convinced more conventional newsmagazines to switch their format. *Newsweek* in 1990 featured political or world leaders on its covers but by 1997 put celebrities on one-third. The same for their competitor *Time*, which had only two celebs on their cover in 1990—David Lynch and Bart Simpson—but had almost a dozen during 1999.

Another aspect of America's culture of entertainment was the presidency of Bill Clinton. The constant barrage attacking him from his first day in office, his continual self-inflicted wounds, created a relentless stream of national noise. As commentator Frank Rich put it when the president retired:

Rational—and irrational—people may differ over the merits of Bill Clinton's presidency, but few can dispute that he was without peer as our entertainer in chief. He turned the whole citizenry . . . into drama fiends. When he left office, the cliché had it that late-night comics, after eight years of sure-fire punch lines, would miss him the most. Now it turns out we're all junkies for the fast-paced, round-the-clock theatrics that defined the Clinton years. . . . Americans' hunger for raucous theater did not end with Mr. Clinton's term of office; if anything, it has intensified. . . . Americans are more addicted to combative entertainment than ever.[2]

The rapid development of the internet in the nineties demanded new legislation to erect some rules and regulations. The last time the government became involved was six decades earlier and was the legislative response to the rise of radio in the 1920s, the 1934 Communications Act. Thus, in 1996 Congress passed and President Clinton signed the Telecommunications Act. It was a major change in American telecommunication law, since it was the first time that the internet was included in broadcasting and spectrum allotment. "The goal of this new law," wrote the Federal Communications Commission, was to establish policies for the internet, broadband, cell phone connections, and create "fair rules for this new era of competition."

What actually happened was very different. What ensued was a fight for market shares between telephone and internet companies, many of them that merged. Rather like the railroads of the nineteenth century, where Great Northern and Central Pacific didn't build competing railroad lines between two major cities, telecommunication corporations staked out their claim to certain districts of a city, a state, even the nation, and in effect built a monopoly. Thus, Verizon, AT&T, Sprint, Time Warner Cable, and T-Mobile built the cell phone and internet infrastructure and after various mergers with smaller companies developed as enormous corporations earning billions in revenue and controlling large portions of the digital industry, while Google eventually controlled much of the search engine business.

Moreover, Section 230 of the act provided a legal shield and thus helped to launch Big Tech. It enacted a free speech rule different from print or media broadcasts, which can be held liable for false or malicious slander; internet cannot, for the web is not treated legally as a speaker or publisher.

The Telecommunications Act also had an impact on the radio industry, for it eliminated a limit on nationwide station ownership and allowed a company to own up to four stations in one market. Consequently, critics pointed out that in the five years after the law went into effect, radio station ownership dropped from about 5,100 owners to 3,800. And that meant mergers and buyouts. Thus, Texans Lowry Mays and Red McCombs began purchasing smaller stations and developed the largest radio corporation in the nation, iHeart-Media. By 2020 it had more than 860 stations in over 150 markets in America; the behemoth bragged on their website that they were "reaching 9 out of 10 Americans every month."

Monopolies, of course, had been a long-term problem for America, and so was health care. Of all the industrialized nations in the world, the United States had the most uninsured citizens, and the health care situation was one reason that voters had elected Clinton. In his first term the president had put together a team to pass health care reform, universal health care insurance, but Senate Majority Leader Dole fought the bill, and it collapsed in the Senate. Yet all was not lost, for Democratic senator Edward Kennedy and Republican senator Nancy Kassebaum pushed through a bill guaranteeing that workers who changed jobs would not lose their health insurance. Also important was the Children's Health Insurance Program, CHIP. In 1997 the president signed CHIP, and it provides federal matching funds to states to provide health coverage to children in families with incomes too high to qualify for Medicaid but too low to afford private coverage. All states expanded children's coverage significantly through their CHIP programs, and the *New York Times* editorialized that the bill was "the largest expansion in federal health care since the Medicare and Medicaid programs were established in 1965."

More quietly, Clinton went to work on the environment. With the Republican control of Congress in mid-decade it was obvious to the president and his allies that they would not be able to pass environmental legislation. GOP support seemed to evaporate after President Bush signed the 1990 Clean Air Act. "We spent the better part of the first three years," admitted Secretary of the Interior Bruce Babbitt, "in a very defensive posture." But Gingrich's shutting down of the federal government in late 1995 and early 1996 also closed the national parks, which not only was very unpopular but according to one environmental official was "a call to arms."

At question in 1996 was the Grand Canyon, more specifically that national park's ecosystem in the area of southern Utah. Those acres held one of the largest known coal reserves in the nation, and a Dutch company was planning an enormous mining operation, supported by most politicians in the state. Babbitt convinced the president that he could preserve that area, and many others, by invoking the 1906 Antiquities Act, first used by President Teddy Roosevelt. "This was not about getting congressional approval," said Babbitt, it was "about the use of his authority." Accordingly, with the stroke of a pen the president could turn federal lands into national monuments.

Clinton helicoptered to the rim of the Grand Canyon. With the picturesque background, he stood at the podium and signed into existence the largest national monument in US history, the Grand Staircase Escalante National Monument. It was the size of Delaware, and just the beginning. The president in his second term established eleven national monuments, all in western states, and completed cleanup of over five hundred polluted Superfund sites, more than in the Reagan and Bush administrations combined. He also banned roadbuilding and logging on almost sixty million acres of public land, almost the size of Oregon. And he brokered a plan to repair the nation's premier wetlands, the Everglades. "Clinton left office," declared the *Washington Post*, "with what may be the most substantive environmental legacy of any president since Theodore Roosevelt."

There was another thing domestically that Clinton could boast about, and did, during his second term—the federal budget. In 1997 the federal budget was balanced—for the first time since 1969, LBJ's last budget. Better yet, at the end of the fiscal year on September 30, 1997, the president announced that for the first time in twenty-nine years the federal government ran a surplus, and this one was $70 billion. Clinton's budget continued to produce surpluses. They averaged about $140 billion a year, soaring to $236 billion his last year in office, for a total surplus in his second term of almost $560 billion. "Tonight," the president crowed in his last State of the Union address, "I stand before you to report that America has created the longest peacetime economic expansion in our history."

"Too Good to Be True?" asked *Time* in 1997. The "U.S. is enjoying its best economic and social health in 25 years." And that same year Clinton signed a bill that significantly helped citizens' retirement funds, the Roth Individual Retirement Accounts. Senators William Roth and Bob Packwood developed this bill to allow people to put $2,000 away annually, later increased, and pay no taxes on this income when they retired and started withdrawing that money. The Roth IRA was very popular, and by the end of the decade some forty-six million Americans had invested and were saving over two trillion dollars for their retirements.

Clinton's budget act was one of many reasons why the economy was running on overdrive. Another reason, as we have seen, was the dot.com revolution, and there were two other indicators that pushed the economy, which actually had their origins decades earlier. "You can't talk about the '90s without talking about the sudden availability of excellent coffee," Kurt Andersen wrote, "all over America. This was thanks to Starbucks." The three original owners opened their first store in 1971 on Pike Street in Seattle and named it after the first mate, Starbuck, in Herman Melville's classic novel *Moby Dick*. The coffee chain had a good growth rate in the 1980s, and after Howard Schultz took it public in 1992 it skyrocketed from about one hundred outlets in the United States to two thousand at the end of the decade, making it the largest coffee shop chain in the world.

Nor could you talk about the nineties without mentioning Nike. In the early 1960s Phil Knight ran for coach Bill Bowerman's track and field team at the University of Oregon, and the two eventually decided to design a better running shoe. They did and named it Blue Ribbon Sports, wisely changing the name in the 1970s to the ancient Greek goddess of victory, Nike. A design student created the swoosh logo for a mere $35, and with more advertising, sales climbed. Knight took control of the company and in 1980 took the company public; the IPO immediately made Knight worth almost $180 million. By 1988 the company was advertising with the slogan "Just Do It" and enlisting the first of many superstar endorsements—Michael Jordan— and later Tiger Woods, Lebron James, and Kobe Bryant.

Jordan played college basketball for the University of North Carolina's Tar Heels. In his first year he was a member of UNC's 1982 team that won the NCAA national championship. Two years later he was drafted by the Chicago Bulls and quickly emerged as a league star, not only because of his tough defensive play but also because of his incredible leaping ability: Air Jordan. Nike signed him in 1984 and launched the Air Jordan and Air Max Nike shoe series, while Jordan took the Bulls to one championship after another, six during the nineties! The superstar was the most famous athlete of the decade, winning ten NBA scoring titles and six NBA Finals Most Valuable Player Awards. When he retired in 1999 the *Chicago Tribune* headlined "END OF AN ERA," labeling Jordan the "most popular athlete in the world and undoubtedly the most popular in American sports history," while a Japanese newspaper headlined "JORDAN RETIRES! SHOCK FELT AROUND THE WORLD."

As Air Jordan and the economy soared, so did immigration and population. In fact, the nineties became the decade with the highest number of legal immigrants in American history—which also meant that the nation's population increased by a ten-year record, almost thirty-three million, and easily surpassed the baby booming 1950s: the emerging Millennial Generation.

Previously, the immigration record was held by the first decade of the twentieth century, but immigration acts in the 1920s erected a quota system that cut newcomers and favored white northwestern Europeans. President Lyndon B. Johnson changed that with his 1965 act that based immigration on family relations and needed skills, not quotas, which opened the gates. The nation's foreign-born population during the nineties grew four times faster than the native-born, and by the 2000 census legal foreigners were 10 percent of the US population. This trend was even more dramatic in major cities. In New York at the millennium foreign-born was an astonishing 40 percent. Because of family relatives, the greatest numbers came from the Pacific islands and Central and South America. Spanish-speakers increased rapidly throughout the nation, which had a tremendous impact on education, food, music—on a changing American culture and creating what some called the "Browning of America."

Others called it "Post-ethnic America" as interracial marriages and births, which had been climbing since the 1960s, ascended in the nineties as the multicultural generation headed to the altar. The 2000 census found that Hispanics supplanted African Americans as the second-largest ethnic group in America. The shade of Americans would continue to tan, many predicted, because in advertisements, show business, and on television, "Transracial America sells."

This alarmed many conservatives. "Our own country," Patrick Buchanan proclaimed, "is undergoing the greatest invasion in history, a migration of millions of illegal aliens yearly from Mexico." As bilingual programs and classes proliferated, a number of states proposed or passed legislation that made English the "official language."[3]

English (and Gaelic) were the official languages in Ireland, where Clinton's 1995 visit had jump-started serious negotiations. The president picked former US senator George Mitchell to mediate, and he kept at it for more than two years, mediating between the British and Irish governments and eight political parties from Northern Ireland.

It was a long and difficult road, with government changes, occasional bombings, and recrimination. The IRA's cease-fire was tenuous, lapsing, then in 1997 they resumed it and Sinn Féin returned to the talks. Mitchell told the various parties that they had until Good Friday to agree to a settlement. "I had no authority to impose it," he recalled, but two years of listening had paid off. He had gained their trust, one leader said, "He listened us to agreement." In April 1998 all sides signed the Good Friday Agreement. That accord created a fair and inclusive Northern Ireland Assembly based on power-sharing between Irish and British communities and established cross-border cooperation and consultations between Ireland and Northern Ireland. In May both North and South held referendums. The agreement was approved by over 90 percent in Ireland and over 70 percent in Northern Ireland. Eventually the IRA disarmed, and the UK gave direct rule to the new Northern Ireland Assembly. Finally, the Time of Troubles ended. As Mitchell often said, the negotiations had "seven hundred days of failure and one day of success."

Clinton's gamble, his visa for Gerry Adams, "brought about the historic August 1994 IRA ceasefire," wrote journalist Niall O'Dowd. "The American president's unorthodox, outside-the-box maneuver had played a massive role in bringing an end to the violence in Northern Ireland."

The 1998 Good Friday Agreement made Clinton very popular in all parts of the Emerald Isle; that was not the case in Iraq. After Saddam Hussein attempted to assassinate the Emir of Kuwait and former president Bush in April 1993, and after Clinton responded with twenty-three Tomahawk missiles, most countries lost interest in Baghdad. The dictator continued to obstruct UN inspections as the economy deteriorated. Because of international concern about starvation and possible epidemics, the UN modified its sanctions, developing the "food for oil" program, which began in 1996. Iraq was allowed to sell a limited amount of petroleum with the understanding that two-thirds of proceeds were to be spent on its people's humanitarian needs; three years later the nation could sell as much as it wanted, which helped the struggling economy. All the while United Nations Special Commission (UNSCOM) officials complained that Saddam was not opening all sites to inspections, prompting tough talk from the Clinton administration. "One way or the other," declared Clinton in February 1998, "we are determined to deny Iraq the capacity to develop weapons of mass destruction and the missiles to deliver them. That is our bottom line." In an attempt to defuse the tension, UN Secretary-General Kofi Annan visited Baghdad. Annan and Saddam worked out an agreement; if Iraq would allow another round of inspections, then Annan would try to end all UN sanctions.

Nevertheless, Saddam's behavior had irritated the US Congress, and they voted for the Iraq Liberation Act. It declared that "it should be the policy of the United States to support efforts to remove the regime headed by Saddam Hussein from power," and it pledged almost $100 million to opposition groups to overthrow the dictator. Saddam responded by suspending cooperation with UNSCOM, which prompted Clinton to retaliate with Operation Desert Fox. In December he went on television and addressed the public. He had no idea if Saddam was building WMDs inside Iraq, but he was under intense pressure and an impeachment vote because of his sexual indiscretions with Monica Lewinsky, so Clinton played tough guy: "For nearly a decade, Iraq has defied its obligations to destroy its weapons of terror and the missiles to deliver them. America will continue to contain Saddam. . . . And mark my words, he will develop weapons of mass destruction. He will deploy them, and he will use them."

The American president and British prime minister Tony Blair ordered Desert Fox. The Anglo-American assault lasted four days, with 650 air sorties and 415 cruise missiles—almost 100 more than were used during the entire 1991 Gulf War. They and some 600 bombs hit almost 100 sites in Iraq that UNSCOM had been prevented from inspecting. Many were damaged, some destroyed, and the attack shook Saddam. He panicked during the attack, ordering arrests and executions that backfired and destabilized his regime for months.

The timing of Desert Fox raised Republican suspicions. "I cannot support this military action in the Persian Gulf at this time," declared Senate Majority Leader Trent Lott, and a Republican representative from California called the strike "an insult to the American people."

Clinton's strike also raised Arab concerns. They approached General Anthony Zinni, commander of US Central Command, which included the Middle East, and began asking questions: If you Americans overthrow Saddam, what will come next? Who is going to be the bulwark against the old threat, Iran? Who would help out during possible economic dislocations and care for the subsequent massive exodus of Iraqi refugees? "An implosion is going to cause chaos," Arabs said to Zinni. "You're going to have to go in . . . do you guys have a plan?" The general admitted, "It shocked the hell out of me."

Desert Fox was Clinton's last action toward Saddam. Although the world did not know it at the time, the attack was very successful, destroying any remaining ability the Iraqis had to make WMDs; that would be revealed in 2003 after the American invasion. But because of Desert Fox, by the end of 1998 the dictator had banned further inspections and broken off relations with UNSCOM. Thus, for the next few years, the international community did not have knowledge of Iraq's potential for making weapons of mass destruction. In addition, the American attack provoked international condemnation from France, China, Russia, most of the Arab world, and members of the United Nations. As conditions inside Iraq deteriorated, more nations called for an end to sanctions, especially after one UN official resigned and claimed that the sanctions caused "four thousand to five thousand children to die unnecessarily every month."

By the end of the nineties, then, most nations had given up on enforcing sanctions and many were trading freely with Iraq, including France, Germany, and Russia. In 2000, representatives of forty-five countries defied the ban on commerce and attended the Baghdad International Trade Fair. By then, only Britain and the United States were still trying to enforce sanctions, which gave Saddam an opportunity. With control of the media, he blamed Israel, Saudi Arabia,

Kuwait, and especially the United States for the poverty and malnu-
trition of the Iraqi people. That message was continually broadcast, so
by the beginning of the new millennium Iraqis were hardened against
the Americans. When one seasoned US journalist arrived in Baghdad
a woman snarled at her, "I will teach my children to hate Americans
forever."[4]

Bill Clinton lost interest in Saddam as he sank deeper into the
quicksand of various sex scandals and the impeachment proceedings.
"When 1998 began," he later wrote, "I had no idea it would be the
strangest year of my presidency, full of personal humiliation and dis-
grace. . . . This time the darkest part of my inner life was in full view."

Clinton was correct—on January 17, 1998, the Drudge Report
made an announcement to its 85,000 subscribers over the internet:
"*Newsweek* Kills Story on White House Intern: 23-Year-Old, Sex
Relationship with President" screamed the headline posted by Matt
Drudge, the maverick internet editor. As the BBC later wrote, "It was
in the wilds of cyberspace—not the morning newspaper—that the
story of Bill Clinton's alleged affair with a young White House intern,
Monica Lewinsky, first unfolded."

Four days later the mainstream print media caught up, and in
Anything Goes America articles flowed on Ms. Lewinsky, igniting the
greatest media buzz in three years—since O.J.

During the 1992 campaign citizens had known about Gennifer
Flowers, the Arkansas state employee and cabaret singer who claimed
that she had a twelve-year affair with Clinton. That receded during
his first term, but then there was Paula Jones. She met then-governor
Clinton in 1991, and she claimed in 1994 that he had exposed himself
and sexually harassed her. She filed a suit, *Jones v. Clinton*, and it slowly
worked its way through the courts, with a federal appeals court ruling
that a sitting president could be tried. He appealed to the Supreme
Court, and in 1997 the court ruled unanimously against him. The case
could go to trial, and the date was set for 1998.

Three years earlier, during summer 1995, Monica was a twenty-one-year-old intern at the White House. But she was not just any intern. Lewinsky was a flirtatious young woman with a flair for getting attention; she was twenty-seven years younger than Clinton. She had met the president at a party, caught his attention, and was hired as a regular White House staff member. Soon thereafter they began their relationship. She made it a point to appear in the West Wing whenever possible, and during Gingrich's government shutdown she volunteered at the White House to keep the administration open; the usual staff of 430 had shrunk to only ninety. Monica and the president began their affair on November 15, 1995; they continued their sexual encounters in a private study just off the Oval Office for about two years. Eventually, staff members in the West Wing noticed her hanging around the area too much and convinced the president that she should be reassigned, and she left for a position at the Pentagon.

A colleague at both locations, Linda Tripp, befriended Monica and they talked a lot, sometimes over the phone. Tripp, who was nearly

White House photo of intern Monica Lewinsky posing with President Bill Clinton. Courtesy Clinton Presidential Library.

fifty, disliked Clinton and was very interested when Monica began telling her of the sexual relationship with the president. Secretly, Tripp recorded at least ten phone conversations, which included "graphically recounted details of an . . . affair she said she had with Clinton."

Then the sexual and legal affairs became more complicated. Previously Paula Jones's lawyers subpoenaed Tripp; they were trying to locate any and all alleged paramours of the president to bolster their sexual harassment case against Clinton. At the request of Paula Jones's attorneys, Lewinsky signed an affidavit on January 7, 1998, stating that she never had a sexual relationship with Clinton. But a few days later Starr's office received the tapes from Tripp, which seemed to contradict Monica's affidavit. Consequently, nine days later a court of appeals panel gave Starr the green light to add the Clinton–Lewinsky allegations to his portfolio to see if she lied under oath, while Tripp informed Jones's lawyers about Lewinsky's affair with the president.

Starr's new expanded role caught White House officials off guard, and when asked about the issue Clinton's lawyer declared, "The president adamantly denies he ever had a relationship with Ms. Lewinsky, and she has confirmed the truth of that. . . . This story seems ridiculous, and I frankly smell a rat."

So did another woman smell a rat—Kathleen Willey. When Tripp worked at the White House in 1993, she said she saw "a woman emerge from the Oval Office after she allegedly had a romantic encounter with Clinton. . . . Willey, another White House aide, appeared in the hallway with her makeup smeared and clothing askew." She apparently went to the president to ask for a better job, but he grabbed her, "started kissing and groping her and said, 'I've always wanted to do that.'"

Journalists went ballistic. "Diary of a Scandal," declared *Newsweek*. "Last weekend, there were two extraordinary dramas playing out in Washington," wrote Michael Isikoff. "Clinton was being questioned, under oath, by Paula Jones's lawyers as a media army waited outside. Clinton was asked if he had ever had a sexual encounter with Jones. As he has before, Clinton denied it. But unknown to the reporters in the street, the president was also asked about a woman named Monica Lewinsky." Jones's attorneys were eager to prove a pattern of sexual harassment, looking for other women who might have had contact with the president. Clinton denied ever having had a sexual relationship with Lewinsky.

In another part of the capital, Starr's lieutenants were questioning Lewinsky on the Paula Jones case. Recall that Monica had signed an affidavit swearing that she never had a sexual relation with Clinton, but Linda Tripp had supplied the prosecutors with the telephone tapes, which suggested that Monica was lying and that she might be guilty of perjury, even obstruction of justice. The men wanted to know: Had the president advised Monica to lie about their relationship? If so, then Clinton could not only be guilty of perjury but also obstruction of justice.

Clinton was in a pressure cooker. Stories and rumors ran amok. There were other women, scores of them, and Monica had a blue dress that had been stained by Clinton's semen. Finally on January 26 Clinton went on television and denied the affair, declaring what became perhaps the most memorable line of the scandal: "I did not have sexual relations with that woman, Miss Lewinsky."

Damage control continued the next day. The First Lady went on the *Today* show and attacked Starr as a "politically motivated prosecutor" who had spent four years looking at every "call we've made, every check we written, scratching for dirt." Hillary rejected the allegations as a "vast right-wing conspiracy that has been conspiring against my husband since the day he announced for president."

Late-night talk show hosts had a field day. Jay Leno quipped, "Macy's had a sale for Presidents Day. All men's pants were half off."

"They took a poll of American women and asked, 'Would you have an affair with Bill Clinton?' 70 percent said Never Again!"

"Dan Quayle, Newt Gingrich and Bill Clinton went to the Emerald City to see the Wizard of Oz. Quayle said, 'I'm going to ask for a brain.' Newt, 'I'm going to ask for a heart.' Clinton, 'Where's Dorothy?'"

"These comedians are killing me," Clinton said to an aide. "Have you seen Letterman's Top 10 White House Jobs That Sound Dirty? 'Giving the President an Oral Briefing?' Do you know what Leno said? 'Another President brought down by Deep Throat?'"

But late-night humor didn't help Clinton—the Monicagate rollercoaster careened out of control. *Time* ran a Special Report: "Clinton's Crisis: Truth or . . . Consequences," declaring the "worst week of Clinton's presidency brought tales of sex and cover-ups that threatened to sink even the Comeback Kid." With allegations of inviting Monica "into a private study off the Oval Office for oral sex," penned journalist Nancy Gibbs, "Last week even his apologists didn't know where to begin. . . . Monica Lewinsky's story was so tawdry, and so devastating, it was hard to know which was harder to believe: that she would make up such a story, or that it actually might have happened." Many Americans, she continued, were beginning to view

> the White House as a harem, the President as a lecher and the govern-
> ment as a hostage to his libido. No matter what he does, the President
> now faces a steady flow of ugly leaks from the conversations Tripp re-
> corded or recalled having with Lewinsky. . . . Clinton . . . had a strict
> rule: oral sex only. . . . Lewinsky jokes that if she ever got to leave her
> job at the Pentagon and return to the White House, she would be made
> "Special Assistant to the President for b___ j___."

Clinton recoiled, responded with lawyer double talk, and double negatives. "I didn't ask anybody not to tell the truth," while his lawyers asked, was oral sex really sex?

Starr struck back, hard. The independent prosecutor had been investigating Clinton for four long years, at a cost of close to $40 million, and so far he had uncovered very little. In July 1997, his office actually announced that Vincent Foster's 1993 death was a suicide, which physicians, lawyers, and FBI agents had ruled three years earlier. Then, Tripp's tapes appeared: Bingo. By summer, with Monica still in the headlines, he was ready to test the power of the White House. In July, he served a subpoena to the sitting president.

Starr demanded testimony from numerous administration officials—the Oval Office secretary, Secret Service detail, uniformed officers—seeking additional evidence against Clinton. He found little, but the big show was Monica. That same month Starr's subordinates met with Ms. Lewinsky's lawyers to work out an immunity deal for her, dismissing her lie about sex with Clinton. If she cooperated and gave testimony, the special prosecutor's office agreed that she would not be charged. Linda Tripp had told Monica not to dry clean the blue dress, in case she needed evidence of the affair. Monica gave them the blue dress, and the stain matched Clinton's DNA.

The administration announced that the president would appear voluntarily on August 17 to give testimony in the White House. Clinton became the first sitting president to give a statement before a grand jury in which the president was the focus of the grand jury investigation, *Jones v. Clinton*, claiming sexual harassment. That evening—*eight* long months after the story broke—Clinton went on television, admitting, "I did have a relationship with Ms. Lewinsky that was not appropriate. In fact, it was wrong. It constituted a critical lapse in judgment and a personal failure on my part for which I am solely and completely responsible."

CNN and Fox News announced enormous viewer ratings, and then the print media pounced. *New York Post*: "'I misled people,' the President said. No, he didn't mislead people. He lied to them. By using the word 'misled' instead of the word 'lied,' the President lied to the American people. Again." "It is almost beyond comprehension," wrote the *Des Moines Register*, "that Clinton is so lacking in self-discipline, so reckless, that he engaged in a sordid liaison with a youthful intern . . . at a time he was under scrutiny for alleged sexual misconduct." "For the nation," penned the *Houston Chronicle*, "it's a sort of Super Bowl of sordidness, complete with off-color analysis, play-by-play commentary and endless—endless—on-the-field mayhem."

Tabloids piled on. "Humiliated," declared the *New York Post*. "LIAR, LIAR," screamed the *Daily News*, while the *Star* proclaimed, "Bill's Eight Other White House Women," and with a picture of the intern declared "Monica's Story," complete with the made-up words, "I'm Not A Fat, Cheesy Slut."

Clinton's excuses, lies, lawyer-speak, over eight months had exhausted America. Many agreed with humorist Garrison Keillor, who editorialized, "Can We Get On to Something Serious?"

> Never before has so much been said by so many about so very little. . . . What we now know is approximately what we knew at the start. He did it; we're sorry he did; he must be sorrier than anyone else that he did it. . . . And I suppose that Monica Lewinsky, in her pain, has promised herself never again to get romantically involved with a sitting President. And I imagine it has dawned on Mr. Starr that he may go down in history as a rather small and obsessive figure who spent $40 million for a stained dress. And I imagine that by now all of the Monicas in America wish they were Cheryls or Ambers.

By the time that the president made the speech virtually everyone had made up their mind about Bill Clinton. Interestingly, the sordid affair had little impact on the opinion polls. During the spring and summer most people thought he had the affair and that he was lying, and before his speech a Time/CNN survey found that if Clinton were to confess and then apologized to the American people, almost 70 percent thought that Starr's investigation should end. By August, 73 percent of women and 64 percent of men thought Starr should terminate the inquiry. The president's popular approval rating hovered between 60 and 65 percent.

Many citizens were tired of the entire affair, and that included techies and progressives Joan Blades and Wes Boyd. They employed the internet and created the first online petition concerning American politics and emailed it to friends, "Censure President Clinton and Move On to Pressing Issues Facing the Nation." Within days they had hundreds of thousands of signatures, stunning other progressives who joined them to form Moveon.org.

At the same time Clinton admitted, "No one wants to get this matter behind us more than I do, except maybe all the rest of the American people."

But not Kenneth Starr. In September he sent his enormous report to Congress alleging Clinton had eleven impeachable offenses. Whitewater, the original reason for a special prosecutor, was mentioned twice; sex was mentioned more than five hundred times. The media focused on the report, as the midterm elections loomed. The *New York Times* called the report "devastating," others called for Clinton's resignation, while pundits declared that the Democrats would take a beating in November. Jokes circulated that Clinton had an "Achilles' tendon in his groin."

Starr's report also elicited another response from the public—against Starr. Polls indicated that less than 20 percent viewed the prosecutor as favorable, while over 40 percent viewed him as unfavorable. A "federally paid sex policeman," a Democratic congressman called Starr. Many citizens agreed, viewing the minister's son as the "relentless, self-righteous inspector . . . a humorless moralist, a Puritan in Babylon, out of touch with contemporary attitudes. A zealous ideologue."

During this feeding frenzy Clinton continually tried to change the narrative—the booming economy, Middle East, Good Friday Agreement, congressional elections. Most Democrats and independents thought the correct congressional path was simply to vote a motion to censure the president. Nevertheless, the Republican-dominated Judicial Committee began the impeachment inquiry and started calling witnesses.

Meanwhile, and at the same time, the Clinton administration was mediating between the Israelis and Palestinians. The nation's first female secretary of state, Madeleine Albright, had been working for months to get Israeli prime minister Benjamin Netanyahu and Palestinian Liberation Organization leader Yasser Arafat to the negotiating table, and on October 15 they arrived at the Wye River Conference Center in Maryland. Negotiations were tough, and there were many issues separating the parties, so after five days the president invited King Hussein of Jordan and his American-born wife, Queen Noor, to join the gathering. Hussein had cancer and was being treated at the Mayo Clinic in Minnesota. The weakened king arrived and surprisingly energized the meeting, telling the parties that the divisions still remaining were trivial and the benefits of peace were enormous, especially for future generations and their children. That motivated additional wrangling for another few days, and the last negotiating session lasted all night.

Clinton presented Netanyahu and Arafat on October 24 at the White House. As cameras snapped, the two arch enemies shook hands. The Wye Accords included a security agreement designed to curb violence and strengthen Israeli security. The Israelis gave the Palestinians control of 13 percent more of the West Bank, released 750 Palestinian prisoners, allowed an airport, and began discussion of a seaport in Gaza. In return Palestinians agreed to change their national charter to delete language calling for the destruction of Israel. Both nations agreed to opening corridors of safe passage between Gaza and the West Bank. The United States would provide financial aid to both parties.

The Wye agreement was signed ten days before the midterm elections. Republicans bashed Clinton on his extramarital affair and possible impeachment and actually ran an ad against gay marriage—just a couple weeks after two homophobic men beat to death a University of Wyoming student, Matthew Shepard, and left his bloody body dangling on a fence. That horror repulsed most Americans, and eleven years later Congress passed, and President Obama signed, another legacy of the nineties—the Matthew Shepard and James Byrd Jr. Hate Crimes Prevention Act.

On November 3, 1998, the nation went to vote, and Democrats let out a sign of relief. The party didn't lose a seat in the Senate and picked up four in the House, the first time since 1934 that the non-presidential party failed to gain congressional seats in a midterm election. Exit and opinion polls demonstrated that only about a quarter of the voters considered Clinton's affair an impeachable offense, while three-quarters were concerned with other domestic issues. Outside a Chicago poll a voter commented, "I don't know any President—maybe Jimmy Carter—who hasn't done a little sleeping around, and

I don't know any 50-year-old man who hasn't lied about it," labeling the Republican Congress's impeachment inquiry "insane." The voters disapproved of Clinton as a person by 60 percent but approved of him as a president by over 60 percent, while the same percentage wanted Congress to drop impeachment proceedings. Almost 80 percent thought the impeachment had been more about politics than about investigating possible crimes. "Yes, he lied, yes, he can't keep his zipper zipped," said a Republican woman in Houston. "But I don't think it affected how he ran the country. Republicans are acting like it was the crime of the century."

Garrison Keillor was right—the nation was tired of the Monica story, the majority wanted it dropped, and since 1992 citizens had known about the moral flaws of Bill Clinton. Most Americans had moved on.[5]

So did Newt Gingrich. Three days after the election Newt stunned the nation by resigning his speakership, and two months later he resigned from the House. He took the blame for the poor Republican electoral showing. Also, the House had reprimanded him for ethics violations, and he was under pressure from the right in his party who thought that he had been too moderate in negotiations with the president. "His contempt for fund-raising laws and House ethics and his role in the 1995 Government shutdown frightened the public enough to make him one of the nation's most unpopular figures," the *New York Times* editorialized. Republican congressmen "forced out the leader who took them to control of the House in 1994. It was a fitting if unpredictable end for a man who always saw politics as blood combat."

Moreover, in the months while Newt was hammering Clinton for moral lapses, after he proclaimed that he would not give a speech in the House without mentioning Monica, the speaker was having his own sexual affair—with Callista Bisek. She was from Wisconsin, twenty-three years his junior, and when they met in 1993 she was working as an aide to a Republican congressman. The liaison began that year when Newt was still married to his second wife, Marianne, and he began a six-year affair until he divorced his wife in 1999 and married Callista.

Many Republican congressmen were aware of the affair and kept quiet. Instead, they went after Bill Clinton—at a time when his approval rating was increasing, and his party had picked up seats in the still Republican-controlled Congress. Ten days after the election, Paula Jones dropped her sexual harassment appeal against Clinton in return for $850,000. Clinton paid but made no apology or admission of guilt. Also in November, Kenneth Starr delivered a two-hour address to the House, outlining what he believed were the charges against the president, "High Crimes and Misdemeanors," needed for impeachment. On December 8, the House Judiciary Committee recommended that an impeachment inquiry commence. It was a strictly partisan vote. The House adopted two articles of impeachment, charging the president with perjury in his *Jones v. Clinton* grand jury testimony by denying he had sexual relations with Monica, and obstructing justice in his dealings with various potential witnesses. Next day, the Republican-controlled House approved the two articles of impeachment by narrow partisan majorities and sent the issue to trial in the Senate.

The president responded three days later, appearing in the Rose Garden and apologizing to the nation: "I am profoundly sorry for all I have done wrong in words and deeds. I never should have misled the country, the Congress, my friends or my family. Quite simply, I gave in to my shame. . . . Mere words cannot fully express the profound remorse I feel for what our country is going through."

Then Clinton launched an attack, not on his Republican opponents, but on Saddam Hussein. Clinton and British prime minister Tony Blair commenced Operation Desert Fox, firing cruise missiles into Baghdad.

The operation ended on December 19, and the nation quickly changed focus that day to Congress, which was becoming even more bizarre. Newt's designated successor as the next Speaker of the House,

Louisiana congressman Bob Livingston, announced he would step down—sexual misconduct.

"There have been so many bombshells," said a congressman. "We have bombshells in Baghdad, and we have bombshells in the House of Representatives. You can't turn your back for 10 seconds."

Two months earlier Larry Flynt, the flamboyant publisher of the pornographic magazine *Hustler*, took out a full-page ad in the *Washington Post* offering up to $1 million to any woman who could prove that she had a sexual relationship with a high government official or a member of Congress. The ad was vintage Flynt, for he had done the same thing twenty years earlier and caught two congressmen in sex scandals. The publisher had made a career out of raging against "sexual hypocrisy," with as much publicity as possible. "Every day, you'd open the paper and he was doing something outrageous," a biographer said. "One day he'd be running for president, the next he would show up in a courtroom wearing a diaper. After that, he'd pay his fines with garbage bags loaded with one-dollar bills, delivered by hookers. He just kept topping himself, as if he was addicted to getting in the news."

Again, Flynt was in the news—and so was Livingston. The Speaker-designate stunned his colleagues by announcing his resignation, saying he had "on occasion strayed from my marriage." Although *Hustler* never published the article, the editors said they were investigating Livingston "as a result of receiving tips from four different women."

The hypocrisy was overwhelming. "When it seemed . . . that the world couldn't spin any further out of control," wrote *Time*, "here was Speaker-elect (although not for long) Bob Livingston announcing that because he wasn't 'running for saint,' his occasional affairs shouldn't be held against him. He called what he did 'straying,' said he had 'sought spiritual counseling,' and 'received forgiveness' from his family. Sound familiar?"

The American people knew it, and rewarded Clinton. A Gallup poll on December 21 reported that the president's approval ratings jumped ten points to an all-time high of 73 percent, while the GOP's plunged into the 30s, its lowest in years. Sixty-eight percent believed the Senate trial should not convict Clinton, while support for his resignation dropped to 30 percent.

One would think those polls would end the political carnival, but this was Anything Goes America: what did the Republicans do? They charged ahead with the impeachment trial. On January 7, 1999, the Senate began its hearing, the first president to be impeached by the House since Andrew Johnson in 1868. It was a forgone conclusion. A two-thirds majority, or sixty-seven senators, was needed to convict, and the Republicans never would get twenty-one Democrats to cross the line and vote against their president; none did. After deliberating behind closed doors, the Senate voted on February 12, 1999, to acquit Clinton.

The president again apologized to the nation but later wrote about his impeachment: "This was about power, about something the House Republican leaders did because they could." And the same could be said about Bill. He got himself involved with Monica because he could. Clinton went down in history for being the first president to be impeached for lying about sex.

Enough already, said Texas liberal columnist Molly Ivins. An iconoclast who once said that her two greatest honors were when the *Minneapolis Star and Tribune* named their mascot pig after her, and when Texas A&M banned her from speaking on campus, she poked fun at Clinton, who she labeled "weaker than bus-station chili. But the man is so constantly subjected to such hideous and unfair abuse that I wind up standing up for him on the general principle that some fairness should be applied. Besides, no one but a fool or a Republican ever took him for a liberal."

In retrospect, there are a few takeaways from Clinton's scandal and impeachment. First, it damaged the president's standing and tarnished his reputation, and future historians never would judge him very high in presidential rankings; he would be in the middle of the executive pack. The affair also demonstrated that political compromise and civility, which had been in decline since Clinton's election, especially after Newt took control of the House, would become a more permanent part of American politics. The two parties moved into stiffer ideological postures. The impeachment also revealed that American values had changed remarkably since the women's and sexual liberation movements of the late 1960s and the 1970s. While older and more conservative Americans were angered that the president would have a sexual affair out of wedlock, most baby boomers and especially the younger Hip-hop Generation and Gen Xers, were not concerned: chill, Dude.

Finally, and since the O.J. trial, it soon became obvious that the nation's capacity for commercialization of sex and sensational "news" events seemed infinite. During spring 1999 Barbara Walters interviewed Monica on the *20/20* show and some fifty million viewers tuned in, a record for a TV news program. ABC ran commercials that included Victoria's Secret lingerie, a promotion for the film *Cleopatra* with the voice-over "when she was twenty, she seduced the most powerful leader in the world," and a Maytag washing machine ad boasting that the product "actually has the power to remove stains."[6]

So in February 1999, the impeachment issue was over, and Clinton's attention returned to America's business—and on the front burner were domestic and foreign policy issues.

In April two seniors at Columbine High School in Colorado, Eric Harris and Dylan Klebold, took homemade bombs and deadly weapons to their school. Both had shotguns; Harris had a 9 mm Hi-Point 995 carbine with thirteen 10-round magazines, and Klebold had a Harris 9 mm semi-automatic TEC-9 pistol with three magazines each holding from 28 to 52 rounds. With the Assault Weapons Ban in place they were too young to buy these weapons, so coworkers at their pizza shop bought them at gun shows, a loophole in the law.

At about 11 a.m. Harris and Klebold rushed the west entrance of the school, firing and killing one student and wounding another. The killers dashed into the building and fired at other students, many who thought it was a prank with paint ball rifles—until they were hit. The assailants next went to the cafeteria and began shooting students at early lunch. One of the teachers heard the commotion and also thought it was a practical joke, until she was shot in the shoulder; lying on the floor, she warned students and called 911. It was only three minutes into the attack. While teachers and custodians were helping students to evacuate, Harris and Klebold entered the library, where more than fifty students and teachers were hiding. They declared that they would shoot anyone wearing a white ball cap, a symbol of a school athlete, and began shooting at people and at computer screens and bookshelves.

It was a massacre. Harris and Klebold saw one African American, called him a "nigger," and fatally shot him in the chest. They walked down aisles of books, shooting at terrified students, yelling, "Who's ready to die next?" During seven horrifying minutes in the library, they killed ten people and wounded twelve.

Police outside shot at the two when they appeared at windows— but did not attack. After creating almost fifty minutes of terror, Harris and Klebold shot themselves in the head, ending the carnage. At that time, Columbine was the deadliest school shooting in American history.

No one "wanted to accept the idea that this might actually be murder," recalled a journalist on the scene. "I was sure it wasn't going to be murder, until, at 4:00, when the sheriff announced them. . . . And that's when the world did change, because we weren't ready to accept anything this horrific."

"Columbine changed everything because they realized that . . . people will get killed while you're waiting," said Robert J. Louden, a criminal justice and homeland security expert. Since then, the police have increasingly emphasized speed: You go in now, with what you got. Neutralize a shooter as soon as possible because lives can be lost so quickly. Later, in 2012, at Sandy Hook Elementary School, twenty-six people were killed in six minutes before police arrived, and in 2017 in Las Vegas, fifty-nine people died at an outdoor concert in twelve minutes before the police got to the gunman's hotel room.

Clinton rushed out to Columbine to console parents and relatives, simply saying what has been true since, "The heart and soul of America is on the line."

Much less lethal was another domestic issue, the bipartisan aim to deregulate the economy, in this case the banking and financial industry. In the Great Depression, when hundreds of banks were collapsing along with the public's confidence in those institutions, the federal government responded by passing the Glass–Steagall Act. The law separated commercial banking from investment banking and created federal insurance for a client's deposits through the Federal Deposit Insurance Corporation. That stabilized banks and restored public trust, which lasted until 1999 when the Texas Republican senator Phil Gramm proposed the Gramm-Leach-Bliley Act. "In the 1930s," the senator declared at the signing ceremony, "it was believed that government was the answer. . . . We have learned that freedom and competition are the answers." Clinton again demonstrated that he was a New Democrat with his signature, saying, "This historic legislation will modernize our financial services laws, stimulating greater innovation and competition in the financial services industry." The bill repealed Glass–Steagall, deregulating the banking industry, allowing commercial and investment banks to combine. The mergers commenced. In 1990 there were over thirty large financial institutions; a decade after the Gramm Act there were only four that were worth over a trillion dollars—and then the housing bubble broke.

The foreign policy issues were Kosovo, the expansion of NATO, and mounting Islamic terrorism. After the bloodshed in Bosnia and the subsequent Dayton Accords in November 1995, ethnic tensions simmered in the former Yugoslavia, now composed of only the former provinces of Serbia and Montenegro. In the south, there had been generations of hatred and resentment between Serbs and Albanians and the area between them, the Muslim area of Kosovo. The Yugoslavian government discriminated against the people of

Kosovo, who were 90 percent ethnic Albanians, denying them education and employment opportunities; the Kosovo Albanian population had an unemployment rate of over 70 percent. In response, the Kosovo Liberation Army organized and began attacking the mainly Serbian police, Albania shipped arms to the KLA, and Yugoslavian president Slobodan Milošević responded by ordering his army to attack Kosovo. His troops went into towns and villages uprooting populations, sending massive numbers of refugees fleeing, and massacring civilians.

Clinton had other worries in 1998—the Monica scandal, impeachment, the elections—and paid little attention to Kosovo, but the UN that year passed economic sanctions and a resolution condemning Milošević's violence. But the carnage continued, until the Serbs again outraged Europeans and Americans. On January 15, 1999, Serbian forces rounded up forty-five Kosovo men, women, and teenagers from their homes in the village of Racak. The security forces marched them to the hills above the village, beat them, and murdered them. Next day a US diplomat inspecting the area for the UN labeled the action "a crime against humanity."

The Racak massacre provoked the hesitant Western allies to intervene. In March 1999 NATO began bombing Serbia and their forces in Kosovo, as hundreds of thousands of the Kosovo population took to the roads and headed out of the province. The Serbs continued executing remaining locals, NATO kept bombing, and after seventy-eight days the Serbs agreed to withdraw. NATO sent 50,000 peacekeepers, and a half million refugees began returning home; peace came to Kosovo.

The Kosovo War had an impact on NATO, at a time when former Soviet satellites and Warsaw Pact members Poland, Hungary, and the Czech Republic had formed a coalition; for economic and security enhancement they wanted to join the European Union and NATO. The original NATO rule was that any nation could become a member if all the current members voted in favor, but the meaning of the organization had changed since the collapse of the Soviet Union. NATO was formed in 1949 against a different enemy, the USSR.

Stalin's dictatorship and enormous nuclear-armed military was a considerable adversary; Russia, much less so. Most Americans supported the expansion, but there were others who wondered about the enormous expense to US taxpayers for arming those Eastern European nations, and then, if attacked, going to war to defend them.

During the Kosovo War in April 1999, NATO members assembled for the fiftieth anniversary of the organization in Washington, DC. The chairman of the Senate Foreign Relations Committee, Joe Biden, had supported the expansion of NATO, saying that turning the former Warsaw Bloc foes into allies would mark the "beginning of another 50 years of peace" for Europe. Russia, of course, opposed the expansion, but to no avail as the members approved, and Poland, Hungary, and the Czech Republic joined NATO—placing the Western military alliance closer to Russia's borders.

The expansion of NATO created a great debate, yet during 1999 the Clinton administration had another foreign worry—Islamic terrorism. After a number of attacks on US military installations, by February 1998 Osama bin Laden was making plans for al Qaeda's first attack on American soil. He and other terrorists signed the "International Islamic Front for Jihad Against Jews and Crusaders," which was published by an Islamic paper in London. Accordingly, American troops in Saudi Arabia, its embargo toward Iraq, and its support for Israel amounted to a "war on God, his messenger, and the Muslims." Therefore, bin Laden and his associates issued a fatwa, a theological order: "to kill the Americans and their allies—civilian and military—is an individual duty for every Muslim."

Six months later al Qaeda attacked—not yet America—but in Africa. On August 7, on the eighth anniversary of the arrival of American troops in Saudi Arabia, the terrorist organization hit the US embassies in Kenya and Tanzania. The 2,000-pound truck bombs collapsed buildings and demolished most of the embassies. Both attacks injured almost 5,000 people, mostly local inhabitants, killed 257, including twelve Americans. Al Qaeda faxed a claim of responsibility to London. "No matter what it takes," Clinton told the grieving relatives at the ceremony, "we must find those responsible for these evil acts and see that justice is done." The FBI placed bin Laden on its Ten Most Wanted List, and Clinton ordered the military to prepare operations to "kill bin Laden."

The embassy bombings shifted Clinton's response to terrorism into high gear. The president called a meeting with the principals. Clarke, the FBI, and the CIA confirmed that al Qaeda was responsible for the bombing, and Clinton signed memoranda that "authorized killing" bin Laden and his lieutenants and approved shooting down any private plane carrying the al Qaeda leader. National Security Adviser Sandy Berger held another meeting, and the CIA claimed that the terrorist was attempting to acquire or produce dangerous weapons, including chemicals, gases, and possibly a nuclear device. Cabinet members discussed an attack at one of bin Laden's factories in Sudan, possibly where toxic gas was being produced. When someone objected, Berger asked, "What if we do not hit it and then . . . nerve gas is released in the New York City subway? What will we say then?"

During that August, bin Laden was somewhere in Afghanistan, a guest of the Taliban regime. His exact location was a mystery, for he traveled most of the time to meetings with other terrorists, such as al Qaeda's number-two man, the Egyptian doctor Ayman al-Zawahiri, and the organization's third man, Mohammad Atef. The jihadists met at bin Laden's compound in Kandahar and his camp out of town, Tarnak Farm, a walled facility of about one hundred acres, where satellite pictures revealed women and children and training facilities for terrorists.

"I want boots on the ground in Afghanistan," Clinton told General Hugh Shelton, chairman of the Joint Chiefs of Staff. "I want to scare those terrorists out of their camps, and eliminate bin Laden." The president wanted Special Forces dropped into Afghanistan, but Shelton talked to Pentagon colleagues who did not think the operation was a good idea, nor did the commander of the Central Command, General Zinni, who would have had to direct the campaign. It was almost impossible to locate bin Laden, there was no good staging area in the region, it would be hard to tell friend from foe, and it might require tens of thousands of troops. Clinton relented and instead signed an executive order that imposed economic sanctions on bin Laden, al Qaeda, and eventually the Taliban. He also ordered the navy to fire cruise missiles at two targets, the chemical plant in Sudan and a camp in Khost, eastern Afghanistan. The CIA had learned that bin Laden was meeting other terrorists at that camp on August 20; an attack on that camp, wrote CIA director George Tenet, was a "no brainer."

That evening, after the missiles had been fired, Clinton informed the nation, "With compelling evidence that the bin Laden network of terrorist groups was planning to mount further attacks against Americans and other freedom-loving people, I decided America must act." The navy launched the missiles from the Red Sea, destroying the plant in Sudan, but it was a more difficult operation in Afghanistan. In order to hit bin Laden, the US Navy had to fire the missiles over Pakistan and inform that government, which apparently leaked the information to the Taliban government and to bin Laden. The navy launched about seventy missiles. At 400 mph, they took two hours to reach the Khost camp, killing about twenty people, but most of the men had evacuated about an hour before the missiles struck, including bin Laden.

"We survived the attack," Zawahiri declared. "Tell the Americans that we aren't afraid of bombardment, threats, and acts of aggression. We suffered and survived the Soviet bombings for ten years in Afghanistan, and we are ready for more sacrifices. The war has only just begun; the Americans should now await the answer."

The answer arrived at the end of the millennium. Terrorist Czar Clarke, CIA director Tenet, and CIA Counterterrorism Center director Cofer Black all knew that al Qaeda could not miss a chance to strike the West at the end of the second Christian millennium. A year earlier, in December 1998, Tenet had sent Clinton a Presidential Daily Briefing titled "Bin Laden Preparing to Hijack US Aircraft and Other Attacks," so during December 1999, Clarke sent out warnings to all US embassies, military bases, and police agencies in the United States.

That month Tenet and Black told the president that bin Laden was planning between five and fifteen attacks worldwide. "This set off a frenzy of activity," Tenet later wrote. The "CIA launched operations in fifty-five countries against thirty-eight separate targets." Apparently, al Qaeda had planned attacks the last day of the millennium for the Los Angeles International Airport, the Amman Radisson Hotel in Jordan, Israeli holy sites, and a navy destroyer docked in a Yemen port. But the strike on US soil was foiled by one alert customs agent who noticed a man acting nervously in the line coming into Washington State from British Columbia. She pulled him aside; Ahmed Ressam's car held explosives, along with a map of the Los Angeles International Airport. On heightened alert, authorities apprehended conspirators in eight countries, and all of the attempted attacks were thwarted, including the one in Jordan. "We have stopped two sets of attacks planned for the Millennium," Berger declared at a principals meeting, warning that bin Laden would attempt more in the future. "I spoke with the President and he wants you all to know . . . this is it, nothing more important, all assets. We have to stop this fucker."

One way to stop him was to get the Taliban to hand over bin Laden to the United States, so during 1999 the administration began sending messages to that government demanding that it turn over the Saudi. They refused, claiming it was impossible because of Pashtun traditions.

Meanwhile, al Qaeda continued attacking US interests; their next strike was an unusual target—an American warship, the USS *Cole*. The guided missile destroyer had been built with the most advanced technology to fight the Soviet navy, but the enemy arrived at 11 a.m. on October 12 in a fiberglass fishing boat. The *Cole* was anchored in Aden's harbor in Yemen. Two sailors watched the boat come amidship; they waved to the fishermen. Then the boat exploded, ripping an enormous hole in the ship, wounding thirty-nine sailors and killing seventeen. "The destroyer represented the capital of the West," bin Laden said, "and the small boat represented Mohammed."

The *Cole* was the last terrorist strike of the Clinton years. By that time, the CIA's Tenet later wrote, the "principal policy makers of the

Clinton Administration understood fully the nature of the threat we were facing." As for the president, he continued to push the Pentagon and the national security team to get bin Laden. Wrote Clinton, "I was very frustrated, and hoped that before I left office we would locate bin Laden for a missile strike."[7]

That was not to be, but at Fin de Siècle and as the new century commenced, so did the presidential campaign, and it would result in perhaps the strangest presidential election in American history.

Throughout 2000, opinion polls demonstrated voters were most interested in health care topics and insurance, prescription drug costs for the elderly, and school violence after the Columbine High School massacre. Conservatives were focused on moral values after Clinton's impeachment trial. The Democratic nominee was Vice President Al Gore, who easily won the nomination and who called for "continued peace and prosperity." Gore avoided campaigning with a president despite his 60 percent approval rate, even going alone to states that the president had carried in the previous election—Arkansas, Louisiana, Missouri, Kentucky, Florida, and his own state of Tennessee.

A third-party candidate tossed his hat in the ring—longtime champion of public interest and corporate regulation Ralph Nader. He became the nominee of the Green Party, and, as usual, he argued that there were no differences between the Democratic and Republican candidates. Nader concerned the Gore camp by stating that the vice president "offers no real hope for changing the concentration of power by the few over the needs of the many." Many politicos began to wonder how many votes Nader would pull away from Gore.

The Republican candidate was Governor of Texas George W. Bush, and he also tried to be a moderate centrist, proclaiming that like his dad he was a "compassionate conservative," while making "values" one of his main themes. A born-again Christian, Bush roused the Republican faithful at the convention: "And so, when I put my hand on the Bible, I will swear to not only uphold the laws of our land, I will swear to uphold the honor and dignity of the office to which I have been elected, so help me God."

Throughout the campaign Bush pledged to "bring respect back to the White House." As president he would unite Americans, and he continually said, "We need a uniter, not a divider." After Clinton's divisive impeachment trial, the governor declared, "I have no stake in the bitter arguments of the last few years. I want to change the tone of Washington to one of civility and respect."

Gore campaigned on the robust economy, job creation, and the typical New Democrat initiatives, but pundits often commented that Clinton's moral lapses would cause Gore's defeat. Thus, the president called his vice president and declared that he would stand out in public—and let Gore lash him with a bullwhip. Gore deadpanned, "Maybe we ought to poll that." Clinton replied, "Let's see whether it works better with my shirt on or off."

Concerning foreign policy, Bush was asked about his "guiding principles" during the second presidential debate and responded, "What's in the best interests of the United States? . . . Peace in the Middle East is in our nation's interests. . . . Strong relations in Europe is in our nation's interest." On another occasion he criticized Clinton's use of troops to stabilize the governments of Haiti and Bosnia, declaring, "I would be very careful about using our troops as nation-builders. . . . If we don't stop extending our troops all around the world in nation-building missions, then we're going to have a serious problem down the road. And I'm going to prevent that."

Like most campaigns in prosperous times, it came down to which candidate was the most likeable, personalities not policies. Bush appeared as an easy-going Texan governor. Lots of bubbas said that they'd rather have a beer with him than Gore, which was strange because born-again Bush didn't drink. Gore was more wooden in his speeches, and the media pounced on his statement that when he was in Congress, "I took the initiative in creating the Internet." The statement was true if one is talking about the legislation Senator Gore sponsored. Vinton Cerf, one of the "Fathers of the Internet," said that Gore's "initiatives led directly to the commercialization of the Internet. So he really does deserve the credit." But that history and clarification was not interesting to many in the media, who claimed Gore told a whopper, so they continued repeating it throughout the campaign.

On November 7 the public's blasé attitude was apparent. Only 55 percent showed up at the polls. Neither candidate's campaign had inspired the nation, some saying it was an election between "Gush verses Bore." Others said the contest was the "Seinfeld election"—it was about nothing, and it didn't matter.

The subsequent election was first confusing, then bizarre. The count came in, and it was disappointing for Gore, who not only lost his own state of Tennessee but also Clinton's Arkansas; either one would have delivered him the election. The vote was feverishly close in Oregon, New Mexico, and Florida. Officials commenced recounts. Oregon and New Mexico fell into the Gore camp, bringing his total to 267 electoral votes—just three short of victory. As for Nader, he won over 97,000 votes in Florida and over 27,000 votes in New Hampshire, considerably more than Bush's lead of about 1,000 in the first and a lead of some 7,000 in the second. Most pundits noted that if Nader had not run, those voters either would have stayed home or they would have supported Gore; either state would have given him the presidency.

Gore won a half million more popular votes than Bush, but not the Electoral College. The vote counting dragged on in Florida. Some TV networks first called the state for Gore and then reversed themselves; Gore conceded the election, only to call Bush later and withdraw his concession. As comedian Jon Stewart said about network declarations: "Gore's the winner. Gore's not the winner. Bush is the winner. Bush is not the winner, nobody's the winner. The media declared two people president, and then declared no one president." After the election CNN journalists bluntly labeled TV coverage a "news disaster."

Florida was too close to call, a situation that had not happened in a presidential election since 1876, resulting in the Compromise of 1877. So, the counting and recounting continued on and on—for thirty-six days. Wild charges mounted of voter fraud and suppression, and Americans learned new terms for Florida's elections, including "butterfly ballot" and "hanging chads." Lawsuits ensued and then challenges, and more recounts eventually made it appear that Bush was ahead in the state by just 537 votes. The election ended up in the Florida Supreme Court. Outside, Florida Republicans picketed with Democratic placards that were Gore/Lieberman for the election now turned to Sore/Loserman.

The election was so close that a recount was mandated by Florida law, so the Florida Supreme Court ordered a recount in all of Florida's sixty-seven counties, but the main battleground became heavily Democratic Miami-Dade County. As the recount began, Gore quickly was boosting his total votes.

To stop that recount Republicans filed *Bush v. Gore*, and the case headed to the US Supreme Court. The Rehnquist Court had moved slightly to the left when Clinton nominated, and the Senate approved, Ruth Bader Ginsberg and Stephen Breyer. But the Court contained seven Republican-nominated justices and two Democratic. For years many of the conservatives had been advocating curbing federal oversight and boosting states' rights, and they had been talking about being "originalists" and "strict constructionists," meaning that they would interpret the Constitution strictly, as the Founding Fathers intended, and not "legislate from the bench," as they charged liberal justices had been doing since the Warren Court of the 1960s.

On December 12—just a few days after the Florida Supreme Court ordered a recount—the US Supreme Court ruled 5 to 4 that the recount had to stop. It was the first time in American history that the Supreme Court intervened and determined the outcome of a presidential election. The ruling gave Florida and the presidency to Bush. All five justices had been appointed by Republican presidents Reagan or Bush.

Associate Justice Antonin Scalia wrote the opinion, claiming that it was not "an ordinary election" in which the federal government would have no input on the outcome and citing the "irreparable harm" that could befall a possible President Bush, as the recounts would cast "a needless and unjustified cloud" over Bush's legitimacy. In dissent, Republican-nominated Justice John Paul Stevens wrote that "counting every legally cast vote cannot constitute irreparable harm."

In most legal circles *Bush v. Gore* was condemned as one of the worst decisions of the Supreme Court, and they compared it to the 1857 *Dred Scott* decision that ruled a free Black man was not a US citizen, the 1896 *Plessy v. Ferguson* decision that upheld Jim Crow racial segregation, and the *Korematsu* case that allowed the internment of Japanese American citizens after Pearl Harbor. "The Unbearable Wrongness," Harvard law professor Laurence Tribe labeled the case, and even one defender admitted the case "quite startling, and transparently dishonest." Conservative legal scholar Terrance Sandalow called the decision "incomprehensible" and "an unmistakable partisan decision without any foundation in law." Many academics noted the case seemed in contradiction to the "equal protection" clause of the 14th Amendment, while others observed that Article II of the Constitution gives state legislators the authority to appoint presidential electors. Others wondered where in the Constitution is it written that the Supreme Court had the power to stop a state's vote or recount? It doesn't. So much for strict construction and states' rights. "If I had to pinpoint the moment when George W. Bush became president," wrote satirist Andy Borowitz, "I'd choose December 12, 2000, the day the Supreme Court elected him."

Bush v. Gore diminished the reputation and stature of the Supreme Court. "We do risk a self-inflicted wound," said dissenting Justice Stephen Breyer, "a wound that may harm not just the court but the nation." Opinion polls recorded that only 9 percent of citizens thought the 1996 presidential election was "unfair," but 37 percent thought that in 2000, and Gallup polls showed the Court's usual 60-plus percent approval rating slipping to a low 40 percent in 2005. Justice Scalia was hounded for the rest of his life about the decision; his usual reply was "Get over it." Late-night hosts joked that George Bush won the "Black vote," the vote of Clarence Thomas. Perhaps the most accurate statement was by Justice Stevens: "Although we may never know the winner of this year's presidential election, the identity of the loser is perfectly clear. It's the nation's confidence in the judge as an impartial guardian of the rule of law."

The millennial election became the last spectacle of Anything Goes America. All the ingredients reappeared, first shown with the O.J. trial and then with Monica Lewinsky and impeachment. Networks had talking heads pontificating around the clock during their televised coverage, first of the election, then the exit polls, then the ridiculous Florida butterfly ballots and hanging chads, and finally the farcical Supreme Court decision.

Nevertheless, the nineties era ended as the Clinton presidency closed, at a time of peace and prosperity in America. Gore gave a gracious concession speech, and citizens wondered what was in store for the Bush presidency. The Clintons, however, could celebrate one aspect of the election. As the president's political career was ending, his wife's was beginning. Hillary won a US Senate seat in New York, and that was the first time a First Lady had won an election.

Overseas in the Middle East, the Israelis and Palestinians were talking, not fighting. In Iraq, the US and British air forces were patrolling that nation's No Fly Zone. The Anglo-American policy was containing Saddam, who was not threatening his neighbors. In Afghanistan, the Taliban had consolidated its power and controlled all but the northern part of the country, while bin Laden and his men were training new members for al Qaeda. Relatively speaking, at the dawn of the new millennium the world was at peace.

Few Americans, few people in the world, realized the foreign threat that was looming.[8]

Epilogue

9/11

Thursday, September 11, 2001, began as a beautiful, clear blue morning on the East Coast. Suddenly, that day—and America—was shattered, ending the nineties and beginning a new era of war.

During the first seven months of the new Bush administration, governmental officials began warning about a possible attack from Osama bin Laden and his group, al Qaeda. In January, Terror Czar Richard Clarke briefed each of his old colleagues from the first Bush administration—Condoleezza Rice, Steve Hadley, Dick Cheney, Colin Powell—with a blunt message: "al Qaeda is at war with us, it is a highly capable organization, probably with sleeper cells in the U.S., and it is clearly planning a major series of attacks against us; we must act decisively and quickly." On January 25, Clarke sent a memorandum to Rice: "We *urgently* need . . . a Principals level review on the al Qaeda network," noting the "imminent al Qaeda threat."

Rice said that the principals would not meet until their deputies had reviewed the issue. After many delays the deputies met in April. Clarke began the briefing, "We need to target bin Laden," to which Deputy Secretary of Defense Paul Wolfowitz responded, "I just don't understand why we are beginning by talking about this one man bin Laden." When Clarke reminded him about al Qaeda's attacks and that its terrorist network "alone poses an immediate and serious threat to the United States," Wolfowitz responded, "Well, there are others that do as well, at least as much. Iraqi terrorism for example." Clarke, thinking of the attempt on former president George H. W. Bush's life in Kuwait, responded, "I am unaware of any Iraqi-sponsored terrorism directed at the United States . . . since 1993 and I think FBI and CIA concur in that judgement." The deputy CIA director agreed: "We have no evidence of any Iraqi terrorist threat against the U.S." Wolfowitz ignored that, commenting, "You give bin Laden too much credit. He could not do all these things . . . not without a state sponsor." Clarke again warned, "al Qaeda plans major acts of terrorism against the U.S. It plans to overthrow Islamic governments and set up a radical multi-nation Caliphate, and then go to war with non-Muslim states."

The new administration was not listening to its terrorism czar, nor to the CIA. In February, CIA director George Tenet told the Senate: "The threat from terrorism is real, it is immediate, and it is evolving. . . . Osama bin Laden and his global network of lieutenants and associates remain the most immediate and serious threat. . . . He is capable of planning multiple attacks with little or no warning." The CIA chief also met with key administration officials. On May 30, Tenet, his counterterrorism chief Cofer Black, and Clarke met with Rice. "The mounting warning signs of a coming attack . . . were truly frightening," he reported to her, and again on June 28 Tenet and Black presented Rice with "ten specific pieces of intelligence about impending attacks." By July 10, the CIA's counterterrorism team had intercepted al Qaeda communications and other intelligence and presented it to Tenet. He was so alarmed that for the first time in seven years as CIA director he picked up the phone and requested an immediate meeting at the White House.

Twenty minutes later he, Black, and an undercover agent met Rice, Clarke, and Steve Hadley. Tenet began the meeting bluntly: "There will be a significant terrorist attack in the coming weeks or months!" The attack would be "spectacular" and designed to inflict mass casualties against US facilities and interests. "Multiple and simultaneous attacks are possible, and they will occur with little or no warning." This was an urgent problem that had to be addressed immediately, including covert or military action to thwart bin Laden. Rice asked Clarke if he agreed, which he confirmed, but she brushed off the warning, and the men left her office frustrated. They wanted to "shake Rice," as Black later said. "The only thing we didn't do was pull the trigger to the gun we were holding to her head."

The administration also refused to heed the warnings of outgoing Clinton administration experts Daniel Benjamin, who had been director for counterterrorism on the National Security Council staff, and Brian Sheridan, former assistant secretary of defense for special operations. Nor did they listen to the outgoing deputy National Security Adviser, Lieutenant General Don Kerrick. He sent a blunt memo to the NSC after Bush's inauguration, "We are going to be struck again."

"They never responded," Kerrick continued. Terrorism "was not high on their priority list. I was never invited to one meeting." Nor did they respond to warnings from the Chairman of the Joint Chiefs of Staff, General Henry Shelton, who tried to warn the Defense Department. Secretary Donald Rumsfeld did not think that counterterrorism was a mission for the US armed forces.

"After 9/11 some senior government officials contended that they were surprised at the size and nature of the attacks," Tenet later wrote. "Perhaps so, but they shouldn't have been. We had been warning about the threat at every opportunity." In fact, between the inaugural in January and September 11, "Bush received 44 morning intelligence reports from the CIA mentioning the al Qaeda threat, and not once did he say . . . 'let's begin a process to stop the attack.'"

The president did not show any interest in his own daily intelligence briefings. The title of his August 6 briefing was alarming: "Bin Laden Determined To Strike in US." It reminded Bush that bin Laden had proclaimed that his followers would "bring the fighting to America." It cited Egyptian sources who had informed American officials that bin Laden was "planning to exploit the operative's access to the US to mount a terrorist strike." The briefing continued, "al-Qaeda members—including some who are US citizens—have resided in or traveled to the US for years, and the group apparently maintains a support structure that could aid attacks." The briefing concluded that the FBI had information that "indicates patterns of suspicious activity in this country consistent with preparations for hijackings or other types of attacks, including recent surveillance of federal buildings in New York."

The president did not respond. In August he went on vacation to his Texas ranch.

On September 4, Rice finally held the principals meeting that Clarke had requested in January. "Tenet and I spoke passionately about the urgency and seriousness of the al Qaeda threat," recalled Clarke. But the discussion turned to the questions of funding a larger anti-terrorist campaign and of attempting to use a new unmanned Predator surveillance aircraft to fire missiles at bin Laden in Afghanistan. The meeting concluded without answers. Clarke sent Rice a memorandum to complain about foot dragging: "Are we serious about dealing with the al Qaeda threat?" he asked. "Is al Qaeda a big deal?" And Clarke emphasized, "Decision makers should imagine themselves on a future day when the CSG [Counterterrorism Security Group] has not succeeded in stopping al Qaeda attacks and hundreds of Americans lay dead in several countries, including the US." Three years later, the 9/11 Commission simply concluded: "The System Was Blinking Red."

Yes it was, but to be fair there was some significant information missing. "Throughout the summer of 2001," said director of the National Security Agency Michael V. Hayden, "we had more than thirty warnings that something was imminent." They usually were intercepted messages, "Something spectacular is coming," but the warnings contained no specific details—no what, where, or when. Thus, even Clarke admitted that no one knew if 9/11 could have been prevented.

Moreover, what American besides Clarke and a few others ever would have thought that nineteen men would be able to take over four airplanes and fly them into buildings, killing themselves? It seemed incomprehensible.

Another warning arrived on September 10, when NSA intercepted two emails that came from a suspected al Qaeda location in Afghanistan: "The match begins tomorrow" and "Tomorrow is zero hour." For the next two days, no one translated the messages.

On that beautiful September 11 morning Mohamed Atta and Abdul Aziz al Omari boarded their 6:00 a.m. flight in Portland, Maine, and at 6:45 arrived at Logan Airport in Boston. They and three others, Satam al Suqami, Wail al Shehri, and Waleed al Shehri, checked in and boarded American Airlines Flight 11 bound for Los Angeles and scheduled to depart at 7:45. In another Logan terminal, Marwan al Shehhi, Fayez Banihammad, Mohand al Shehri, Ahmed al Ghamdi, and Hamza al Ghamdi checked in and boarded United Airlines Flight 175, also bound for Los Angeles at 8:00 a.m. Although they had metal box cutters, none of the men were stopped by security. Nor were four other men at Newark International Airport in New Jersey. Saeed al Ghamdi, Ahmed al Nami, Ahmad al Haznawi, and Ziad Jarrah walked through security for their United Airlines Flight 93 to Los Angeles and took their seats in the business class cabin. Over three hundred miles southwest, Khalid al Mihdhar, Majed Moqed, Hani Hanjour, and two brothers, Nawaf al Hazmi and Salem al Hazmi, were going through security for their flight at Dulles International Airport in the Virginia suburbs of Washington, DC. Two of them set off the alarm, but Mihdhar did not set off the alarm the second time and he passed through. Moqed did, so a screener wanded him, and he passed this inspection. The men boarded their flight for Los Angeles.

By 8:00 a.m. on September 11, nineteen men were aboard four flights. They had defeated all the security layers that the airlines had in place to prevent hijacking. The terrorists were armed with knives, mace, box cutters, and probably some fake bombs, all stored in their carry-on baggage, yet they were not stopped by airport security. At that time, the walk-through metal detectors were calibrated to detect items with at least the metal content of a .22-caliber handgun. Moreover, security then was operated by private firms contracted by each airline, which did not want to inconvenience customers, especially those who bought more expensive tickets. Except for two hijackers, all flew business or first class, seats closest to the cockpit.

The men also had defeated any attempts to track them as potential terrorists. They had attended flight schools, rented apartments and cars, used credit cards—all with their own names. The nineteen had entered the United States a total of thirty-three times, through more than ten different airports, without ever being stopped or detained. Only one, Mohamed al Kahtani, had been refused entry in August 2001 by a suspicious immigration inspector at Florida's Orlando International Airport. The nineteen had no criminal records and had not been identified by intelligence agencies for special scrutiny. As late as January 2004, a former Immigration and Naturalization Service commissioner commented, "Even under the best immigration controls, most of the September 11 terrorists would still be admitted to the United States today."

In Boston, American Flight 11 took off at 7:59 and climbed to 29,000 feet. At 8:14 air traffic control gave the pilot navigation instructions, which he acknowledged, and sixteen seconds later told the aircraft to climb to 35,000 feet—which was not acknowledged. Five minutes later a flight attendant in coach, Betty Ong, was on an airphone: "the cockpit is not answering, somebody's been stabbed in business class—and I think Mace—that we can't breathe—I don't know, I think we're getting hijacked." "Nobody move," one of the hijackers said over the plane's intercom at 8:25. "Everything will be okay. If you try to make any moves, you'll endanger yourself and the airplane." The speaker did not realize that he also was broadcasting that message over the air traffic control channel, alerting Boston. Two minutes later the Boeing 767 turned south, and Ong reported that it was "flying erratically." At 8:41 air traffic controllers declared that American 11 had been hijacked and that they thought it was headed toward Kennedy International Airport in New York City. They alerted the airport to prepare and planes in the area to stay clear. At 8:43 flight attendant Madeline Amy Sweeney called the American Flight Services Office in Boston: "Something is wrong. We are in rapid descent . . . we are all over the place." An American official asked her to look out the window to see if she could determine where they were, and Sweeney responded: "We are flying low. We're flying very, very low. . . . Oh my God, we are way too low." At 8:46 American 11 crashed into the North Tower of the World Trade Center.

By that time, United Airlines 175 had lifted off from Logan Airport and had reached its cruising altitude of 31,000 feet. At 8:42 the cockpit crew reported that a few minutes earlier they had heard a "suspicious

Hijacked airliner approaching the south tower of the World Trade Center. AP Photo/Carmen Taylor.

transmission" from another plane, which turned out to be American 11. That was the last communication the Boeing 767 had with air traffic control, but flight attendants and passengers were calling loved ones on cell phones: "I think they intend to go to Chicago or some- place and fly into a building," Peter Hanson said to his father. "If it happens, it'll be very fast—My God, my God," and then the phone went dead. At 9:03 United 175 slammed into the South Tower of the World Trade Center.

Earlier, at 8:20, American 77 had taken off from Dulles International Airport and by 8:46 had reached its cruising altitude of 35,000 feet. Five minutes later the Boeing 757 made its last report to air traffic controllers. At 8:54 the aircraft deviated from its course, and fifteen minutes later American Airlines Headquarters alerted all of their flights. At 9:32 air traffic controllers at Dulles observed a "radar target tracking eastbound at a high rate of speed," which was American 77. The plane was headed in the direction of the White House but then made a 330-degree turn as the pilot pushed the throttles to maximum power. At 9:37 American 77 was going 530 miles per hour when it smashed into the Pentagon.

In Newark, United 93 was late. Scheduled to take off at 8:00, it sat on the ground in heavy traffic for over forty minutes until it lifted off the runway. The crew of the Boeing 757 was unaware of the three hijackings, but by 9:00 United, American, and the Federal Aviation Administration were alert, and the two airlines began grounding all their flights in the United States. At 9:23 a United official warned their flights, "Beware any cockpit intrusion—Two a/c hit World Trade Center." At 9:26 the pilot of United 93 was puzzled by the message and asked for confirmation, but within two minutes the hi- jackers attacked. "May-day!" the captain yelled. There were sounds of struggle in the cockpit, and seconds later, "get out of here—get out of here." Four minutes later the hijackers were in control and told the passengers: "We have a bomb on board. So sit." The new pilot then turned the plane back to the east, as two flight attendants and ten passengers made calls from cell and airphones and learned about the World Trade Center. Alarmed, the thirty-three passengers in coach decided to vote—and to attack the terrorists. "Everyone's running up to first class," one female passenger shouted into her phone, "I've got to go." Realizing the assault, the pilot rolled the plane violently, left, right, down, but the attack continued, as air traffic controllers listened on the ground. "Roll it!" But they kept coming. "Pull it down! Pull it down!" came from the cockpit, and as the plane flew out of control, "Allah is the greatest! Allah is the greatest!" At 10:02, United 93 plowed into an empty field in Pennsylvania at 580 miles per hour, about twenty minutes flying time from the probable targets, the Capitol or White House.

Firemen and other first responders rushed to the World Trade Center and Pentagon as administration officials received news of the tragedy. The president was reading a book to children at an elementary school in Sarasota, Florida, and was slated to give a talk on education when his chief of staff, Andrew Card, whispered to him: "A second plane hit the second tower. America is under attack." The vice president was at the White House and was told to turn on television, wondering, "how the hell could a plane hit the World Trade Center?" By 9:45 Bush had more information, had returned to Air Force One, and called Cheney: "Sounds like we have a minor war going on here, I heard about the Pentagon. We're at war . . . somebody's going to pay." The president wanted to return to the capital, but Card and Cheney opposed that idea, so his plane took off for an unknown destination, eventually landing at Offutt Air Force Base in Nebraska, the underground headquarters of the US Strategic Command. The bunker there was built to withstand an atomic bomb. Meanwhile, the White House was warned that American 77 was approaching Washington, and the Secret Service took the vice president to the White House bunker, where a few minutes later he learned that the Pentagon had been hit. Just after 10:00 the Secret Service reported an inbound aircraft, which was United 93, and at about 10:15 a military aide asked the vice president for authority to engage the aircraft. Cheney had discussed this possibility with the president, and he immediately authorized fighter aircraft to engage the inbound plane. The plane already had crashed in Pennsylvania.

The nation's air defenses had been overwhelmed, for there never had been such an attack on the United States. Confusion abounded. By 10:38 Air National Guard fighters lifted off from their base in Maryland and began patrolling the skies over Washington and a few minutes later were joined by NORAD fighters that had scrambled out of Langley, Virginia. The first group had received instructions to engage incoming planes and, if necessary, shoot them down, but the second was operating under different rules of engagement. About that same time, Cheney contacted Rumsfeld at the Pentagon telling the secretary that he had given the order to shoot down hijacked planes, adding "it's my understanding they've already taken a couple of air-craft out."

Confusion reigned, and perhaps the most appropriate comment about what happened during September 11 was made by an officer at NORAD's defense sector in Rome, New York: "This is a new type of war." The first major attack cost about 2,800 American lives, more than the December 7, 1941, attack on Pearl Harbor.[1]

September 11 changed the course of America—and the world.

Conclusions

Why the Nineties Matter

"Well, how did I get here?"

"Once in a Lifetime," Talking Heads

A fine historian, David M. Pletcher, once said to me that in order to be a historian one has to have stereoscopic vision: one eye on the past, and the other one on the present. That seems particularly true when writing conclusions for contemporary America; it is a chore fraught with peril because we live in a divided nation participating in endless culture wars amplified by screaming social media. With a world changing at warp speed in the internet age, one could continually be rewriting conclusions. Nevertheless, it is time to connect the dots between the nineties and the 2020s and answer: Why the Nineties Matter.

The 9/11 tragedy ended the nineties and began a new era: a generation of distant wars. Like the 1993 World Trade Center bombing and the 1995 Murrah Federal Building detonation, 9/11 again demonstrated that Americans had entered a new era—we were vulnerable, either to domestic or foreign terrorists.

Americans united as at no time since Pearl Harbor. President Bush took charge and demanded that Afghanistan's Taliban government hand over Osama bin Laden. They refused. The president then ordered an invasion, and the first team in were CIA operatives. By mid–October Special Operation troops drawn from all services and US Special Forces were on the ground, enlisting, and bribing, anti-Taliban ethnic groups in the Northern Alliance to mount a military campaign. With American GPS air and drone support, along with a few thousand US Marines, the Northern Alliance warlords soon had the Taliban on the run. The world rallied around America. For the first time NATO invoked Article 5: "An attack on one is an attack on all." The Taliban government collapsed in December.

Yet where was the world's number-one terrorist? Bush did not listen to his CIA operatives on the ground near Tora Bora, who warned him of bin Laden's possible escape from that complex, and on the night of December 15 he and his entourage fled into Pakistan. Americans would have to wait until May 2011, when the CIA found the terrorist and President Obama issued the order to kill him, which US Navy SEAL Team 6 executed in a daring nighttime raid. The terrorist's body was dumped in the sea—there would be no shrine.

Meanwhile, and in one of the worst blunders in US military history, Bush and his administration misled the nation about Saddam Hussein having weapons of mass destruction, and in 2003 he ordered the invasion of Iraq: Bush's Vietnam. It resulted in a long slog in that Middle Eastern nation and massively complicated the war effort in Afghanistan. Both conflicts ended unsuccessfully, decreasing America's standing in the world. President Obama withdrew US Armed Forces from Iraq in 2011, and in 2021 President Biden did the same from Afghanistan. Finally, America's longest military conflicts, what had become known as the Forever Wars, were over.

Back at home, 9/11 resulted in the establishment of the Department of Homeland Security, which worked to keep the nation and its citizens safe and in conjunction with other departments and agencies has prevented another major attack. The DHS by 2020 would have a budget over $50 billion and employ about 240,000 personnel in a combined department that included the US Coast Guard, Cybersecurity and Infrastructure Security Agency, Customs and Border Protection,

Citizenship and Immigration Services, FEMA, and the Transportation Security Administration (TSA).

The TSA changed travel for Americans and the world. Screening devices were improved, cockpit doors reinforced, travelers were vetted before boarding planes, and air marshals flew onboard, meaning that the number of airplane hijackings, once a problem, plummeted as TSA agents took pistols, knives, and other weapons out of carry-on luggage.

The younger Bush also continued a significant effort started and continued by his father and Clinton—attacking HIV/AIDS, but this time for the world. In 2003, as poorer nations were struggling to contain the virus, Bush announced the President's Emergency Plan for AIDS Relief, or PEPFAR. Over the next twenty years it became the largest health commitment ever made by any country, by 2023 totaling more than $100 billion in more than fifty countries. "It's been an amazing program," said Kellie Moss of the Kaiser Family Foundation. "It's been incredibly, wildly successful beyond anyone's expectations."

Speaking of the Bush presidencies, the older Bush signed legislation that made a difference and changed America.

The Clean Air Act of 1990 cut pollution. The EPA declared that because of it "emissions of the six principal air pollutants decreased by more than 41 percent" by 2010 and that conservation measures did not hurt the economy. Moreover, by that year the cleaner air prevented more than 200,000 premature deaths and about 700,000 cases of chronic bronchitis. Acid rain from coal-fired power plants was cut, while atmospheric ozone levels were improved.

As part of the environmental push in the late nineties, automobile corporations began producing gas-electric hybrid vehicles. In 1997 Toyota introduced its Prius in Japan, and it became the world's first mass-produced hybrid car; three years later the manufacturer released the Prius worldwide. The car used a nickel metal hydride battery, a technology derived from research at the US Energy Department. Toyota had a monopoly on the market for only two years, for in 1999

Honda introduced its hybrid, the Insight, and they began arriving at US ports.

Elon Musk was watching from Silicon Valley. He announced in 2006 that his startup, Tesla Motors, would manufacture luxury electric cars that had a range of more than two hundred miles on a single charge. During the Obama administration the Department of Energy loaned Tesla $465 million to build a factory that would become the largest vehicle manufacturer in California. Tesla eventually repaid the loan, and its success inspired General Motors to produce the Chevy Volt and Nissan the LEAF. More were on the way as the world was moving toward electric vehicles, EVs.

President George H. W. Bush was correct on that hot day in July 1990 when he signed the Americans with Disabilities Act, declaring it a "Declaration of Independence" for disabled Americans. For "too many generations," the president continued, discrimination "separated Americans with disabilities from the freedom they could glimpse, but not grasp. Once again we rejoice as this barrier falls for claiming together we will not accept, we will not excuse, we will not tolerate discrimination in America." Since he signed the legislation, courts began to narrow the act, so in 2008 his son signed the ADA Amendments Act, which clarified and expanded the definition of disability and thus the number and types of citizens who are protected by the ADA. That law also became the inspiration and model for other countries to pass similar legislation and for the UN Convention on the Rights of Persons with Disabilities.

Other Bush domestic policies had an impact. The Clery Act resulted in colleges and universities sending emails, texts, or other notifications to current students, staff, and faculty reporting man-made or natural disasters such as tornadoes, emergency situations such as shootings, or inappropriate or illegal behavior: "CRIME ALERT: Indecent Assault / Fondling." The university police department "received information regarding an indecent assault." Such instant communication helped to keep the campus community safe. The EB-5 or Golden Visa has been one of the most popular in the world with economic investors. At the start of the program in 1992 the US government gave out only fifty-nine Golden Visas, but by 2014 that soared to more than 10,000 annually. During the twenty-six years from 1992 to 2018 the total number of EB-5 visas was more than 83,500 investors and their families, with the most coming from China, South Korea, Taiwan, and the United Kingdom.

The Bush-Clinton North American Free Trade Agreement had a major impact on the economies of Mexico, Canada, and the United States. H. Ross Perot was right about the "great sucking sound," and during the nineties hundreds of thousands of manufacturing jobs moved south of the border where US corporations relocated and employed Mexican workers who earned a fraction of American labor. Others contend that NAFTA only accelerated that process and that most of those jobs would have been lost to other countries during rapid globalization, especially to China. That undercut unions, and US companies began threatening workers with closing plants and moving south if workers demanded increases in wages and benefits. For the most part, American wages have not kept up with the cost of living and unions have been in decline, which began during stagflation in the 1970s and during the Reagan years.

Nevertheless, trade between the United States, Canada, and Mexico increased sharply, more than quadrupled in the last twenty-five years, from less than $300 billion in 1993 to more than $650 billion in 2000, to a whopping $1.3 trillion in 2018. The two neighbors buy more than one-third of US merchandise exports; about 80 percent of Mexico's exports go to the United States as those two countries supplanted China as America's greatest trading partners. Naturally over the years, the pact needed upgrades in the internet age. The Trump administration renegotiated it, and in July 2020 USMCA came into force, the United States-Mexico-Canada Agreement.

Economists and other commentators will argue for years over the impact of NAFTA. But one thing they agree on is that in terms of combined US, Canadian, and Mexican Gross Domestic Products, NAFTA created the world's largest trading bloc.

As a biproduct of the original negotiations, Mexico in 1993 changed its restrictive property laws and allowed noncitizens to buy within 50 km of the coast or 100 km of an international border. To protect mostly American and Canadian buyers, a NAFTA clause declared that the Mexican government could not expropriate foreigners' property except for a public purpose like road building, same as in the United States. The result was stunning. The Mexican middle class surged as tourism flourished with new resorts, hotels, and restaurants. Northerners retired in many areas such as Baja California, Puerto Vallarta, Cancún, and the Mayan Riviera.

While the Bush administration was negotiating NAFTA in 1991, the Soviet Union was collapsing, and that meant the emergence of only one superpower and the end of the Cold War. The Soviet Union disintegrated and became fifteen independent republics. Without any background in capitalistic democracy, most of those new nations became capitalistic oligarchies. Both Bush and Clinton enlarged NATO, first with the new unified Germany joining and then in 1999 expanding the alliance closer to Russia's borders with Poland, Hungary, and the Czech Republic. The expansion continued when talks began in 2002 and in 2004 resulted in seven Central and Eastern Europeans nations joining the alliance: Bulgaria, Estonia, Latvia, Lithuania, Romania, Slovakia, and Slovenia. Albania and Croatia joined in 2009, and in 2017 Montenegro and 2020 North Macedonia joined. During the next two years three other nations expressed their interest in joining NATO: Bosnia and Herzegovina, and two former Soviet states—Georgia and Ukraine.

The expansion of NATO prompted a great debate. In 1999 when Poland, Hungary, and the Czech Republic joined the alliance, the *New York Times*'s foreign affairs commentator Thomas L. Friedman called the nation's elderly "Father of Containment," George F. Kennan, formerly America's greatest expert on Russia. The journalist asked Kennan what he thought of the expansion, and the former diplomat answered:

I think it is the beginning of a new cold war. I think the Russians will gradually react quite adversely and it will affect their policies. I think it is a tragic mistake. There was no reason for this whatsoever. No one was threatening anybody else.

For the next two decades Kennan was correct. The next US administrations had their own problems fighting in Afghanistan and Iraq, coping with the Great Recession of 2007–9 and economic recovery, and then the COVID-19 pandemic.

In Moscow, Vladimir Putin succeeded Boris Yeltsin in 1999 as president of the Russian Federation. At home, the new president became increasingly dictatorial, curtailing the press, attacking news outlets, even attempting to kill political opponents. Abroad, Putin felt that his country was entitled to exert influence over the former Soviet states, especially ones on Russia's borders. Yet these nations had been free of Moscow's control for a dozen years and grown their own ways, and most of those non-Russian peoples had no interest being aligned with the Kremlin.

In the first decade of the new century, Putin began interfering on his southern border, launching a conflict and other diplomatic and economic pressures with Georgia. "Russia has invaded a sovereign neighboring state and threatens a democratic government elected by its people," declared President Bush in August 2008. "Such an action is unacceptable in the 21st century." Yet his administration did not seize international leadership; instead of forceful action to confront Putin, the president sent humanitarian aid and relied on European allies to negotiate and monitor a ceasefire—which left Russian troops in about 20 percent of Georgia. The relatively weak Western response apparently gave license to Putin, so in March 2014 the Russian dictator once again invaded a neighboring state. Responding to a perceived "fascist coup" in Kyiv, disguised Russian military personnel seized control of the Ukrainian province of Crimea, once home to the Soviet Union's Black Sea Fleet. Putin quickly held a referendum in the split Russian–Ukrainian peninsula, which had an ethnic breakdown that year of about two-thirds Russian. Moscow officials reported that an unbelievable 97 percent cast ballots to join Russia, creating the appearance of legitimacy for Russia to formally annex the province and the city of Sevastopol. The Obama administration and some European states protested, and they started relatively weak sanctions against the Putin regime.

"Beyond economic sanctions, Putin faced little consequence for this 2014 power play," wrote historian Lynne Hartnett, "and his geo-political machinations surged. Russian interference in the 2016 U.S. presidential election and Donald Trump's subsequent derision of NATO probably convinced Putin of his ability to extend Russia's global sway without substantial obstacles."

Until 2022, for that year President Joe Biden proved Kennan wrong. Obviously thinking that it would be an easy campaign with little interference from the West, Putin invaded Ukraine. It was an eighteenth-century land-grab in the twenty-first-century globalized internet world, where Ukrainian defenders were communicating with cell phones, taking videos of Russian brutalities, and using drones and Google Maps to locate and counterattack the invading army. To justify the invasion, Putin used the same argument as George W. Bush did on June 1, 2002, when he was preparing to start an unnecessary war in Iraq. "We must take the battle to the enemy, disrupt his plans, and confront the worst threats before they emerge," declared Bush; he advocated "preemptive action when necessary to defend our liberty and to defend our lives." Putin mimicked that in his May 2022 Victory Day speech. "The danger was rising by the day," Putin said. "Russia has given a preemptive response to aggression. It was forced, timely and the only correct decision."

Not to the Ukrainians. They had been free from the Kremlin's control for over thirty years, had held a number of elections, and had no interest in living under Putin's thumb. They put up a stiff resistance, and Biden rallied the European Union and NATO, which quickly developed a powerful counterpunch. France, Britain, Germany, Poland, and others joined the United States in the defensive effort, and soon massive amounts of US and NATO arms flowed into the invaded nation, as their forty-four-year-old president Volodymyr Zelensky rallied Ukrainians. The Ukrainians gut-punched Putin.

As Winston Churchill said, "Generals are always prepared to fight the last war," and in a sense the great British prime minister was correct. After a conflict the military leadership studies what went right and wrong in the last war as they prepare for the next one, and that begs the question of what went wrong in America's previous conflicts—Afghanistan, Iraq, and Vietnam. They turned out to be failures, and while there were many different reasons for the losses, there was one overwhelming similarity: America's allies, the host nations' governments, were not up for the long fight.

After twenty years of US military training and support of the Afghanistan army, once most US troops withdrew and the Taliban enemy attacked, the Afghan president flew out of Kabul and the Afghan army evaporated, like the South Vietnamese army in 1975. The improbable country, Afghanistan, a "nation" the British pasted together with five different quarreling ethnic groups, did not make a good ally, and neither did Iraq. Bush's war of choice in Iraq, another British concoction with three distrustful ethnic groups, resulted in a failed state with a weak central government. The conflicts made Americans wary of foreign adventures and weakened international faith in US aims and ability.

But Ukraine was different. In a historic miscalculation Putin thought his army could roll into his neighbor and capture the capital in a few days. Instead, Zelensky united the nation—and Ukrainians surprised the world by putting up a cohesive front and stiff resistance. The solid opposition convinced Western democracies that Ukraine was the time and place to stop appeasing and start confronting Putin. The Biden administration saw that they would have a worthy ally, and the president assembled the usually sleeping giant, the European Union, and NATO members to supply massive amounts of weapons to fight the Russian Bear.

Putin accomplished exactly the opposite of what he wanted to do—he momentarily unified the politically polarized United States and the fractured West. Biden asked Congress to reinstate that relic of World War II that supplied arms and supplies to our allies, Lend Lease, but this time for Ukraine. The Senate passed it on a voice vote—unanimously—and it passed overwhelmingly in the House. In Europe, and after seven decades of maintaining neutrality, Sweden and Finland declared that they were interested in joining NATO, and the latter was admitted to the world's largest alliance in April 2023. Both nations provide ports for the US Navy, and Finland's membership added 830 miles of NATO allies on Russia's border, putting St. Petersburg almost within artillery range. Four months after the invasion, NATO met and deemed Russia a "significant and direct threat" to the alliance, and the group declared that it was increasing its rapid reaction force in Europe from 40,000 to 300,000 troops. "We're stepping up," said Biden, "sending an unmistakable message . . . that NATO is strong and united."

The Russian dictator created a lose-lose situation. In the 1980s the Soviet Union became embroiled in a long war in Afghanistan, which proved to be one reason for the disintegration of the USSR. In 2022 Putin got Russia involved in another long slugfest, like Afghanistan but on its doorstep—Ukraine. He also created a new Cold War. Democratic leaders lined up behind Ukraine, while more authoritarian regimes either remained silent, neutral, or supported Russia.

Again, the invasion raised questions about the expansion of NATO. Did placing NATO closer to Russia's borders provoke Putin to invade Georgia, Crimea, and Ukraine? Recall that the Russian dictator labeled "The breakup of the Soviet Union . . . the greatest geopolitical tragedy of the 20th century." Since coming to power he has acted like a czar expanding the power and influence of old Imperial Russia. He has emphasized the "Motherland," nationalism, and in a 2012 speech declared that the nation must reconnect with its glorious past since they have "a common, continuous history spanning over 1,000 years."

Former secretary of defense Robert Gates agreed with Kennan. "U.S. agreements with the Romanian and Bulgarian governments to rotate troops through bases in those countries was a needless provocation," wrote Gates. "Trying to bring Georgia and Ukraine into NATO was truly overreaching."

Clinton disagreed, and after the 2022 invasion the former president joined the argument:

> It wasn't an immediate likelihood of Ukraine joining NATO that led Putin to invade Ukraine . . . but rather the country's shift toward democracy that threatened his autocratic power at home, and a desire to control the valuable assets beneath the Ukrainian soil. And it is the strength of the NATO alliance, and its credible threat of defensive force, that has prevented Putin from menacing members from the Baltics to Eastern Europe.

Others stated that Putin began foreign adventures because his economic policies at home created a tiny billionaire class while failing to produce a growing economy for the massive number of average Russians.

It will be a very long debate, but not debated was that Russia was committing war crimes in the Ukraine. Thanks to the nineties digital revolution, war in the Ukraine became the most watched conflict in world history. The Age of Digital Witness began as the Russian army withdrew from the outskirts of Kyiv. The defenders moved back into Bucha—only to find a mass grave of more than a hundred civilians; the same horror was discovered in other areas held by the Russians, such as Vynohradne, Balaklia, Izium, Borodianka, and Irpin. Like the 1995 Srebrenica massacre in Bosnia and the 1999 Racak massacre in Kosovo, Bucha sounded alarm bells, and by summer 2022 the International Criminal Court had dispatched investigators, while Poland interviewed refugees. Ukraine's judicial system began investigating war crimes, with its prosecutors collecting evidence throughout the war-torn nation. Their top prosecutor said that they had documented some 20,000 cases involving accusations of torture, rape, executions, and the deportation of thousands of Ukrainians, even children alone, to Russia. Nine months later, in March 2023, the ICC accused Putin of war crimes and issued a warrant for his arrest. It increased his isolation and restricted his travel to countries that supported his war; he could be arrested in other nations. As in Bosnia and Kosovo, the investigation and eventual trials will take years.[1]

Also not debated was the respect most Americans give the armed forces since the Persian Gulf victory. "Thank you for your service" has been the common refrain, and when the troops came home on commercial airlines and landed at airports in 1991, they often were greeted with applause from a grateful nation.

Yet the thanks began to ring a little hollow during the long Afghanistan and Iraq wars. With no Selective Service, the armed forces since 1973 have been an all-volunteer force, and that has meant that in subsequent conflicts they became the "one percent" wars, only that small percentage of citizens were involved. One percent defending the nation in a distant—and eventually forgotten—conflict. "We went to war," said a US Army soldier in Iraq, "Americans went to the mall."

While the one percent were fighting the nation's wars, only a small percentage of Americans have been focused on confronting climate change. Recall that in 1989 Bill McKibben wrote what many consider the first book on global warming, *The End of Nature*, and the next year and throughout the decade Al Gore had been calling on the nation to begin curbing carbon emissions. Along the way Gore received a startling amount of pushback, as climate deniers appeared in Congress, many of them from states producing fossil fuels, stalling progress. Big Oil sowed distrust in climate change. Exxon's scientists knew for years that global warming was real, but CEO Lee Raymond denied it; as late as 1997 he declared, "First, the world isn't warming. Second, even if it were, oil and gas wouldn't be the cause." That stance continued on; in 2005 ExxonMobil CEO Rex Tillerson again cast doubt: "We just don't know," for there are "holes in science."

There were no holes, as demonstrated in 2006 by Al Gore's documentary *An Inconvenient Truth*, which won the Academy Award for Best Documentary Feature. That had an impact. The term climate change, which detractors said always was changing, became global warming, which was much easier to prove. Soon some Republicans joined

Democrats. Gingrich in 2007 agreed the climate was getting warmer, and in 2012 Republican John McCain supported cap and trade.

When accepting the Academy Award, Gore said, "My fellow Americans," which brought laughs, and then:

> People all over the world, we need to solve the climate crisis. It's not a political issue. It's a moral issue. We have everything we need to solve it, with the possible exception of the will to act. That's a renewable resource. Let's renew it.

Almost two decades later the climate crisis is looming and is acknowledged by about 95 percent of meteorologists. President Obama signed legislation that subsidized building renewable energy sources, solar and wind, allowing homeowners to add solar panels and take tax credits. But President Trump mocked climate change as a hoax, supporting policies that accelerate it, and his administration treaded water for four years on one of the most significant issues facing the nation and the world. Thirty years after *Time* published a cover story, "Planet of the Year: Endangered Earth," the magazine produced an entire issue on just one topic, "The Fight for Earth."

Many others were sounding the alarm. "Record carbon dioxide levels alarm scientists," wrote the *Financial Times* in a 2022 article, and later that year the UN Secretary-General emphatically proclaimed, "We're on the highway to climate hell with our foot on the accelerator." The *New York Times* published a disturbing article, "Carbon Dioxide Levels Are Highest in Human History," and a senior scientist at the National Oceanographic and Atmospheric Administration starkly declared, "There is more carbon dioxide in the atmosphere now than at any time in at least 4 million years." It was way past time to act, to move to a global effort to switch to renewable energy. "For climate change isn't something that will happen decades in the future," wrote columnist Paul Krugman, "its effects are happening as you read this."

Finally, in August 2022, Congress acted. Senate Democrats pushed through the Inflation Reduction Act, which regardless of its name was the nation's first major climate bill, moving the country away from fossil fuels and toward solar, wind, and other renewable energy. The bill did not impose a carbon tax on polluters and instead relied on incentives to cut America's greenhouse gases by roughly 40 percent below 2005 levels by 2030. It passed the Senate by a 50–50 vote with Vice President Kamala Harris breaking the tie, and it passed the House and became law with Biden's signature. Not one Republican voted for the act. "Finally, now we have crossed a major threshold," said Al Gore, adding with the understatement of the year, "I did not for a moment imagine it would take this long."

Another problem that seemed to take forever to confront was gun violence. In 2004 Clinton's Assault Weapons Ban expired. By that time the Republicans controlled Congress and the White House, and they were not interested in renewing the legislation. The National Rifle Association (NRA) had become one of the most powerful lobbying organizations in Washington, DC, and supported the GOP with massive funding for their campaigns; in 2016 they gave Trump's presidential campaign over $30 million; more in 2020.

The nation stood by as gun sales soared; with a population of about 335 million in 2022 there were 400 million guns in America. ATF reported that same year that since 2000, gun production had tripled in the United States.

Bloodshed ensued, and below is just a partial list of some of the most tragic mass shootings (four or more dead) after the Assault Weapons Ban expired. In 2005 a sixteen-year-old student killed his grandfather and his friend at his Minnesota home before going to Red Lake High School and killing five students, a teacher, and a security guard. Two years later a college student killed thirty-two people at Virginia Tech and wounded two dozen others. In 2012 a nineteen-year-old in Newtown, Connecticut, stormed Sandy Hook Elementary School and killed twenty first-graders and six educators. Three years later a man killed nine at the Umpqua Community College near Roseburg, Oregon, and in 2017 a man on the 32nd floor of a Las Vegas hotel opened fire on a country music festival happening below him outside, killing sixty people and injuring 867. Later that year a gunman approached the First Baptist Church in Sutherland Springs, Texas, and killed two people outside before entering and shooting at the congregation, killing twenty-six people and injuring twenty-two. The next year, a twenty-year-old attacked Marjory Stoneman Douglas High School in Florida and killed fourteen students and three staff members. That same year a teenager opened fire at Santa Fe High School in Houston, killing ten, and an antisemite opened fire at the Tree of Life synagogue in Pittsburgh, killing eleven people and injuring six others. In 2019 a racist targeted El Paso, Texas, killing twenty-three and injuring twenty-three others at a Walmart, the deadliest attack on Latinos in modern American history. More recently, a racist clad in body armor opened fire at a Tops supermarket in Buffalo, New York, killing ten African Americans and wounding three. A week later, as classes were about to recess for the summer in 2022, an eighteen-year-old with an assault weapon opened fire at Robb Elementary School in Uvalde, Texas, killing nineteen children and two adults. On Chinese New Year weekend, 2023, two different Asian men slaughtered eleven at a dance studio in Monterey Park, and seven at Half Moon Bay, California, in the deadliest attacks since Uvalde. And in March a woman with an AR-15 style rifle slaughtered six at the Covenant Presbyterian School in Nashville, Tennessee.

"Why are we willing to live with this carnage?" asked President Biden after the Robb Elementary School massacre. "Why do we keep letting this happen?" Clearly emotional, he continued, "Where in God's name is our backbone to have the courage to deal with it and stand up to the lobbies? It's time to turn this pain into action."

Since Columbine in 1999, more than two thousand people have been killed or injured in mass shootings—by far more than in any other developed nation. From 1998 to 2019 the United States had 101 mass shootings. The next highest country was France with eight, then Germany with five. Canada, a neighbor filled with hunters, had only four. Although US opinion polls continually reveal that between 65 and 90 percent of Americans support national commonsense gun control—being licensed to carry, background checks, red flag legislation, with two-thirds supporting a new assault weapons ban—Congress can't or won't pass the necessary legislation. Republicans supported by the NRA generally oppose, while Democrats generally support such legislation. "I am here on this floor, to beg, to literally get down on my hands and knees and beg my colleagues," pleaded Connecticut Democrat Chris Murphy in the Senate, who had done the same after the Sandy Hook massacre, to "find a way to pass laws that make this less likely."

The primary killer has been a person shooting the AR-15 prototype assault weapons, which can shoot shells three times faster than handguns, some sixty rounds a minute as shooters change the 15-round magazine in five seconds. As we have seen with the passage of the Assault Weapons Ban in 1994, the public, even an eighteen-year-old in many states like Texas, could buy these weapons at gun shows and even over the internet—no background check needed. These weapons were opposed by President Reagan, who supported the original ban. In fact, during the ten years when the ban was in effect, gun massacres resulting in six or more deaths fell by more than one-third; after the ban expired, they nearly tripled.

The deadly beat goes on. After the Murrah Federal Building bombing in 1995, journalist Joe Klein declared the "Nervous Nineties. Life—by any rational standard—is good. The economy is good. We are not at war. But we are not quite at peace, either. We are beset by amorphous threats." The same is true today. After each school massacre parents are fearful taking their kids to school, and teachers practice drills for the new "lockdown generation." Outside the Nashville Covenant School mourning students held signs: "Will I Live If I Go to School," "Protect Kids and Teachers, Not Guns." Nothing changes. We cringe, fearing the next shooting. "Insanity," wrote columnist John Micek, "is doing the same thing over and over again, and hoping for a different result. And that's the story of our lawmakers' ongoing inability to pass even the simplest of gun violence reduction measures."

With the vast majority of Americans shouting "Do Something!," Congress finally worked out a bipartisan bill after the Buffalo and Uvalde slaughters and passed a weak firearms bill. The new law strengthened background checks but only for eighteen- to twenty-one-year-old buyers, restricted firearms from domestic violence offenders, and provided funds to states to enact red-flag laws. Biden signed the bipartisan effort, saying it would "save lives."

It hasn't. CBS News reported on the first 150 days of 2023, May 31, that 263 mass shootings have been reported in the United States, killing 327 victims, "the highest ever recorded this early in a year." More Americans are wondering: Who have we become?

More successful since the nineties has been a legacy of the Anita Hill testimony against Clarence Thomas, which was one of many factors that stimulated the Me Too movement.

In 2007, African American Tarana Burke, a sexual violence survivor, was working as an activist in Philadelphia with young women who also had the same painful experience. "I was 7 years old the first time I was raped," she later wrote. "I have spent every single day . . . trying to forget." Burke was searching for a way to let the Philadelphia women know that they weren't alone, so she told them: "Me too."

On October 15, 2017, Burke added a hashtag, #MeToo on Twitter, and twelve million responded in twenty-four hours. As she wrote, "millions of people around the world made a courageous decision to reveal their darkest secrets. The sheer number . . . ensured that the stories could not be ignored."

Women stepped forward, sharing their accounts, naming names. In one of the more spectacular cases, actresses such as Wedil David, Paz de la Huerta, Lucia Evans, and others in 2017 said that Hollywood film producer and cofounder of Miramax Films, Harvey Weinstein, sexually assaulted and raped them. Weinstein was one of the most famous and powerful film producers, and his films had received more than three hundred Oscar nominations and secured over eighty wins for such films as *Pulp Fiction*, *Sling Blade*, and *Shakespeare in Love*. More women came forward, and eventually some eighty women claimed sexual abuse by the film producer. He was tried, found guilty, and sent to prison, boosting the #MeToo movement. "For every Harvey Weinstein, there's three or four thousand other pastors, coaches, teachers, uncles, cousins and stepfathers who are committing the same crimes," said Burke. "We have to keep that in focus and we have to keep talking about it."

The movement quickly spread throughout the world. Within days after the Weinstein verdict, Burke went from being a grassroots community organizer to a national figure, and the movement "erupted into a global rallying cry that brought down the careers of dozens of powerful men accused of sexual misconduct . . . in more than 80 countries."

The next year sexual abuse returned to the Supreme Court. In July 2018, President Trump nominated US Court of Appeals Judge Brett Kavanaugh to the Supreme Court, a man who in the mid-1990s worked for Kenneth Starr's investigation of Bill Clinton. That nomination provoked a California psychology researcher, Christine Blasey Ford, to write a letter to Judicial Committee member Senator Dianne Feinstein accusing Kavanaugh of sexual assault in 1982, when they were both in high school. When news of the alleged assault was revealed, the committee held days of questioning the judge in September, postponing a final vote. Blasey Ford appeared at a Senate hearing, while two other women accused the judge of past sexual assault. The FBI began an investigation. The hearing turned into a morality play, in which there were "obvious parallels to Anita Hill and Clarence Thomas," wrote *Time*. "Twenty-seven years later, another professor with misgivings about coming forward had leveled allegations against a conservative Supreme Court nominee on the eve of his confirmation."

Kavanaugh rejected the charge. "I categorically and unequivocally deny this allegation," he declared. "I did not do this back in high school or at any time." Like in 1992, the White House stood by their man. "What is being attempted here is a smear campaign to destroy his reputation as a decent man." His opponents, now with almost three decades of charges of sexual harassment, knuckled down. "We've had enough," said the female director of NARAL. "We're not going to take any more."

Time to vote. The Judicial Committee voted 11 to 10 to forward the nomination to the Senate. The FBI delivered a hastily prepared investigation into the allegations. The Senate voted by the thinnest of margins, 50–48, to confirm Kavanaugh's appointment to the Supreme Court.

The Anita Hill–Clarence Thomas episode altered male behavior and gender roles in America, while in 2022 Congress reauthorized a tougher Violence against Women Act that guaranteed that people who experience sexual harassment at work can seek recourse in the courts, which the Associated Press called "a milestone for the #MeToo movement." Previously, citizens had to settle sexual harassment or assault cases through forced arbitration that usually benefited the employers and kept misconduct allegations private and secret. This was publicized in 2016 when former Fox News anchor Gretchen Carlson brought a lawsuit against her boss, the former chairman of Fox News Roger Ailes, and it had to go to forced arbitration because of that clause in her contract. This bill banned those arbitration clauses, and since then the alleged victims could have their day in court. Senator Lindsey Graham, Republican of South Carolina, cosponsored the bill with New York Democratic senator Kirsten Gillibrand, and she labeled the new law "one of the most significant workplace reforms in American history."[2]

Gender roles were transformed by the nineties, and race was modified by South Central. Black resentment simmered with an uptick every time a white racist or policeman attacked an African American. In 2016 the Marshall Project asked Jesse Jackson about the significance of South Central, and he responded:

> I think when you look at Rodney King, and that was awful, you look at Trayvon Martin [17 year-old shot to death by a white man in Florida], and that's sad, and you look at Ferguson [Missouri race riots], and at some point the question becomes, do black lives matter? You're beaten

or killed and it's on tape, and the killer walks free? The logic of Black Lives Matter grew out of a number of very concrete situations.

More recently that would include police brutality and the death of George Floyd. The forty-six-year-old African American in Minneapolis tried to pass a counterfeit $20 bill in a convenience store, the cashier reported it, and police came to the scene. The police hand-cuffed Floyd, who was acting erratically, and Officer Derek Chauvin got him down on to the street next to the cruiser. Chauvin held his knee on Floyd's neck for more than nine minutes while the suspect gasped for air: "I can't breathe."

Floyd died at the scene—as a teenage girl nearby used her cell phone to videotape the deadly encounter. It went viral. The peaceful "city of lakes" exploded, and like South Central almost three decades before, riots and burnings ensued, and the governor had to call in the National Guard.

Floyd's unnecessary death outraged most Americans. In May 2020, during the COVID-19 pandemic, activists took to the streets in New York City, Washington, DC, Los Angeles, Philadelphia, even small towns like Juneau, Alaska, and Bryan, Texas. Protesters set fires inside Reno's city hall. Police had to launch tear gas at combative demonstrators in Fargo, North Dakota. Protesters in Salt Lake City flipped over a police car, set it on fire, while in Ferguson, Missouri, activists threw stones and hit and hurt six officers. Overnight curfews were imposed in more than a dozen major cities nationwide, including Atlanta, Denver, Los Angeles, San Francisco, Seattle, and, of course, Minneapolis.

Millions across America joined Black Lives Matter marches—the largest marches in the nation since the 1960s. These events also raised questions about Confederate statues, public monuments, and names of professional sports teams. "We're sick of it. The cops are out of control," declared one protester in Washington, DC. "I can't breathe" was spray-painted on numerous buildings. In twenty-two cities police arrested nearly 1,700 people, the most in Los Angeles, where fires burned across the city and the governor mobilized the National Guard—like the riots in 1992. After mentioning numerous African Americans who have died at the hands of the police, Black columnist Leonard Pitts asked, "How long can we see our sons and sisters murdered with impunity? . . . How long can we be backstabbed by the American Dream?"

The Minneapolis Police Department fired Officer Chauvin and the three other officers on the scene and charged them with crimes. After a long trial, Chauvin was convicted of murder in April 2021 and was sentenced to twenty-two years in prison, while the other officers were charged and found guilty of failing to intervene and violating the suspect's civil rights. After Chauvin's verdict was announced, one of Floyd's brothers said, "We are able to breathe again," and President Biden praised the verdict. It is "too rare," said Biden, but it was a step to deliver "basic accountability" for African Americans.

Besides racial resentment, another cultural conflict has been percolating since the nineties, mostly among white Americans. The debate over political correctness and diversity had been greatly stimulated in the nineties, and during the next generation conservatives would shift the term to "woke," being very or too aware of injustices, prejudices, and discrimination, and to "cancel culture." In 2021 the Babylon Bee, a conservative Christian news satire website, published its *Guide to Wokeness*, which aimed to instruct someone how to be a "good person—and also to avoid getting canceled and having your life ruined by a Twitter mob." In the internet age bloggers could fuel a public backlash against a prominent political figure, celebrity, even athlete who expressed woke views.

Woke, cancel culture, and PC, of course, are as old as human speech, but they seem to have been put into warp speed by social media and became a mostly Republican battle cry during the 2020 presidential election season. Like President George H. W. Bush's rail against PC in the 1992 campaign, in 2020 President Trump traveled to Mount Rushmore and delivered a speech condemning a "new far-left fascism" that is "driving people from their jobs, shaming dissenters and demanding total submission from anyone who disagrees."

That from a president who continually tried to intimidate media by calling any reporting he didn't like "fake news," publicly disagreeing with his own scientists over COVID-19, and criticizing those wearing face masks as being PC.

Since the nineties, there continues to be a hardening of ideological arteries. Of course, the decline of cross-party cooperation predates the internet and social media, but the ideological distance between the two parties began increasing faster with the 1994 Republican victory. Newt's party stiffened its stance—maximalist opposition to virtually all Democratic proposals—which Fox News broadcasted 24/7. Add Rush and other conservative talk show hosts to the mix, and they all kept the political fires raging.

Recall that in Bill Clinton's first weeks as president he forgot about his middle-class tax cut and instead advocated legislation to reduce the deficit—usually part of the traditional Republican agenda. The plan received no votes from Republicans in the House or the Senate, only passing when Vice President Gore broke a 50–50 Senate tie. This Republican stance of course only magnified when Newt became Speaker with the large incoming class of '94, resulting in the longest government shutdown up to that time. The next Democrat faced the same obstacles. During President Obama's first weeks in office during the Great Recession he pushed for legislation to halt the financial meltdown and stimulate the economy. Again, it received no votes from House Republicans and only three from Senate Republicans. Obamacare included many conservative ideas originating from former Massachusetts Republican governor Mitt Romney, but top Republicans led by Senator Mitch McConnell thought that any support of the bill would strengthen Obama and weaken them. After the Tea Party Republicans won control of the House in 2011, new Senate Majority Leader McConnell declared his main goal was not to pass legislation but to make Obama "a one-term president." In 2021 Joe Biden went to the White House. During the COVID-19 pandemic he urged passage of the American Rescue Plan Act of 2021 that spent billions on vaccines, reopening schools, unemployment, and increasing Supplemental Nutrition Assistance Program (SNAP) benefits and the Child Tax Credit. Again, no Republicans voted for the emergency legislation, but some did vote in 2021 for Biden's bipartisan Infrastructure Law, which poured funding into both Democratic and Republican congressional districts.

The hardening of ideological stances continued during the winter of 2018 and 2019. In December and January, President Trump shut down the government when the Democratic Congress refused to fund his border wall—it became the longest shutdown in American history. As pressure mounted, on the thirty-fifth day Trump relented, and Congress quickly funded a reopening without money for the wall. The president got hammered from both sides. "It's the most stupid shutdown I've ever seen in my life," declared Democratic senator Jon Tester while conservatives labeled the president's behavior "inconsistent" and "erratic." Conservate pundit Ann Coulter unleashed a wicked tweet. "Good news for George Herbert Walker Bush: As of today, he is no longer the biggest wimp ever to serve as President of the United States."

The shutdown was "a landmark in U.S. political history," wrote NPR correspondent Don Gonyea, when Trump's surpassed the 1995–96 closure. The reporter continued that the Gingrich shutdown birthed "a new era of American gridlock that arguably led to the sharp partisanship that has gripped the nation" ever since.

Sharp partisanship created gridlock. In response to President Obama and his Affordable Care Act that barely passed Congress, without one Republican vote, the voters elected the Tea Party Patriots. Obama called the 2010 election a "shellacking," and it was, as sixty-three new GOP Republicans headed to retake control of the House of Representatives; in 1994 the GOP picked up fifty-four seats. The new Speaker was John Boehner, the former point man for Newt, and he decided to have a meeting with this group who never had sat in Congress. "I had to explain how to actually get things done," wrote

Boehner. "A lot of that went straight through the ears of most of them. . . . Incrementalism? Compromise? That wasn't their thing. A lot of them wanted to blow up Washington. That's why they thought they were elected." The Speaker continued that "they didn't really want legislative victories. They wanted wedge issues and conspiracies and crusades." To the Tea Party, Boehner's attempts to pass legislation meant that he was a "liberal collaborator."

Increasing intransigency in the Republican Party "began long before Donald Trump," wrote columnist Paul Krugman. It "goes back at least to Newt Gingrich's takeover of Congress in 1994." It was pumped up by Trump's refusal to concede the 2020 election. "And the cowardice of the Republican establishment has sealed the deal. One of America's two major political parties has parted ways with facts, logic and democracy, and it's not coming back."[3]

Yet in 2022, and after maybe the Age of Newt and lockstep opposition, politics as a blood sport was starting to fade. Both Democrats and some Republicans voted for a major infrastructure bill, veterans' expanded health care, the CHIPS and Science Act, funds to renovate the Postal Service, a law protecting same-sex and interracial marriages, the Emmett Till Anti-Lynching Act, the Electoral Count Reform Act, which clarified that vice presidents cannot change the electoral count, and support for Ukraine, especially after December, when President Zelensky delivered a sterling speech to a joint session of Congress.

Perhaps the future will hold more compromise, but at the same time another toxic ingredient was added to fragile American democracy—social media. Twitter debuted in 2006 and, like Facebook, did not turn a profit until 2009. Both platforms soon became digital juggernauts. Millions joined in, giving voice to people who probably had little agency previously, and they could hold powerful people accountable, or they could spread conspiracy theories—even in the halls of Congress. One of the first examples was the "birther movement," the idea that Barack Obama was born in Kenya or someplace overseas, hence not constitutionally qualified to hold the presidency. The lie became so common that candidate Obama posted his birth certificate online demonstrating that he had been born in Hawaii, but many Republicans tossed that fact out and went on a rampage. When asked about the new president's birthplace in 2009 Sarah Palin said that the public "rightfully is still making it an issue," and Gingrich told Fox News that the president's policies could be understood only by those who understood "Kenyan, anticolonial behavior." By 2011 over half of Republicans believed Obama was foreign born.

Conspiracies continued after the 2017 emergence of QAnon in the fringe corners of the internet. In 2020, as COVID-19 was spreading all over the globe, QAnon supporters flooded social media with false information such as that the pandemic vaccines contain microchips. An NPR and Ipsos poll at the end of the year found that 17 percent of Americans believed the core falsehood of QAnon—that "a group of Satan-worshiping elites who run a child sex ring are trying to control our politics and media." It is hard to imagine that these absurd conspiracies would have that type of following without Facebook, Twitter, and TikTok.

Conspiracies were nothing new in American politics. In 1964 historian Richard Hofstadter published an article that became a book the next year, "The Paranoid Style in American Politics." The "paranoid spokesman," he wrote, "is always manning the barricades of civilization. He constantly lives at a turning point: it is now or never in organizing resistance to conspiracy. Time is forever running out."

Fast-forward fifty years, and what was new was conspiracies *and* social media. The most significant social media operator was Donald Trump. He had been the star of *The Apprentice* for fourteen seasons, and he knew how to generate attention; like Rush Limbaugh, make outlandish statements, insult people, and employ social media. He had over 80 million followers during most of his presidency. "Trump's Twitter account is the greatest bully pulpit that has ever existed," said his former campaign manager.

Many presidents have used new technology. Hubert Hoover installed radio in the White House, and Calvin Coolidge gave the first speech using the new invention. FDR presented his famous "Fireside

Chats" on the radio, and the four-term president also gave the first address on a very weak television signal. Clinton's behavior was revealed and analyzed endlessly on the internet. Obama had Facebook and Twitter accounts, but without a doubt the Tweeter-in-Chief was Donald J. Trump. One professor collected all his tweets between June 2015 when he announced his candidacy and January 2021 when Twitter temporarily suspended his account: 20,301. He tweeted the term "fake news" more than eight hundred times. The president had many stories to tell, but the main theme was: "There was a danger to the nation, Trump was uniquely able to protect America and he was righteously supported by 'real' Americans." That continual message "built a high level of loyalty, diverted attention away from negative topics and generally set the agenda for what the American public was discussing."

The Tweeter-in-Chief certainly did build loyalty. A CNBC analysis of his tweets found that his most popular and frequent posts "largely spread disinformation and distrust." Of his ten most popular tweets, four contained false claims related to the 2020 election results. But that made no difference to his supporters, especially to the many angry white men who voted Republican and who did not get their news from mainstream media but from right-wing radio, social media, Breitbart, Newsmax, and Fox News.

Trump also was instrumental in altering the term "conservative," which had changed considerably since the nineties. Originally the term had its root in conserve, preserve, and conservation, and Republicans had been boosters of conservation efforts from Teddy Roosevelt to Nixon—who signed into law the Clean Air Act of 1970, Endangered Species Act, and supported establishing the Environmental Protection Agency. George H. W. Bush signed the last major environmental legislation, the Clean Air Act of 1990. But since, conservatives have lost interest. His son's policy was the Clear Skies Initiative, which scaled back his father's accomplishment by cutting regulations on polluting industries and failing to address global warming. Speaking of which, the George W. Bush administration in its first year in office declared that it had "no interest" in the Kyoto Protocol, which committed signatories to reduce greenhouse gas emissions. The next administration, Obama's, joined the Paris Accords, which put the international community on the path to address climate change and global warning. President Trump withdrew, making the United States the first nation to exit the Paris Accords.

What happened to Republican values? Since the Eisenhower 1950s the Republicans had stood for free enterprise over regulation, limited government, traditional principles and respect for the Constitution, and fiscal responsibility by balancing the federal budget. The saying was that they were the country club and chamber of commerce people who supported business and generally the social status quo. Yet Reagan dented that image with supply-side Reaganomics that resulted in massive federal debt. The GOP had been the party of free trade, but that stance was weakened when Trump took his anger out on foreign governments by piling up tariff barriers with nations that for generations had been our most favored trading partners, even Mexico and Canada. Republicans had believed in strong alliances such as NATO and stood tall against brutal regimes and executive overreach—all diminished in one Trump term. After reading the 2022 Texas Republican Party platform, business journalist Chris Tomlinson lamented, "What I'd give to have the old chamber-of-commerce GOP again."

Since the marches and riots of the 1960s the Republicans also had been the party of law and order, which President Nixon emphasized during the 1968 campaign and until Watergate. That theme was resuscitated during the Reagan and Bush years. But during the second Bush presidency, that theme was tarnished by the administration's questionable actions during his global war on terror, some ruled unconstitutional by the Supreme Court. Trump demolished that theme by becoming twice impeached—the second time for telling his supporters, on videotape, to go to the Capitol and "stop the steal," resulting in six dead, in the greatest attack on the Capitol since the War of 1812.

After the women's, sexual, and gay liberation movements of the 1970s, the GOP emerged as the party of traditional family values. They emphasized that as Clinton was trying to survive during the Monica scandal. Yet that title didn't even last Clinton's impeachment; first Gingrich and then Livingston admitted infidelity and resigned from Congress.

Republicans still stand against restrictions of the Second Amendment, bearing arms, and most are opposed to abortion, which is a change since the Supreme Court in 1973 ruled on *Roe v. Wade*. Then, in general, opinion polls demonstrated that more Republicans supported the decision and were pro-choice than Democrats. That was because a traditional value of conservatives was individual rights, and the ruling allowed a woman to make her own decision. At the same time many Democrats were Catholics, Republicans mostly Protestant. Those views began changing after LBJ signed civil rights legislation and white southerners and social conservatives began moving from the Democratic to the Republican Party, a shift that was completed during the Reagan 1980s. Evangelicals moved to the Republicans, and since then one of their most consistent issues has been opposition to abortion.

Overall, contemporary Republican values are vague outside of abortion, gun rights, and, before the 2024 election, Trump. As conservative Charles Sykes reported in 2018, "Even after a year of juvenile taunts on Twitter and his repeated assaults on truth, 82 percent of Republicans said that Trump shared their values, and four out of five think he 'provides the United States with moral leadership.' The percentage of Republican voters who thought sexual misconduct by a president was an important issue dropped from 70 during Bill Clinton's presidency to just 25 percent under Trump's."

Many wondered, how did the Party of Lincoln become the Party of Trump? The key to answering that question is "to realize that the Trump presidency was not an aberration but the culmination of more than three decades in the GOP's evolution," wrote historian Julian Zelizer. Longtime Republicans such as Reed Galen, George Conway,

Rick Wilson, Steve Schmidt, Bill Kristol, Sarah Longwell, and others bolted from the party and joined the Lincoln Project or Republican Accountability Project aimed at defeating Trump's 2020 reelection bid. "I personally think that the Republican brand is probably destroyed," said Conway. "It's destroyed by it having become essentially a personality cult."

What will become of the Republican Party is hard to say. It still will have a loyal following, and it will win elections in the future. But one wonders, and many were asking, what are conservative ideas? Where will the next Republican administration take America?

That begs another question: since the nineties, what has happened to the Democratic Party? "I am not a member of any organized political party," proclaimed Will Rogers. "I am a Democrat." Since the 1896 election and William Jennings Bryan the Democrats have been a big windy tent that tries to cover everything on the left side of center. By the progressive era and Woodrow Wilson they emerged as the party of reform, which was continued with Democratic presidents from FDR's Social Security to LBJ's civil rights and Medicare to Obamacare. They usually support commonsense gun control and affirmative action or diversity and inclusion, and they generally win backing from college-educated whites, minorities, women, and the LGBTQ+ community. Yet, most political observers agree that in the last generation the Democrats have not shifted ideologically as far to the left as the Republicans have moved to the right. Since the nineties, the center remains fragile.

The Democrats used to get their support from the working class, but Reagan brought many of those white men to the Republican camp. In 2016 Trump beat Hillary Clinton among the white working class by a crushing 28 points.

Perhaps the last word about the two parties goes to the late conservative humorist P. J. O'Rourke. "The Democrats are the party that says government will make you smarter, taller, richer and remove the crab grass on your lawn. The Republicans are the party that says government doesn't work and then get elected and prove it."[4]

Since it began broadcasting in 1996, what has happened to Fox News? During the network's first twenty years it always was conservative but usually attempted some semblance of its slogan, "fair and balanced." What little of that existed evaporated with the campaign and election of Donald Trump. By the beginning of his term Fox News had become the most watched cable news network in the United States, with about one million primetime viewers nightly. Yet former conservative Fox commentators who didn't support Trump left the network—Steve Hayes, George F. Will, Bill Kristol—and instead viewers tuned into Trump devotees such as Jesse Watters, Tucker Carlson, Sean Hannity, and Laura Ingraham. After the 2020 election and the subsequent January 6 insurrection at the Capitol the last moderates left Fox News. After nearly two decades working at the network Chris Wallace departed. The son of Mike Wallace, who reported for CBS for five decades, Chris said, "I'm fine with opinion: conservative opinion, liberal opinion. . . . But when people start to question the truth—Who won the 2020 election? Was Jan. 6 an insurrection?—I found that unsustainable."

Fox News hosts and executives lost credibility during and after the election when it aired numerous falsehoods that Dominion voting machines loaded with Smartmatic software changed votes from Trump to Biden. Smartmatic and Dominion Voting Systems sued Fox. The network settled with Dominion minutes before the 2023 trial began for $787,000,000. "The truth matters," said Dominion's lawyer, "lies have consequences."

In 1796 President George Washington published his Farewell Address, and he cautioned that American democracy was fragile. He worried about the safety of the eight-year-old Constitution. He believed that the stability of the Republic was threatened by the forces of geographical sectionalism, political factionalism, and interference by foreign powers. He warned his fellow citizens, "Cunning, ambitious, and unprincipled men will be enabled to subvert the power of the people and to usurp for themselves the reins of government."

Washington was correct, for 224 years later Donald Trump attempted to subvert American democracy. "Make no mistake," the former president declared, "this election was stolen from you, from me and from the country." As Republican Liz Cheney stated in the televised January 6 Committee hearings, he oversaw a "plan to overturn the presidential election and prevent the transfer of presidential power. . . . Trump's intention was to remain president of the United States."

Six months later, in Cheney's concluding remarks of the January 6 Committee in December 2022, she quoted Ronald Reagan's 1981 inaugural address: "The orderly transfer of authority as called for in the Constitution routinely takes place, as it has for almost two centuries, and few of us stop to think how unique we really are. In the eyes of many in the world, this every-4-year ceremony we accept as normal is nothing less than a miracle." Cheney concluded, "Every President in our history has defended this orderly transfer of authority, except one. January 6, 2021, was the first time one American President refused his Constitutional duty to transfer power peacefully to the next."

Except for Trump's MAGA supporters, the condemnation was widespread. The conservative editorial board of the *Wall Street Journal* summarized, "The President spread falsehoods about the election. He invited supporters to Washington on Jan. 6, tweeting on Dec. 19 that it 'will be wild!' He riled up the crowd and urged it to march on the Capitol. After violence began, he dawdled instead of sending help. Mr. Trump bears responsibility for the mayhem."

Instead, Trump declared that the January 6 insurrection "represented the greatest movement in the history of our country." When the January 6 Congressional Committee issued its report based on over 1,000 interviews and 140,000 documents, the former president tweeted, "WITCHHUNT!"

Regardless of Trump's tweets, by spring 2023 state and federal prosecutors were conducting five separate investigations of the former president's behavior during the 2016 and 2020 elections and of his company's business practices. In April 2023 a New York City grand jury confronted Trump with a 34-count felony indictment—the first former president ever to face criminal charges. By August he faced three other indictments, guaranteeing that he would be spending much of his future in legal battles.

What happened on January 6 had been brewing since Ruby Ridge, the Waco siege, and the Oklahoma City bombing. The eleven-day standoff at Ruby Ridge in August 1992 between federal agents and the Weaver family was the "precursor for the last couple, three decades of extremism because it combined two things: white supremacy and rage against the government, and that is exactly the same two movements on the far right that has animated extremism on the far right," said Heidi Beirich of the Southern Poverty Law Center. Domestic terrorism expert Daryl Johnson added, "The modern-day militia movement owes its existence to Waco."

Ruby Ridge and McVeigh's execution did not end the movement of the far right. Over the years various Alt Right groups believed "white identity" was under attack by multicultural forces with the aim of undermining "their" civilization, and they would have other run-ins with authorities: the Montana Freemen in 1996; the Republic of Texas in 1997; Nevada rancher Cliven Bundy in 2014; Alt Right marchers in Charlottesville, Virginia, in August 2017, and those who protested the state lockdowns during the COVID-19 pandemic in state capitals such as Sacramento, Austin, and Lansing; the Oath Keepers, Proud Boys, and the Michigan Liberty Militia "demonstrators with swastikas, Confederate flags and some with long guns inside the Capitol."

The Center for Strategic and International Studies analyzed 893 terrorist plots and attacks in the United States between 1994 and 2020 and found that "far-right terrorism has significantly outpaced terrorism from other types of perpetrators, including from far-left networks and individuals inspired by the Islamic State and al-Qaeda." The right wing accounted for the majority of all terrorist incidents during those years and was growing significantly.

Then came the attack on the Capitol. "January 6 was not an isolated event," said FBI director Chris Wray in 2021. "The problem of domestic terrorism has been metastasizing across the country for a long time now and it's not going away anytime soon." In fact, the director continued, "The domestic terrorism caseload has exploded," and it "is the most lethal facing the United States."

Fortunately, the 1995 O.J. trial was less dangerous to the nation, but it had a significant impact on television and viewers. Not just Americans, but also international viewers followed "every turn of the case so closely," wrote *Time*, "that the trial would permanently change the news cycle and media patterns. Americans had never been so consumed by a single news story." They turned off daytime television dramas to watch months of O.J.'s soap opera. Magazines and newspapers profiled the officers, attorneys, witnesses, and virtually anyone associated with the case, instantly turning many of them into celebrities. Court TV, launched in 1991, got a tremendous boost in ratings as they, along with CNN, covered every detail of the trial live, which was unprecedented. Judge Ito read the verdict live from the courtroom, *Time* continued, creating powerful stimulus for "the current 24-hour news cycle and sowed the seeds for the reality television boom to follow."

The O.J. trial certainly helped create the Infotainment that has dominated nightly news since, and celebrity news has been popular and cost effective for the mainstream networks. All have announcers and camera crews on the payroll in Los Angeles, along with New York and Washington, DC, so it costs the networks little to cover Infotainment, while it costs thousands of dollars a day to put an announcer, camera crew, and their security in foreign destinations such as Ukraine. Moreover, American and international viewers seem to have a bottomless pit for celebrity news and trash television. Little wonder that the reality shows that followed the O.J. trial were popular, or that the host of *The Apprentice* became president of the United States. As Jerry Springer tweeted after one 2016 presidential debate, "Hillary Clinton belongs in the White House. Donald Trump belongs on my show."

A month before the 2016 presidential election nominee NBC's *Access Hollywood* video exposed "an extremely lewd conversation about women" in 2005 between announcer Billy Bush and candidate Trump. In the video, Trump bragged about grabbing and kissing women, single or married: "I don't even wait. And when you're a star, they let you do it. You can do anything. . . . Grab 'em by the pussy. You can do anything."

That video before the nineties would have doomed a candidate, and it did. In 1987 it was rumored that the Democratic front-runner, Colorado senator Gary Hart, was a "womanizer" having an extramarital affair. The senator told reporters, "Follow me around. . . . I'm serious. If anybody wants to put a tail on me, go ahead. They'd be very bored." Reporters followed him, and they eventually took a picture with Hart and his mistress, the attractive young model Donna Rice, sitting on his lap. Behind the couple was a yacht where they had spent the night, appropriately named: Monkey Business.

Hart ended his campaign, but not Trump in 2016, for the nation had gone through Anything Goes America. By the end of the nineties the electorate was numb to sex and scandal. The Trump campaign told his supporters that this mostly Democratic outrage over the video was another example of "politically correct" liberals coming after him and other "real" American men.

In fact, in the 2016 election Trump did surprisingly well with the white women's vote against the first female presidential candidate, Hillary Clinton, winning a little over half. But a majority of all female voters did not support the president-elect. The night after the election a retired woman in Hawaii got on the internet and called for a rally in Washington. When she woke up the next morning more than ten thousand people had replied, and others joined in—shortly thereafter a white, Black, Muslim, Latina leadership team announced the Women's March on Washington. On January 21, 2017, the day after Trump's inauguration, generations of feminists appeared in more than 600 US cities, some 3.3 million, one of the largest single-day protests in American history.

While a majority of American women opposed Trump, that was not the case with evangelicals. The president-elect won an astonishing 80 percent of that white vote. When journalists asked leading pastors how their flock could vote for a man with a video stating such crude views on sex and women, their answers were the same psalm, "We're all sinners."

Trump won in 2016 because he understood the Republican electorate—and they turned out. "His version of conservative populism played into the nativism, racism, sexism, insular xenophobic nationalism, and white rage that all had deep histories in this country," wrote historian Julian Zelizer. "Trump just took it to another level and did so without any sense of hesitation or shame."

Another accelerated theme of the nineties was demographic; the era eclipsed all previous decades in population growth, even the 1950s, creating the Millennial generation, which is slightly larger than the previous record holder, the baby boomers. What was surprising about the Millennials was the percentage of foreign born, and what some have labeled "The Browning of America," as massive numbers arrived who were Spanish-speakers, Asians, and Pacific Islanders. The Census Bureau reported in the 1990 census that Hispanics or Latinos were about 12.5 percent of the total US population, just edging out African Americans as the second-largest ethnic group. By 2000 Latinos were 13 percent, and in the next two decades their numbers dramatically increased, from about thirty-five million in 2000 to sixty-two million by 2020, or almost 19 percent of the population. White citizen numbers grew, of course, between 1990 and 2020, but their percentages decreased from about 74 to about 58 percent. By 2022 Hispanics edged out white Anglos in Texas to become the largest ethnic group, 40 to 39 percent, Texas becoming the third state with Hispanics as the largest ethnic group, joining New Mexico and California.

There were many results from this demographic change, and most apparent is the proliferation of ethnic restaurants. When the *Houston Chronicle* publishes official governmental notices, they not only are in English and Spanish but also in Vietnamese and Chinese. Airports

often have "Welcome" and "Bienvenidos" signs. Grocery stores usually have an aisle or more for various ethnic spices and foods. Bilingual
education is common in schools, and Americans fluent in a second
language often are the first hired, like residents of other countries
who have mastered English. A trend that Clinton emphasized, a diverse cabinet, has become the norm in Democratic and Republican
administrations.[5]

Like President George H. W. Bush, Clinton also sponsored significant legislation that changed America. To many citizens, Clinton's
most significant legislation was the Family and Medical Leave Act.
"In the next eight years in office," Clinton wrote, "more people
would mention it to me than any other bill I signed." Indeed, during
Clinton's two terms more than thirty-five million Americans utilized
FMLA. Over the years up to 2020 some 20 percent used it for the
birth or adoption of a child or to take care of the health of a child,
spouse, or parent. Some half used it for their own medical condition,
and three-quarters employed it for their own or a family member's
illness. Rather stunning, since Clinton signed the bill, FMLA has been
employed more than 100 million times, fifteen million in just 2022.

The New Democrat's policy to "end welfare as we know it," limiting it to five years, had a sizable impact on welfare mothers and
children. They declined from about fourteen million to less than six
million when Clinton left office. "Recipients of Welfare are Fewest
since 1969," wrote the *New York Times* three decades later. One researcher at the Brookings Institute found "Welfare caseloads began
declining. . . . Between 1994 and 2004, the caseload declined about 60
percent, a decline that is without precedent." Most women went to
work and that lowered the poverty rate, especially for Black children.
His conclusion on the policy, "It Worked."

The Children's Health Insurance Program was popular, and it continued to grow in the number of children served and the federal
expenditure. Between 2000 and 2020 CHIP increased serving from
about three to nine million children, and funding increased from $3
billion to $21 billion.

Although seen as a failure in 1993, "Don't Ask, Don't Tell" got the nation thinking about who could serve in the armed forces. "In the short run," wrote Clinton, "I got the worst of both worlds." But Clinton's policy also began a national debate that would continue for the next seventeen years and eventually bring about a sea change concerning sexual preference. In 2010 federal courts ruled the military ban on gay, lesbian, and bisexual service personnel unconstitutional. At the end of that year Congress passed and President Obama signed the act that repealed the policy, ending restrictions on service by gay and lesbian personnel in September 2011. "Our military will no longer be deprived of the talents and skills of patriotic Americans just because they happen to be gay or lesbian," Obama said at the White House.

The repeal of "Don't Ask, Don't Tell" was an important development in the gay rights movement, for at the same time six states had legalized same-sex marriage, Massachusetts being the first in 2004. How far the nation had come since 1996, when only 27 percent supported same-sex marriage and Clinton signed the Defense of Marriage Act, which established a legal definition of marriage as "a union between one man and one woman." Then in 2015, the US Supreme Court's ruling *Obergefell v. Hodges* struck down all state bans on same-sex marriage, legalized it in all fifty states, and by 2022 over 70 percent approved gay marriage. The ruling, said Obama, "reaffirmed that all Americans are entitled to the equal protection of the law . . . regardless of who they are or who they love."

In the long run Clinton's policy had started a discussion that led to significant gay rights. "If it wasn't for the debate over gays in the military," said Keith Meinhold in 2018, a gay sailor who in 1992 was discharged from the Navy, "we wouldn't have gay marriage today."

Less successful was an act Clinton signed into law that was a bipartisan attempt to deregulate the banking and financial services industry. At the signing ceremony Texas Republican senator Phil Gramm declared that government was not the answer as had been believed in the Great Depression. "We have learned that we promote economic growth, and we promote stability by having competition and freedom."

Yet what actually happened was not freedom but the Great Recession—the worst economic downturn since the Great Depression. It was fueled by low interest rates, easy credit, insufficient regulation, exaggerated confidence that the economy would continue growing as in the late nineties, and so-called subprime mortgages; those were loans to home buyers with low credit ratings whose moderate incomes could not possibly afford a large home. Unscrupulous moneymakers on Wall Street played fast with the few remaining rules, and bankers loaned money to home buyers who had convinced themselves that the value of housing would continue to grow and buyers would sell and make a profit. In fact, the loan verification process was so lax that it drew its own nickname: NINJA loans, No Income, No Job, No Assets. In December 2007 the housing bubble burst, the market collapsed, and homeowners defaulted, bringing the economy with it. In the next eighteen months the Gross Domestic Product fell over 4 percent, the largest decline since the 1930s. In 2009 the unemployment rate reached 10 percent, and home foreclosures skyrocketed to almost three million that year.

The Great Recession, along with Bush's war in Iraq, led to a Democratic sweep in the 2008 election—and the first African American president, Barack Obama. With a Democratic Congress the president was able to push through a significant health care law, the Affordable Care Act, or Obamacare, and to address the recession with the Dodd-Frank Act. It renewed regulations and restrictions on the financial industry and created more consumer protections, which in 2018 were reduced by the Trump administration.

Clinton, like his predecessor, had some substantial foreign policy achievements. He helped to end the Time of Troubles in Ireland and bring about peace. He joined NATO nations and the European Union to craft the compromise Dayton Accords, which helped to bring an end to the genocide, ethnic cleansing, and rape in Bosnia.

For a generation Southeast Europe has been peaceful. He expanded NATO, which as we have seen stimulated an endless debate.

Not debatable any more was Clinton's granting recognition to our former enemy Vietnam. As president he visited the nation, during Obama's administration their leader visited the White House, and it has become one of our top trading partners. Despite the strained history, by 2014 Vietnam had become one of the most pro-American countries in Southeast Asia; three-quarters of their people view America favorably, and US Navy ships hold maneuvers and training sessions with the Vietnam People's Navy. USN ships often pull into Da Nang for liberty call, including the guided-missile destroyer USS *John S. McCain*.

The nineties Anything Goes America has become the mainstream culture. Language, films, books, and other art forms that would have shocked Americans in 1990 no longer raise an eyebrow. Pornography, ho hum. There has been no end, and by 2020 cybersecurity company Webroot reported, every day in America professionals create about three dozen porn videos, send or receive 2.5 billion such emails, and conduct almost 70 million search queries related to pornography, an astonishing one-quarter of total searches. "Have SEX Again," ads to treat erectile dysfunction, litter daily newspapers in larger cities, while television viewers are bombarded with ads of people undressing and jumping into bed, or gays kissing. As for music, hip-hop, which surged in the nineties, continued rapping. "Like it or not," wrote music critic Toure in 2020, "Hip-hop is the most popular music in America. Believe the hype." Two years later, the Super Bowl, usually watched by 100 million people all over the world, gave the entire halftime show to hip-hop, starring Dr. Dre, Snoop Dogg, Kendrick Lamar, Eminem, and Mary J. Blige.

The evolving businesses of the nineties, Nike and Starbucks, and new digital ones flourished; by 2020 the four most valuable companies in the world were Apple, Microsoft, Amazon, and Google. Previous business leaders, many brick-and-mortar stores who were slow to adopt the digital revolution, have faced hard times or gone out of business such as Sears, Macy's, Ward's, Neiman Marcus, J. C. Penney, Toys R Us, and Circuit City.

Speaking of business, the internet has had an impact on newspapers. It has destroyed many local papers, and according to the Poynter Institute, in just one year, 2020, at least sixty local newsrooms closed, some of them a century old, like the *Eureka Sentinel* in Nevada, the *Mineral Wells Index* in Texas, and the *Morehead News* in Kentucky. "Newspapers dying off at rate of two per week," reported the Associated Press. Yet, the internet has boosted business for those outlets that quickly jumped into the digital revolution and went online in the nineties, which greatly enlarged their national and international audiences. The *Washington Post, The Atlantic*, and others are thriving, and the *New York Times* reported that it never has had as many subscribers or readers—or employed as many journalists; in fact, the newspaper stated that it had a remarkable 1700 reporters covering the world from 160 countries and about 40 covering the war in Ukraine.

Perhaps a final legacy of the nineties is the impact of *Bush v. Gore* and the subsequent and uneven decline in approval of the Supreme Court. Gallup has been tracking that since the 1970s, and usually the Court is the highest rated of the three branches of government, generally earning over 60 percent approval. The executive branch reflects the sitting president's popularity, and Congress often is around 20 percent.

Of course, the Supreme Court's rating reflects how it rules on certain high-profile cases. Thus after *Obergefell v. Hodges* allowing gay marriage, approval momentarily dropped twenty points.

Nevertheless, the gradual trend of sinking approval was again confirmed in 2022 with a series of controversial rulings, which will be mentioned later. When Gallup asked citizens if they had "a great deal" or "quite a lot" of confidence in the Court, they found that percentage to be 50 in 1998, 40 in 2006, 32 in 2008, and in June 2022 it bottomed out at 25, the lowest on record. When asked about "overall approval," before *Bush v. Gore* in 2000 it was 62 percent, but by June 2022 another record: 53 percent "disapproved" of the Court. Gallup also asked the question another way, finding that citizens who had either a "great deal" or "fair amount" of "trust or confidence" in the judicial system and Supreme Court slid from 80 percent in 1999 to a "historic low" of 47 percent in 2022. The next year an NPR-Marist poll asked about lifetime appointments, and only 30 percent approved while a record 68 percent said they should serve for only a limited time.

Retired Justice Sandra Day O'Conner did not inspire confidence in the Court when in 2013 she admitted that she had voted wrongly in the 5 to 4 *Bush v. Gore* decision that put Bush in the White House. The decision, she said, "stirred up the public" and "gave the court a less than perfect reputation."

The approval level of the Court has prompted many to call for changes—all of which are Constitutional. Some critics want to enlarge the size of the court, which was done six times in the nineteenth century, settling on nine after the Civil War. (For anyone who thinks the Founding Fathers were infallible, they set the size of the first Court at six.) Some in Congress have offered a bill that establishes staggered, eighteen-year terms for justices, so each new president would get at least one nominee. Many critics have wondered, why lifetime appointments? Only one Supreme Court Justice has been impeached, Samuel Chase in 1805, and he was acquitted because like for the president, two-thirds of senators are needed to convict.

With no fear of losing their position, nominees can say virtually whatever they think senators want to hear at their confirmation hearings, get appointed, then reverse course. Justices Neil Gorsuch and Brett Kavanaugh, who under oath in their hearings said *Roe v. Wade* should be upheld under the court's doctrine of stare decisis, which means the court stands by what it previously decided, "settled law," then voted to overturn, calling *Roe* "wrongly decided." Since Clarence Thomas stonewalled the Senate Judiciary Committee in 1991 by not answering about his legal views and instead talking about himself, other nominees have been as vague as possible for a lifetime appointment, one that often determines the behavior of fellow Americans.

Crumbling approval was not surprising, for in 2022 the most conservative Supreme Court since the early 1930s published several controversial decisions, many of which were unpopular, on the nation's most contentious issues—guns, religion, climate change, abortion, and the next year affirmative action.

In *New York State Rifle & Pistol Assn., Inc. v. Bruen* the Court found New York's 111-year-old gun control regulations unconstitutional— just five weeks after the horrific mass shooting in Buffalo. The NRA hailed the decision, calling it the "most significant Second Amendment ruling in more than a decade," while New York Democratic governor Kathy Hochul called it "shocking" and "frightful in its scope."

Concerning religion, the Court ruled in *Kennedy v. Bremerton School District.* Coach Joseph Kennedy was fired by the school district for praying with the team at the 50-yard line after each game. He sued. Previously the Court had ruled to uphold separation of church and state, but this time it ruled 6 to 3 that the coach had a constitutional right to hold prayers. To most legal observers *Kennedy* seemed to expand Christian religion in public life.

As Americans—and the world—were becoming more concerned than ever about carbon capture, pollution, and global warming the Court ruled on *West Virginia v. Environmental Protection Agency* decreasing the agency's regulatory power. Republicans from fossil-fuel producing states were delighted, while Speaker Nancy Pelosi said the court's conservative majority had decided to "let our planet burn."

Perhaps most controversial was the Court's decision in *Dobbs v. Jackson Women's Health Organization.* "The Constitution makes no reference to abortion, and no such right is implicitly protected by any constitutional provision," Justice Samuel Alito wrote for the majority. True, said Court observers, but the Constitution does not mention many things that citizens have taken for granted, the "privacy rights" guaranteed by the 14th Amendment of "life, liberty and the pursuit of happiness"—the right to marry, travel, homeschool your children, use contraception, engage in romance with whomever you want regardless of race or gender.

Dobbs did not end abortion in America. There were a million illegal abortions a year before the *Roe v. Wade* decision in 1973, and since then about 1.3 million legal abortions every year. Moreover, by 2020 most abortions in the nation were medical ones, not surgical. But because of *Dobbs* it was no longer a national right, and all fifty states began writing their own laws—some would ban, and others would allow abortion.

While abortion has been a hotly debated issue in the nation since before *Roe*, the *Dobbs* decision again threw gas on the smoldering fire, which was not demanded by the *Dobbs* case. The Mississippi law banned abortion after fifteen weeks, and the Court upheld that 6 to 3. That could have been the decision, but then the Court reintroduced *Roe*, and the justices struck down the five-decade ruling 5 to 4 with Chief Justice Roberts voting with the liberals and against 5 other conservatives.

Dobbs resulted in confusion in all fifty states, a bonfire of discord, as the Court joined in and enflamed America's cultural wars—and like *Bush v. Gore* the decision decreased the public's confidence in the institution. What Republican nominee Justice John Paul Stevens wrote in his opinion of *Bush v. Gore* in 2000 deserves repeating. "Although we may never know the winner of this year's presidential election, the identity of the loser is perfectly clear. It's the nation's confidence in the judge as an impartial guardian of the rule of law." In that same decision Democratic nominee Justice Stephen Breyer added, "We do risk a self-inflicted wound, a wound that may harm not just the court but the nation."[6]

Were the nineties "our retreat from seriousness, our Seinfeld decade of obsessive ordinariness," according to conservative Charles Krauthammer, "the most inconsequential decade of the 20th century"? Or were those years more momentous and as cultural writer Kurt Andersen declared, "The Best Decade Ever"?

As has been demonstrated, the nineties changed the course of the nation concerning politics, gender, race, foreign policy, technology, business, entertainment, and the continual fight for justice and democracy. It also changed what it means to be an American. And that is Why the Nineties Matter.

Notes

A NOTE ON NOTES, AND ABBREVIATIONS

One of the legacies of the nineties was the development of the internet and search engines, the most famous being Google, and the development of websites like Wikipedia. This has had a profound impact on historical research, especially for recent history. Instead of running to an archive or library looking through the *Reader's Guide* (remember that?), one can look it up on Google, which has become so popular that it has become a verb, to search. As for citing quotes, many times the reader can simply put the name and quote together on a search engine—bingo, and read the article online. That has meant that this volume has kept the endnotes to a minimum. The Select Bibliography lists most of the books consulted.

AP	Associated Press
Bush PL	George H. W. Bush Presidential Library, College Station, Texas
Clinton PL	Bill Clinton Presidential Library, Little Rock, Arkansas
FT	*Financial Times*
HC	*Houston Chronicle*
LAT	*Los Angeles Times*
NYT	*New York Times*
UPI	United Press International
WSJ	*Wall Street Journal*
WP	*Washington Post*

PREFACE

1. Johnson, *Best of Times*, xi–xii. Charles Krauthammer, "Clinton Writ Small," *WP*, June 25, 2004, and "Bill Clinton Is Fighting to Have Some Historical Relevance," *WP*, February 1, 2008. Kurt Andersen, "The Best Decade Ever? The 1990s, Obviously," *NYT*, February 6, 2015.

INTRODUCTION

1. Brezhnev to a colleague in Westad, *Global Cold War*, 316–36, and Leffler, *Soul of Mankind*, 332. John F. Burns, "Soviet Food Shortages: Grumbling and Excuses," *NYT*, January 15, 1982. Gates, *From the Shadows*, 508–9, 471. Gorbachev from Beschloss and Talbott, *Highest Levels*, 4, and Leffler, *Soul of Mankind*, 430. Scowcroft in Ambrose and Brinkley, *Witness to America*, 579, and Bush and Scowcroft, *World Transformed*, 564. Tillerson in Woodward, *Rage*, 9–10. Reagan, *American Life*, 683.

2. https://www.c-span.org/video/?12861-1/nelson-mandela-arrival-white-house. See Anderson, *Bush's Wars*, 32–41. Minutes of the NSC Deputies Committee on Iraq, August 1, and from the National Security Council meeting, August 2, both 1990, Richard Haass Series, Bush PL. King Fahd from Parmet, *George Bush*, 459. Peter Applebome, "War in the Gulf: Antiwar Rallies," *NYT*, January 27, 1991. Michael Schwartz, "1990s," *Miami Herald,* January 28, 1991. See Rebecca Friedman, "The Long Shadow of the Gulf War," *LISSNER*, February 24, 2016, War on the Rocks.org. https://warontherocks.com/2016/02/the-long-shadow-of-the-gulf-war/.

3. Brands, *The Devil We Knew*. Don Oberdorfer, "Bush's Talk of a 'New World Order' Foreign Policy Tool or Mere Slogan?" *WP*, May 26, 1991. Gates, *Duty*, 150, 157.

CHAPTER 1

1. Quayle and Wattenberg in Troy, *Age of Clinton*, 32–33. *NYT* editorial, "A Law for Every American," July 27, 1990. McKibben, *End of Nature*, 51. Gore, *Earth in the Balance*, 3–5, and Gore, "The Ozone Catastrophe," *WP*, February 9, 1992. Hansen in Dembicki, *Petroleum Papers*, 66–71. Philip Shabecoff, "A 'Marshall Plan' for the Environment," *NYT*, May 2, 1990. "Bush Signs Major Revision of Anti-Pollution Law," *AP*, November 16, 1990. "Lehigh to Pay in Suit Filed over Slaying," *NYT*, July 27, 1988. Nancy Gibbs, "The Clamor on Campus," *Time* cover story, June 3, 1991, and see https://womensmediacenter.com/news-features/date-rape-revisited. "NAFTA's True Importance." *NYT editorial*, November 14, 1993.

2. S. C. Gwynne, "The Long Haul: The U.S. Economy," *Time*, September 28, 1992. Dominick Dunne, "The Verdict," *Vanity Fair*, March 1992. Pelosi in *NYT*, October 8, 1991. *Time* and *Newsweek*, both October 21, 1991. John Cloud, "Clinton's Crisis: Sex and the Law," *Time*, March

23, 1998. https://teachrock.org/wp-content/uploads/Handout-1-Rebecca-Walker-%E2%80%9CI-Am-the-Third-Wave%E2%80%9D.pdf?x96081, Cobbs, *Fearless Woman*, 327–29, and Levenstein, *They Didn't See Us Coming*, 12–17.

3. Karen de Witt, "Huge Crowd Backs Rights to Abortion in Capitol March," *NYT*, April 6, 1992. Stevenson, *Contested Murder of Latasha Harlin*, preface. See *LAT* staff, *Understanding the Riots*, 1992, *The Guardian*, March 22, 1991, and *LAT* staff, "LA Riots: 25 Years Later," April 26, 2017. King in George J. Church, "The Fire This Time," *Time*, May 11, 1992. Martin Walker, "Los Angeles Riots: Rage Takes Over from Aspiration," *The Guardian*, May 1, 1992. "Maxine Waters: '92 L.A. Rebellion Was A 'Defining Moment' For Black Resistance," *HuffPost*, April 27, 2017, https://www.huffpost.com/entry/maxine-waters-la-rebellion-was-a-defining-moment-for-black-resistance_n_58fe2861e4b00fa7de165e18.

4. Quayle in Clinton, *My Life*, 412, and bumblebee backwards in Borowitz, *Profiles*, 64–68. Leno in Kurtz, *Hot Air*, 12. McDougals, see Clinton, *My Life*, 402–3. Told off in Klinker, *Unsteady March*, 310–11, and Sherman in *NYT*, November 1, 1992. Robert McFadden, "Ross Perot, Brash Texas Billionaire Who Ran for President Dies at 89," *NYT*, July 9, 2019, Peter Applebome, "The 1992 Campaign: Independents; Perot, the 'Simple' Billionaire, Says Voters Can Force His Presidential Bid," *NYT*, March 29, 1992, E. J. Dionne Jr., "Perot Leads Field in Poll," *W*, June 9, 1992. That stupid from *Boston Globe*, June 5, 1992. Moynihan from Berman, *Center to Edge*, 17. "Dear Bill: The Classy Letters Left in the Oval Office from One President to Another," *NYT*, January 20, 2021.

5. On PC, see Moira Weigel, "Political Correctness: How the Right Invented a Phantom Enemy," *Guardian*, November 30, 2016. Utah Professor in Richard Bernstein, "The Rising Hegemony of the Politically Correct," *NYT*, October 28, 1990. Sykes, *Nation of Victims*, 5. *Newsweek*, December 24, 1990, and Bush in *NYT*, May 5, 1991. See Ligaya Mishan, "The Long and Tortured History of Cancel Culture," *NYT Magazine*, December 3, 2020. Krauthammer in *WP*, August 15, 1997. Goodman in *Boston Globe*, December 31, 1992. Franken, *Limbaugh*, 247.

6. *Fortune*, December 16, 1991, and *Business Week*, August 26, 1991. Clinton, *My Life*, 483–90. Thurmond in Alejandro de La Garza, "'Don't Ask, Don't Tell' Was a Complicated Turning Point for Gay Rights. 25 Years Later, Many of the Same Issues Remain," *Time*, July 19, 2018. Fallows, *Breaking the News*, 50. "The Pill That Changes Everything," *Time*, June 14, 1993. "The Politics of Paternity Leave," *Newsweek* Staff, September 24, 1995.

7. Richard Lacayo, "Tower Terror," *Time*, March 8, 1993, and N. R. Kleinfield, "First Darkness, Then Came the Smoke," *NYT*, February 27, 1993. See *Terrorists among Us: Jihad in America*, a documentary by Steven Emerson, PBS, 1994. Clarke, *Enemies*, 77–78, 148, 83–84. James Collins, "Bill Clinton: Striking Back," *Time*, July 5, 1993. Bunning in Eric Pianin and David Hilzenrath, "House Passes Clinton Budget Plan by 2 Votes," *WP*, August 6, 1993. NAFTA, see Susan Baer, "Clinton Pounds Unions' Tactics against NAFTA," *Baltimore Sun*, November 8, 1993, and Peter T. Kilborn, "Unions Gird for War over Trade Pact," *NYT*, October 4, 1993.

8. Michael R. Gordon with Thomas L. Friedman, "Details of U.S. Raid in Somalia: Success So Near, a Loss So Deep," *NYT*, October 25, 1993. Keith B. Richburg, "Somalia Battle Killed 12 Americans, Wounded 78," *WP*, October 5, 1993, and see Jonathan Carroll, "Courage under Fire: Re-evaluating Black Hawk Down and the Battle of Mogadishu," *War in History*, July 2022, and his "God's Work in Hell," PhD dissertation, chapter 2. Kerrey in James Gordon Meek, "'Black Hawk Down' Anniversary: Al Qaeda's Hidden Hand," *ABC News*, October 4, 2013. *Time*, May 16, 1994. William Perry Interview, February 21, 2006, William J. Clinton Presidential History Project, Miller Center, University of Virginia, 18–19. Clinton, *My Life*, 593, 554. https://time.com/5682135/haiti-military-anniversary/. Joel Gunter, "Ratko Mladic, the 'Butcher of Bosnia,'" *BBC News*, November 22, 2017.

9. Jaime Fuller, "It's Been 20 Years Since the Brady Bill Passed. Here Are 11 Ways Gun Politics Have Changed," *WP*, February 28, 2014. Emily S. Rueb and Niraj Chokshi, "The Violence Against Women Act Is Turning 25. Here's How It Has Ignited Debate." *NYT*, April 4, 2019. https://nowthisnews.com/videos/politics/even-ronald-reagan-didnt-support-letting-civilians-buy-assault-rifles. La Pierre in Dees, *Gathering Storm*, 74–75.

CHAPTER 2

1. Clinton, *My Life*, 630, and https://www.historyonthenet.com/francisco-martin-duran. Beam in Belew, *Bring War Home*, 54; Col. Sanders in Frank, *Kansas*, 2; Sykes, *Nation of Victims*, 12–15. See also Anderson, *Pursuit of Fairness*, 224–30. Roberto Suro, "Louisiana; Bush Denounces Duke as Racist and Charlatan," *NYT*, November 7, 1991.

2. Evil empire in Balz and Brownstein, *Storming the Gates*, 15. Anne Hull, "Randy Weaver's Return from Ruby Ridge," *WP*, April 30, 2001, and see "Ruby Ridge," *American Experience, PBS*, 2017. Beam in Dees, *Gathering Storm*, 1. Koresh background, see Linedecker, *Massacre at Waco*, chapter

1, and Cook, *Waco Rising,* prologue and chapters 1–3. Nancy Gibbs, "The Branch Davidians: Oh, My God, They're Killing Themselves!" *Time,* May 3, 1993. NRA member in Dees, *Gathering Storm,* 77. Liddy in Kurtz, *Hot Air,* 268. Kenneth S. Stern, "Militia Mania: A Growing Danger," *USA Today* magazine, January 1996. Clinton, *My Life,* 499.

3. Gingrich, see Fried and Harris, *At War,* 90–97. Blankley in https://www.pbs.org/wgbh/pages/frontline/newt/vanityfair6.html. 32 years and left-wing in Adam Clymer, "House Revolutionary," *NYT,* August 23, 1992. Stephanopoulos, *Too Human,* 317. Adam Clymer, "The 1994 Elections," *NYT,* November 10, 1994. Gingrich, *Lessons Learned,* 2–3. Baker in Campbell, *1995,* 9. Also see McKay Coppins, "The Man Who Broke Politics," *Atlantic,* November 2018, and *Time*'s 1995 Man of the Year, Lance Morrow, "Newt Gingrich's World: How One Man Changed the Way Washington Sees Reality," December 25, 1995.

4. Anderson, *Pursuit of Fairness,* 233–35. Dale Russakoff and Serge F. Kovaleski, "An Ordinary Boy's Extraordinary Rage," *WP,* July 2, 1995. Letter in Dees, *Gathering Storm,* 154–55. Lou and Herbeck, *American Terrorist,* 6. https://www.youtube.com/watch?v=hOW9AjskoOo. Anne Hull, "Randy Weaver's Return from Ruby Ridge," *WP,* April 30, 2001.

5. JBS in Sean Wilentz, "Confounding Fathers: The Tea Party's Cold War Roots," *New Yorker,* October 18, 2010. Kirkendall, one of my graduate school mentors, told me this story in 1972. See Molly Yard, "The Rush Hours," *NYT,* December 16, 1990. https://www.rushlimbaugh.com/daily/2011/01/10/this_is_all_about_shutting_us_down/, January 10, 2011. Franken, *Idiot,* 9–24. Oklahoma City from Robert D. McFadden and Michael M. Grynbaum, "Rush Limbaugh Dies at 70; Turned Talk Radio into a Right-Wing Attack Machine," *NYT,* February 18, 2021. https://www.cbsnews.com/news/rush-limbaugh-presidential-medal-of-freedom-state-of-the-union-outrageous-quotes/, CBS News, February 6, 2020. Clinton, *My Life,* 586–87. Scandal-ridden from Fried and Harris, *War,* 101. https://web.archive.org/web/2011112 1163922/http://www.salon.com/2003/03/05/savage_11/singleton/. Black Avenger and others from Richard Corliss, "Look Who's Talking: The Explosion of Radio Call-In Shows Has Created a New Form of Electronic Populism and Demagoguery," *Time,* January 23, 1995. Many quotes from Clyde Haberman, "Roger Ailes, Who Built Fox News into an Empire, Dies at 77," *NYT,* May 18, 2017. Nixon in David Carr and Tim Arango, "A Fox Chief at the Pinnacle of Media and Politics," *NYT,* January 9, 2010, https://www.splcenter.org/fighting-hate/extremist-files/individual/alex-jones. https://nymag.com/intelligencer/2013/11/alex-jones-americas-top-conspiracy-theorist.html, and Merlan,

Republic of Lies, 4. Imus, Stern, and talk show expansion in Richard Corliss, "Look Who's Talking," *Time*, January 23, 1995. Kurtz, *Hot Air*, chapter 1. Baker in Campbell, *1995*, 9.

CHAPTER 3

1. Joe Klein, "The Nervous '90s," *Newsweek*, May 1, 1995. *WP*, May 27, 1983. Christine Gorman, "Invincible AIDS," *Time*, August 3, 1992, and see https://www.amfar.org/thirty-years-of-hiv/aids-snapshots-of-an-epidemic/. Jeffrey Schmalz, "March for Gay Rights," *NYT*, April 26, 1993. Barbara Kantrowitz, "Doctors and AIDS," *Newsweek*, June 30, 1991.

2. *New York Times* editorial, May 17, 1987. James Bates, "Japan's U.S. Real Estate Buying Plunges," *LAT*, February 21, 1992. Glickman in C-SPAN video, August 3, 1991. https://apps.urban.org/features/wealth-inequality-charts/. Margot Hornblower, "Great Xpectations," *Time*, June 9, 1997. Klosterman, *Nineties*, 8–9. Paul Krugman, "For Richer," *NYT Magazine*, October 20, 2002, and other quotes from Klein, *Newsweek*, "Nervous '90s."

3. Nancy Gibbs, "The Trials of Hillary Clinton," *Time*, March 21, 1994. Clinton, *My Life*, 574. David Brock, "Living with the Clintons: Bill's Arkansas Bodyguards Tell the Story the Press Missed," *American Spectator*, January 1994.

4. Patterson, *Restless Giant*, 311–13. Dominick Dunne, "L.A. in the Age of OJ," *Vanity Fair*, February 1995, 48. Johnson, *Best of Times*, 160–61, and see *O.J.: Made in America*, ESPN Films. Jill Smolowe, "When Violence Hits Home," *Time*, July 4, 1994. "The Power of DNA Evidence," *NYT* editorial, May 28, 1995. Fallows, *Breaking the News*, 8. Pam Bellack, "In New York, Many People Anticipated the Verdict," *NYT*, February 5, 1997.

5. Sabina Niksic, "Survivors of Bosnia Massacre Grapple with Horrors, Deniers," *AP*, July 10, 2021. Thomas Ferrick Jr, "1995 Marked by Turmoil Reminiscent of Another Era," *Philadelphia Inquirer*, December 31, 1995. Safire in *NYT*, July 13, Lewis and Holbrooke in *NYT*, July 14, both 1995. Mike Corder, "Bosnian Serb Commander Ratko Mladić Loses Genocide Appeal," *AP*, June 8, 2021. Clinton, *My Life*, 580–81, 686–88. Steven Greenhouse, "Senate Urges End to U.S. Embargo against Vietnam," *NYT*, January 28, 1994.

6. John E. Yang, "Underlying Gingrich's Stance Is His Pique about President," *WP*, November 16, 1995. *New York Daily News*, November 16, 1995. https://www.pewresearch.org/fact-tank/2013/09/30/the-last-government-shutdown-and-now-a-different-environment/.

https://www.npr.org/2019/01/12/683304824/the-longest-governm
ent-shutdown-in-history-no-longer-how-1995-changed-everything.
See Anderson, *Pursuit of Fairness*, 232–45. https://www.c-span.org/
video/?c3874462/user-clip-dornan-outing-gunderson. On ending
welfare see Patterson, *Restless Giant*, 375, and Clinton, *My Life*, 720–21.
On AIDS see *60 Minutes Overtime*, CBS, 1998 and 2020, Steve Wulf,
"Magic Johnson: As If by Magic," *Time*, February 12, 1996, and Liz
Hunt, "'Cocktail' Opens New Chapter on AIDS," *Independent, UK*, July
13, 1996.

7. Steven Erlanger, "Bombing in Saudi Arabia: The Witnesses," *NYT*, June
27, 1996. Kevin Sack, "Bomb at the Olympics: The Overview," *NYT*, July
28, 1996. Clinton, *My Life*, 719–31. Connie Cass and Calvin Woodward,
"Bob Dole, a Man of War, Power, Zingers and Denied Ambition," *AP*,
December 6, 2021, and "Opinion: Bob Dole Led to Get Things Done,"
WP, December 5, 2021.

CHAPTER 4

1. https://www.nasa.gov/content/goddard/hubble-history-timeline, and
Dennis Overbye, "The Hubble Telescope Checks In with the Most
Distant Planets," *NYT*, November 23, 2021. https://www.issnational
lab.org/about/iss-timeline/. Gore, *Earth*, 2. https://www.genome.
gov/human-genome-project. Cook-Deegan, *Gene Wars*, 13–14, 25–28.
Many quotes from "Racing to Map Our DNA," *Time*, January 11, 1999.
Lisa Belkin, "Splice Einstein and Sammy Glick. Add a Little Magellan,"
NYT Magazine, August 23, 1998. Andrew Jacobs, "Bronx Suspect May
Be Rapist of 51 Women," *NYT*, April 8, 1999. BBC, February 22, 1997.
http://news.bbc.co.uk/onthisday/hi/dates/stories/february/22/new
sid_4245000/4245877.stm.

2. Cook-Deegan from Johnson, *Best of Times*, 77. Kurt Andersen, "The
Best Decade Ever? The 1990s, Obviously," *NYT*, February 6, 2015. See
Johnson, *Best of Times*, 20; McCullough, *Internet Happened*, 8; Molly Baker,
"Technology Investors Fall Head over Heels for Their New Love," *WSJ*,
August 10, 1995. Gore in Harrison, *Culture*, 169. McCullough, *Internet
Happened*, 16–20.

3. Isaacson, *Innovators*, 74–79, and for computer history see https://www.
computerhistory.org/timeline/computers/. Isaacson, *Innovators*, 131,
151, and chapter two. Read more: http://www.madehow.com/Vol
ume-2/Integrated-Circuit.html#ixzz6juxGj5fr. Noyce from Isaacson,
Innovators, 197–98.

4. Phil Lemmons, "Apple and Its Personal Computers," *BYTE*, December 1984. https://www.wired.com/2012/12/ff-john-mcafees-last-stand/, and Joshua Davis, "John McAfee Fled to Belize, but He Couldn't Escape Himself," *Wired*, December 24, 2012.

5. Peter Sinton, "Page One — Windows 95 Launch Felt Around World," SFGate. https://www.sfgate.com/news/article/page-one-windows-95-launch-felt-around-world-3025738.php.

6. Berners-Lee, *Weaving the Web*, 2–4, and see CERN history: https://home.cern/about/who-we-are/our-history. McCullough, *Internet Happened*, 22–35. David A. Kaplan, "Nothing but Net," *Newsweek,* December 25, 1995. "High Stakes Winners," *Time* cover story, February 19, 1996. Joshua Cooper Ramo, "Winner Take All: Microsoft v. Netscape," *Time*, September 16, 1996. All on the Web from Campbell, *1995*, 28. McCullough, *Internet Happened*, 81–88, 182–95. Stone, *Everything Store*, 35–38, chapter 2. G. Bruce Knecht, "Wall Street Whiz Finds Niche Selling Books on the Internet," *WSJ*, May 16, 1996. Joshua Cooper Ramo, "Jeffrey Preston Bezos: 1999 Person of the Year," *Time*, December 27, 1999.

7. Kushner, *Player's Ball*, 63. David Kushner, "Recruiting Women to Online Dating Was a Challenge," *Atlantic*, April 6, 2019, and *Player's Ball*, chapter 1. "Battle for the Soul of the Internet," *Time*, July 25, 1994. Craig Bicknell, "The Sordid Saga of Sex.com," *Wired*, April 15, 1999. https://time.com/4013672/ebay-founded-story//. And Adam Cohen, "The Attic of E," *Time*, December 27, 1999. Speed Kills from Joshua Cooper Ramo, "Jeffrey Preston Bezos: 1999 Person of the Year," *Time,* December 27, 1999. https://arstechnica.com/information-technology/2017/12/how-hotmail-changed-microsoft-and-email-forever/.

8. http://www.fundinguniverse.com/company-histories/paypal-inc-history/. McCullough, *Internet Happened*, 197–211, and CrackBerry, 300. https://smartphones.gadgethacks.com/news/from-backpack-transceiver-smartphone-visual-history-mobile-phone-0127134/. http://content.time.com/time/specials/2007/article/0,28804,1638782_1638778_1638772,00.html. https://www.digitaltrends.com/features/the-history-of-social-networking/. https://www.classmates.com/blog/listicle/social-networking-is-20/. Levenstein, *Didn't See Us Coming*, chapter 1, 57, 72, 85–87. On economic growth see Johnson, *Best of Times,* 470–72. "The Net Imperative," *Economist*, June 26 to July 2, 1999. Berry, *Cyberspace*, 209. Klosterman, *Nineties*, 315. Denis Dutton, "It's Always the End of the World as We Know It," *NYT*, December 31, 2009. Timothy L. O'Brien, "Banks Stocked Up on Cash but Hoarders Stayed Away," *NYT*, December 31, 1999.

CHAPTER 5

1. Frank Rich, "Smash-Mouth 1, Civility 0," *NYT*, February 17, 2001, and see his "The Age of the Mediathon," *NYT Magazine*, October 29, 2000. Zappa from https://wiki.killuglyradio.com/wiki/Winter_In_Amer ika. Klosterman, *Nineties*, 38–41. Richard Corliss, "Show Business: X Rated," *Time*, May 7, 1990. 14-year-old hormones from Patterson, *Restless Giant*, 289. Eric Deggans, "Jerry Springer, Talk Show Host and Former Cincinnati Mayor, Dies at 79," NPR *Morning Edition*, and James Poniewozik, "Jerry Springer, American Ringmaster," *NYT*, both April 27, 2023. Kurtz, *Hot Air*, chapter 1. Kurt Andersen, "Blunt Trauma," *New Yorker*, March 30, 1998.

2. Philip Elmer-Dewitt, "Cyberporn," *Time*, July 3, 1995. Politicians see Kushner, *Player's Ball*, 90–91. https://www.complex.com/music/the-best-90s-rappers/. Dave Bry, Alex Russell, David Drake, Dharmic X, and Foster Kramer, "The 10 Best 90s Rappers, Who Dominated Hip-Hop's Golden Era," *Complex*, October 30, 2018, https://www.complex.com/music/the-best-90s-rappers/. Christopher John Farley, "Music: Hip-Hop Nation," *Time*, February 8, 1999. Toure, "Hip-Hop at Middle Age," *AARP Magazine*, December 2019. Public Enemy from Kurt Andersen, "The Best Decade Ever? The 1990s, Obviously," *NYT*, February 6, 2015. Kitwana in Scott Mervis, "From Kool Herc to 50 Cent, the Story of Rap—So Far," *Pittsburgh Post-Gazette*, February 15, 2004, and see Kitwana, *Hip Hop Generation*, xi, preface, chapter 1, Boston women 85–86. "Tough Talk on Entertainment," *Time*, June 12, 1995. Friend, *Naughty Nineties*, 472–73. Frank Rich, "Smash-Mouth 1, Civility 0," *NYT*, February 17, 2001.

3. https://www.fcc.gov/general/telecommunications-act-1996. David Leonhardt, "Big Business Is Overcharging You $5,000 a Year," *NYT*, November 10, 2019. "A Return to Partisanship as Congress Ends Its Session," *NYT*, November 14, 1997. William Booth, "The Green President," *WP* Weekly Edition, January 22–28, 2001. Eric Pooley, "Too Good to Be True?" *Time*, May 19, 1997. Kurt Andersen, "The Best Decade Ever? The 1990s, Obviously," *NYT*, February 6, 2015. https://www.thestreet.com/lifestyle/history-of-nike-15057083. LaFeber, *Jordan*, preface, 24. Buchanan in Patterson, *Restless Giant*, 292.

4. Niall O'Dowd, "On This Day: Bill Clinton's Historic Visit to Northern Ireland," *IrishCentral.com*, November 30, 2015. Anderson, *Bush's Wars*, 43–45.

5. Clinton, *My Life*, 771. "Scandalous Scoop Breaks Online," *BBC*, January 25, 1998. Susan Schmidt, Peter Baker, and Tony Locy, "Clinton Accused of Urging Aide to Lie," *WP*, January 21, 1998. Nancy Gibbs, "Truth or . . . Consequences," *Time*, February 2, 1998. Olivia B. Waxman and Merrill Fabry, "From an Anonymous Tip to an Impeachment: A Timeline of Key Moments in the Clinton-Lewinsky Scandal," *Time*, May 4, 2018. Michael Isikoff, "Diary of a Scandal," *Newsweek*, January 21, 1998. Jeff Greenfield, "Just Keep 'Em Laughing," *Time*, February 9, 1998. Many quotes in Nancy Gibbs, "Ken Starr: Tick, Tock, Tick . . . . . . Talk," *Time*, August 10, 1998. Garrison Keillor, "Can We Get On to Something Serious?," *Time*, August 31, 1998. Francis X. Clines, "At the Polls, Tolerance for Clinton Runs Deep," *NYT*, November 4, 1998. Also see "How It Came to This: A Portrait of a Scandal in 13 Acts," *WP* Weekly Edition, December 21–28, 1998.

6. "The Gingrich Coup," *NYT*, November 7, 1998. Tim Dickerson, "Newt and Callista's Affair 'Was Common Knowledge' on the Hill," *Rolling Stone*, January 26, 2012. Bernard Weinraub, "Hustler Publisher Revels in Role in Livingston Sex Disclosure," *NYT*, December 19, 1998. Margaret Carlson, "The Clinton in Us All: Those Who Hate Him Seem to Bear More Than a Passing Resemblance to Him," *Time*, December 21, 1998. Clinton, *My Life*, 836.

7. Columbine, see https://www.pbs.org/newshour/show/what-we-have-learned-20-years-after-columbine, and Jesus Jiménez, Shaila Dewan, and Mike Baker, "In Mass Shootings, Police Are Trained to 'Confront the Attacker,'" *NYT*, May 27, 2022. Thomas L. Friedman, "This Is Putin's War. But America and NATO Aren't Innocent Bystanders," *NYT*, February 21, 2022. Clinton and Islamic terrorism, Anderson, *Bush's Wars*, 45–53. Clinton, *My Life*, 925, 803–5.

8. 2000 election, Kruse and Zelizer, *Fault Lines*, 238–40. Clinton to Gore, *My Life*, 873. For a 2002 review see Laurence H. Tribe, "The Unbearable Wrongness of Bush v. Gore," *Constitutional Commentary*, 2002, 620. https://scholarship.law.umn.edu/concomm/620. Borowitz, *Profiles*, 118.

EPILOGUE

1. See Kean and Hamilton, *9/11 Report*, chapter 1, 3–23, 60–62, 67–70, and Anderson, *Bush's Wars*, 62–69.

CONCLUSIONS

1. Melody Schreiber, "George W. Bush's Anti-HIV Program Is Hailed as 'Amazing'—And Still Crucial at 20," NPR, February 28, 2023. Lynne Hartnett, "The Long History of Russian Imperialism Shaping Putin's War," WP, March 2, 2022. Valerie Hopkins, "Investigators of War Crimes in Ukraine Face Formidable Challenges," NYT, July 3, 2022.

2. Raymond from Chris Tomlinson, "Exxon Knew about Climate Change; Big Oil Cannot Be Trusted" HC, January 18, 2023. Leslie Hook and Chris Campbell, "Record Carbon Dioxide Levels Alarm Scientists," FT, May 13, 2022. Henry Fountain, "Carbon Dioxide Levels Are Highest in Human History," NYT, June 3, 2022. Paul Krugman, "The Heat Is Already On," NYT, May 24, 2022. Coral Davenport and Lisa Friedman, "Five Decades in the Making: Why It Took Congress So Long to Act on Climate," NYT, August 7, 2022. "Texas Top Cop: Uvalde Police Could Have Ended Rampage Early On," AP, June 21, 2022. Samantha Cooney, "Meet the Woman Who Started #MeToo 10 Years Ago," Time, October 19, 2017. https://case.hks.harvard.edu/leading-with-empathy-tarana-burke-and-the-making-of-the-me-too-movem ent/. Tarana Burke, "To Measure a Movement," Time, October 24, 2022. Molly Ball, "Brett Kavanaugh's Supreme Court Confirmation Is Now the Ultimate Test of Political Power in 2018," Time, September 20, 2018. Michelle L. Price, "Congress Approves Sex Harassment Bill in #MeToo Milestone," AP, February 10, 2022.

3. https://www.themarshallproject.org/2016/03/02/the-rev-jesse-jack son-remembers-rodney-king-and-the-l-a-riots/ Tim Sullivan and Stephen Groves, "'We're Sick of It': Anger over Police Killings Shatters US," AP, May 31, 2020. Leonard Pitts, "George Floyd's Death Raises an Old Question: 'How Long?'," Miami Herald, May 31, 2020. Aja Romano, "Why We Can't Stop Fighting about Cancel Culture," VOX, August 25, 2020, and see Pamela Paul, "Political Correctness Used to Be Funny. Now It's No Joke," NYT, June 1, 2023. Andrew Restuccia, Burgess Everett, and Heather Caygle, "Longest Shutdown in History Ends after Trump Relents on Wall," Politico, January 25, 2019. https://www.npr. org/2019/01/12/683304824/the-longest-government-shutdown-in-history-no-longer-how-1995-changed-everything/. Paul Krugman, "The G.O.P. Is in a Doom Loop of Bizarro," NYT, January 29, 2021.

4. Kevin Roose, "What Is QAnon, the Viral Pro-Trump Conspiracy Theory?," NYT, September 3, 2021. Travis M. Andrews, "Twitter in Chief," WP, October 14, 2020, and see Jonathan Haidt, "Why the Past

10 Years of American Life Have Been Uniquely Stupid," *The Atlantic*, April 2022. Michael Humphrey, "I Analyzed All of Trump's Tweets to Find Out What He Was Really Saying," *The Conversation*, February 8, 2021. Nate Rattner, "Trump's Election Lies Were among His Most Popular Tweets," *CNBC*, January 13, 2021. Chris Tomlinson, "GOP's Bad Ideas Overshadow the Smart Ones," *HC*, June 22, 2022. Frank Bruni, "The Republicans Who Want to Destroy Trump. Their Party's a Lost Cause. America Isn't," *NYT*, July 11, 2020. Sykes, *Lost Its Mind*, xii. Zelizer, *Presidency of Trump*, 28. Wilson, *Trump Touches*, 2. "P. J. O'Rourke Obit," *NYT*, February 15, 2022.

5. "The Evidence of the Jan. 6 Committee. It's a Reminder of the Violence and How Trump Betrayed His Supporters," *WSJ*, June 10, 2022. Meghan Keneally, "Ruby Ridge Siege, 25 Years Later, a 'Rallying Cry' for Today's White Nationalists," *ABC News*, August 18, 2017. Neil MacFarquar, "Oklahoma City Marks 25 Years since America's Deadliest Homegrown Attack," *NYT,* April 19, 2020. Tina Nguyen, "Six Other Times Armed Militias Took on the Government," *Vanity Fair*, January 5, 2016. Moriah Balingit, "Armed Militia Helped a Michigan Barbershop Open, a Coronavirus Defiance That Puts Republican Lawmakers in a Bind," *WP*, May 12, 2020. Johnson in "Waco 30 Years Later, Is Still with Us," *HC* editorial, February 28, 2023. Wray in Reuters, September 21, 2021. Julia Zorthian, "How the O.J. Simpson Verdict Changed the Way We All Watch TV," *Time*, October 2, 2015. James Poniewozik, "Jerry Springer, American Ringmaster," *NYT*, April 27, 2023. Women's march in Levenstein, *Didn't See Us Coming*, 1–2. Zelizer, *The Presidency of Donald J. Trump*, 22–23.

6. Clinton, *My Life*, 720–21. Katharine Q. Seelye, "Recipients of Welfare," *NYT*, April 11, 1999. https://www.brookings.edu/articles/welfare-reform-success-or-failure-it-worked/ Meinhold in Alejandro de la Garza, "'Don't Ask, Don't Tell' Was a Complicated Turning Point for Gay Rights. 25 Years Later, Many of the Same Issues Remain," *Time*, July 19, 2018. Toure, "Hip-Hop at Middle Age," *AARP Magazine*, December 2019. Newspapers in "Daily Briefing," *NYT*, December 1, 2020. https://www.npr.org/2023/04/24/1171352545/poll-two-thirds-oppose-banning-medication-abortion. Andrew Rosenthal, "O'Connor Regrets Bush v. Gore," *NYT*, April 29, 2013.

Select Bibliography

Albright, Madeleine. *Madam Secretary: A Memoir*. New York: Random House, 2003.

Ambrose, Stephen, and Douglas Brinkley, eds. *Witness to America: An Illustrated Documentary History of the United States from the Revolution to Today*. New York: HarperCollins, 1999.

Anderson, Terry H. *The Pursuit of Fairness: A History of Affirmative Action*. New York: Oxford University Press, 2004.

Anderson, Terry H. *Bush's Wars*. New York: Oxford University Press, 2012.

Anderson, Terry H. *The Sixties*. New York: Routledge, 5th ed., 2017.

Andrews, Paul. *How the Web Was Won*. New York: Broadway Books, 1999.

Baker, Peter. *The Breach: Inside the Impeachment and Trial of William Jefferson Clinton*. New York: Scribner, 2000.

Balz, Dan, and Ronald Brownstein. *Storming the Gates: Protest Politics and the Republican Revival*. Boston: Little, Brown, 1996.

Barry, Dave. *Dave Barry in Cyberspace*. New York: Crown, 1996.

Belew, Kathleen. *Bring the War Home: The White Power Movement and Paramilitary America*. Cambridge, MA: Harvard University Press, 2018.

Berners-Lee, Tim. *Weaving the Web: The Original Design and Ultimate Destiny of the World Wide Web*. New York: HarperCollins, 1999.

Beschloss, Michael, and Strobe Talbott. *At the Highest Levels: The Inside Story of the End of the Cold War*. Boston: Little, Brown, 1993.

Blumenthal. Sidney. *The Clinton Wars*. New York: Farrar, Straus and Giroux, 2003.

Brands, H. W. *The Devil We Knew*. New York: Oxford University Press, 1994.

Bush, George H. W., and Brent Scowcroft. *A World Transformed*. New York: Vintage, 1999.

Campbell, W. Joseph. *1995: The Year the Future Began*. Oakland: University of California Press, 2015.

Carroll, Jonathan. "God's Work in Hell: Nation-Building in Somalia, 1992–1995." PhD diss., Texas A&M University, 2023.

Clarke, Richard A. *Against All Enemies: Inside America's War on Terror*. New York: Free Press, 2004.

Clinton, Bill. *My Life*. New York: Knopf, 2004.

Clinton, Hillary Rodham. *Living History*. New York: Simon & Schuster, 2003.

Cobbs, Elizabeth. *Fearless Women: Feminist Patriots from Abigail Adams to Beyoncé*. Cambridge, MA: Harvard University Press, 2023.

Conason, Joe, and Gene Lyons. *The Hunting of the President: The Ten-Year Campaign to Destroy Bill and Hillary Clinton*. New York: Thomas Dunne Books, 2000.

Cook, Kevin. *Waco Rising: David Koresh, the FBI, and the Birth of America's Modern Militias*. New York: Henry Holt, 2023.

Cook-Deegan, Robert M. *The Gene Wars: Science, Politics, and the Human Genome*. New York: Norton, 1994.

Corn, David. *American Psychosis: A Historical Investigation of How the Republican Party Went Crazy*. New York: Hachette Book Group, 2022.

Dees, Morris, with James Corcoran. *Gathering Storm: America's Militia Threat*. New York: HarperCollins, 1996.

Dembicki, Geoff. *The Petroleum Papers: Inside the Far-Right Conspiracy to Cover Up Climate Change*. Vancouver, BC: Greystone, 2022.

Draper, Robert. *Weapons of Mass Delusion: When the Republican Party Lost Its Mind*. New York: Penguin Press, 2022.

Drew, Elizabeth. *On the Edge: The Clinton Presidency*. New York: Simon & Schuster, 1994.

Drew, Elizabeth. *Showdown: The Struggle between the Gingrich Congress and the Clinton White House*. New York: Simon & Schuster, 1997.

Engel, Jeffrey A., ed. *The Fall of the Berlin Wall: The Revolutionary Legacy of 1989*. New York: Oxford University Press, 2009.

Evans, Elizabeth. *The Politics of Third Wave Feminisms: Neoliberalism, Intersectionality, and the State in Britain and the US*. London: Palgrave Macmillan, 2015.

Fallows, James. *Looking at the Sun: The Rise of the New East Asian Economic and Political System*. New York: Vintage Books, 1995.

Fallows, James. *Breaking the News: How the Media Undermine American Democracy*. New York: Pantheon Books, 1996.

Faludi, Susan. *Backlash: The Undeclared War against American Women*. New York: Crown, 1991.

Frank, Thomas. *What's the Matter with Kansas? How Conservatives Won the Heart of America*. New York: Picador, 2005.

Franken, Al. *Rush Limbaugh Is a Big Fat Idiot and Other Observations*. New York: Delacorte Press, 1996.

Fried, Amy, and Douglas B. Harris. *At War with Government: How Conservatives Weaponized Distrust from Goldwater to Trump*. New York: Columbia University Press, 2021.

Friedman, George, and Meredith Lebard. *The Coming War with Japan*. New York: St. Martin's Press, 1991.

Friend, David. *The Naughty Nineties: The Triumph of the American Libido*. New York: Hatchette Book Group, 2017.

Gates, Robert M. *From the Shadows: The Ultimate Insider's Story of Five Presidents and How They Won the Cold War*. New York: Simon & Schuster, 1996.

Gates, Robert M. *Duty: Memoirs of a Secretary at War*. New York: Knopf, 2014.

Gillon, Steven M. *The Pact: Bill Clinton, Newt Gingrich, and the Rivalry That Defined a Generation*. New York: Oxford University Press, 2008.

Gingrich, Newt. *Lessons Learned the Hard Way*. New York: HarperCollins, 1998.

Goldberg, Robert. *Enemies Within: The Cult of Conspiracy in Modern America*. New Haven, CT: Yale University Press, 2001.

Gore, Al. *Earth in the Balance: Ecology and the Human Spirit*. Boston: Houghton Mifflin, 1992.

Guinn, Jeff. *Waco: David Koresh, the Branch Davidians, and the Legacy of Rage*. New York: Simon & Schuster, 2023.

Halberstam, David. *War in a Time of Peace: Bush, Clinton, and the Generals*. New York: Simon & Schuster, 2002.

Harris, John F. *The Survivor: Bill Clinton in the White House*. New York: Random House, 2005.

Harrison, Colin. *American Culture in the 1990s*. Edinburgh: Edinburgh University Press, 2010.

Hemmer, Nicole. *Messengers of the Right: Conservative Media and the Transformation of American Politics*. Philadelphia: University of Pennsylvania Press, 2016.

Hughes, Robert. *Culture of Complaint: The Fraying of America*. New York: Oxford University Press, 1993.

Isaacson, Walter. *Steve Jobs*. New York: Simon & Schuster, 2011.

Isaacson, Walter. *The Innovators: How a Group of Hackers, Geniuses, and Geeks Created the Digital Revolution*. New York: Simon & Schuster, 2014; Kindle edition.

Isikoff, Michael. *Uncovering Clinton: A Reporter's Story*. New York: Crown, 1999.

Johnson, Haynes. *The Best of Times: The Boom and Bust Years of America before and after Everything Changed*. New York: Harcourt Books, 2001.

Johnson, Matthew. *Undermining Racial Justice: How One University Embraced Inclusion and Inequality*. New York: Cornell University Press, 2020.

Kallen, Stuart A., ed. *The 1990s*. San Diego, CA: Greenhaven Press, 2000.

Kaplan, David A. *The Silicon Boys and Their Valley of Dreams*. New York: William Morrow, 1999.

Keen, Thomas H., and Lee H. Hamilton. *The 9/11 Report: The National Commission on Terrorist Attacks upon the United States*. New York: St. Martin's Press, 2004.

Kitwana, Bakari. *The Hip Hop Generation: Young Blacks and the Crisis in African American Culture*. New York: Basic Books, 2002.

Klein, Joe. *The Natural: The Misunderstood Presidency of Bill Clinton*. New York: Broadway Books, 2002.

Klinkner, Philip A., with Rogers M. Smith. *The Unsteady March: The Rise and Decline of Racial Equality in America*. Chicago: University of Chicago Press, 1999.

Klosterman, Chuck. *The Nineties*. New York: Random House, 2022.

Kruse, Kevin M., and Julian E. Zelizer. *Fault Lines: A History of the United States since 1974*. New York, Norton, 2019.

Kurtz, Howard. *Hot Air: All Talk, All the Time*. New York: Times Books, 1996.

Kushner, David. *The Player's Ball: A Genius, a Con Man, and the Secret History of the Internet's Rise*. New York: Simon & Schuster, 2019.

Lacombe, Matt. *Firepower: How the NRA Turned Gun Owners into a Political Force*. Princeton, NJ: Princeton University Press, 2021.

LaFeber, Walter. *Michael Jordan and the New Global Capitalism*. New York: Norton, 2002.

Leffler, Melvyn P. *For the Soul of Mankind: The United States, the Soviet Union, and the Cold War*. New York: Hill and Wang, 2007.

Leffler, Melvyn P. *Confronting Saddam Hussein: George W. Bush and the Invasion of Iraq*. New York: Oxford University Press, 2023.

Levenstein, Lisa, *They Didn't See Us Coming: The Hidden History of Feminism in the Nineties.* New York: Basic Books, 2020.

Linedecker, Clifford L., *Massacre at Waco: The Shocking True Story of Cult Leader David Koresh and the Branch Davidians*. New York: St. Martin's, 1993.

Los Angeles Times Staff. *Understanding the Riots*. Los Angeles: LA Times, 1992.

Maraniss, David. *First in His Class: The Biography of Bill Clinton*. New York: Simon & Schuster, 1996.

Mayer, Jane, and Jill Abramson. *Strange Justice: The Selling of Clarence Thomas*. New York: Plume, 1995.

McCullough, Brian. *How the Internet Happened: From Netscape to the iPhone*. New York: Liveright Publishing, 2018.

Merlan, Anna. *Republic of Lies: American Conspiracy Theorists and Their Surprising Rise to Power*. New York: Metropolitan Books, 2019.

Michel, Lou, and Dan Herbeck. *American Terrorist: Timothy McVeigh and the Oklahoma City Bombing*. New York: Avon Books, 2001.

Milbank, Dana. *The Destructionists: The Twenty-Five-Year Crack-Up of the Republican Party*. New York: Doubleday, 2022.

Miller, Chris. *Chip War: The Fight for the World's Most Critical Technology*. New York, Scribner, 2022.

Moyers, Bill, and Julie Leininger Pycior. *Moyers on America: A Journalist and His Times*. New York: The New Press, 2019.

O'Neill, William. *A Bubble in Time: America during the Interwar Years, 1989–2001*. Chicago: Ivan R. Dee, 2009.

Ott, Brian L., and Greg Dickinson. *The Twitter Presidency: Donald J. Trump and the Politics of White Rage*. New York: Routledge, 2019.

Oxoby, Marc. *The 1990s*. Westport, CT: Greenwood Press, 2003.

Parmet, Herbert S. *George Bush: The Life of a Lone Star Yankee*. New York: Scribner, 1997.

Patterson, James T. *Restless Giant: The United States from Watergate to Bush v. Gore*. New York: Oxford University Press, 2005.

Poniewozik, James. *Audience of One: Donald Trump, Television, and the Fracturing of America*. New York: Liveright, 2019.

Reagan, Ronald. *An American Life*. New York: Simon & Schuster, 1990.

Reich, Robert B. *Locked in the Cabinet*. New York: Vintage Books, 1998.

Reid, Robert H. *Architects of the Web: 1,000 Days That Built the Future of Business*. New York: Wiley, 1997.

Rivlin, Gary. *The Plot to Get Bill Gates*. New York: Random House, 1999.

Rosenwald, Brian. *Talk Radio's America: How an Industry Took Over a Political Party That Took Over the U.S.* Cambridge, MA: Harvard University Press, 2019.

Samuelson, Robert J. *The Good Life and Its Discontents: The American Dream in the Age of Entitlement, 1945–1995*. New York: Random House, 1995.

Shilts, Randy. *And the Band Played On: Politics, People, and the AIDS Epidemic*. New York: St. Martin's Press, 1987.

Stephanopoulos, George. *All Too Human*. Boston: Little Brown, 1999.

Stevens, Stuart. *It Was All a Lie: How the Republican Party Became Donald Trump*. New York: Knopf, 2020.

Stevenson, Brenda E. *The Contested Murder of Latasha Harlins: Justice, Gender, and the Origins of the LA Riots*. New York: Oxford University Press, 2013.

Stiglitz, Joseph E. *The Roaring Nineties: A New History of the World's Most Prosperous Decade*. New York: Norton, 2003.

Stone, Brad. *The Everything Store: Jeff Bezos and the Age of Amazon*. Boston: Little, Brown, 2013.

Sykes, Charles J. *A Nation of Victims: The Decay of the American Character.* New York: St. Martin's Press, 1992.

Sykes, Charles J. *How the Right Lost Its Mind.* New York: St. Martin's Press, 2018.

Troy, Gil. *The Age of Clinton: America in the 1990s.* New York: Thomas Dunne Books, 2015.

Vise, David A., and Mark Malseed. *The Google Story.* New York: Delacorte Press, 2005.

Westad, Odd Arne. *The Global Cold War: Third World Interventions and the Making of Our Times.* Cambridge, UK: Cambridge University Press, 2005.

Wilson, Rick. *Everything Trump Touches Dies: A Republican Strategist Gets Real about the Worst President Ever.* New York: Free Press, 2018.

Wolfe, Alan. *One Nation After All.* New York: Penguin, 1998.

Woodward, Bob. *Rage.* New York: Simon & Schuster, 2020.

Zelizer, Julian E. *Burning Down the House: Newt Gingrich, the Fall of a Speaker, and the Rise of the New Republican Party.* New York: Penguin, 2020.

Zelizer, Julian E., ed. *The Presidency of Donald J. Trump: A First Historical Assessment.* Princeton, NJ: Princeton University Press, 2022.

Index

For the benefit of digital users, indexed terms that span two pages (e.g., 52–53) may, on occasion, appear on only one of those pages.

Note: page numbers followed by *f* refer to figures